THE BLACK ART

Rollo Ahmed

THE BLACK ART

ROLLO AHMED

INTRODUCTION BY
DENNIS WHEATLEY

ILLUSTRATIONS BY
C. A. MILLS

The Black Art

First published in 1936 by John Long Ltd, London

This edition published in 1994 by Senate, an imprint of Studio Editions Ltd, Princess House, 50 Eastcastle Street, London W1N 7AP, England

ISBN 1 85958 048 3
Printed and bound in Guernsey by
The Guernsey Press Co Ltd

INTRODUCTION

IT gives me very great pleasure to introduce this book because, to some extent, I am responsible for it.

Last year my "Black Magic" romance, *The Devil Rides Out*, aroused such widespread interest that Messrs. John Long asked me if I would write a serious book upon the subject for them.

That I could not do. All the data that went into my novel was acquired from old treatises or from conversations with occultists to whom I secured introductions for the purpose of obtaining such information as would enable me to build up an accurate background for my story. To this day my *practical* knowledge of magic remains absolutely nil.

However, the genius of publishing lies in the ability of the publisher to sense and supply a public demand. Messrs. John Long were not put off by my inability to attempt such a book as this, and they asked me if I could suggest a serious student of the subject who would write a full account of the history and practice of the Black Art.

That was altogether a different matter; I had met numerous occultists during my search for genuine local colour for my book, and several of them might have produced a very readable study of this kind, but one stood out beyond all the rest as a man of profound knowledge and one whose very presence radiates power.

In Mr. Rollo Ahmed I introduced to Messrs. John Long no student who has confined himself only to dusty books and minor experiments, but a Master, who has devoted a lifetime to acquiring a first-hand knowledge of that grim "other world" which lies so far from ordinary experience, and yet is so very near for those who have the power to pierce the veil.

Mr. Rollo Ahmed is a member of that ancient race which possessed by far the greatest and longest enduring civilisation of all known antiquity—the Egyptians. They were coupling astrological predictions with exact and scientific astronomical observation when both Greeks and Romans were still skin-clad barbarians. Much of the ancient Egyptian wisdom has been lost, but such portions of it as still remain have been handed down through countless generations to the few, such as Rollo Ahmed, who are its heirs to-day.

In his childhood Mr. Ahmed was taken to the West Indies, which was the home of his mother. He spent many years there and in the little-explored forests of Yucatan, Guiana and Brazil. There he was able to acquire first-hand knowledge, not only of the primitive magic of the native forest Indians but Voodoo and Obeah ; those sinister cults which are still practised by the descendants of the African negroes who were imported as slaves during the seventeenth and eighteenth centuries.

Mr. Ahmed then left South America for a period in Europe, and later for Asia, and settled for some time in Burma to study occult practices in that sorcery-ridden land, where he had many strange experiences.

Having studied the worst aspects of the Black Art in three continents, he eventually sat at the feet of the "white" magicians who lead lives of almost unbelievable asceticism in order that they may acquire power to work for the good of all mankind.

Mr. Rollo Ahmed is himself a practitioner of Raja Yoga, and all those who have heard him lecture upon this subject must envy him his remarkable clarity of exposition.

A little time ago he came to live in Europe, and all those who have been privileged to meet him recognise his brilliant intellect and astounding erudition in all matters connected with the occult.

Such praise as I have received in a most voluminous correspondence from all over the world as to the accuracy of the data in my book, *The Devil Rides Out*, is almost entirely due to my many long conversations with Mr. Rollo Ahmed. With unfailing patience he answered my innumerable questions, and in the most generous manner he placed his profound knowledge entirely at my disposal, in order that I might make my novel a little more than an ordinary fiction book.

It is a very great pleasure to be able to acknowledge my indebtedness to him here, and in the *Black Art* to introduce to the public a really masterly work which I feel certain will prove of the highest interest both to students of the occult and the general reader who, in one volume, now have the opportunity to learn many of the mysteries which have, throughout all ages, fascinated most thinking people.

DENNIS WHEATLEY.

CONTENTS

Part I

Part II

THE BLACK ART

PART I

CHAPTER I

THE EARLIEST RECORDS OF BLACK MAGIC

Traces sorcery back to antediluvian times, and mentions various early evidences and records of its practice.

THE history of man is the history of magic. It is a difficult task to turn to any particular era and say that at this time or that magic made its appearance in definite form, because, although there are very early records of its practice, there are still earlier traces and evidences left behind in the shape of rude carvings, symbols, and so forth, and the legends that have been handed down through generations by word of mouth alone. These traces are to be found among every race and every nation on the globe. Magic was man's first effort to establish contact with the unknown ; the hidden spiritual forces, which he dimly felt to exist and by means of which he hoped to attain his desires and accomplish matters that proved difficult or too much for him by ordinary means. Not all magic was black, but all magic did eventually develop an evil tendency, and magic as a whole grew to imply that which was dark and dubious if not actually evil. In the evolution of thought, magic, as representing a lower intellectual level, probably everywhere preceded religion but, later, ran parallel with it.

Now, the occultist traces black magic much further back than the mere materialist. He goes back to the lost continent of Atlantis, which sank beneath the waves of the Western Ocean and thereby caused the greatest cataclysm the world has ever experienced, referred to in the Bible as the Flood. The people of Atlantis had reached a high state of evolution, physically, mentally, and spiritually, and had attained a vast knowledge of psychic powers. Unfortunately they proceeded to misuse their knowledge, and the initiates of Atlantis fought one against the other for supernatural supremacy, using their powers for the enslavement of their fellow creatures and the race as a whole. They are supposed to have reached an even higher standard of civilisation than man has since attained, but they became adepts of the black art and controlled psychic and elemental forces to dominate the animal and mineral kingdoms. This race is symbolised in the Bible as the Tower of Babel, a civilisation whose base rested on earth and whose summit reached into higher realms than man was yet entitled to penetrate.

In the end, the Atlanteans brought about their own destruction by the perversion of forces which even destroyed the entire continent. Some few of the Atlantean people escaped, by removing themselves to other countries before the final upheaval. The yellow races of to-day are regarded by some as their descendants, and if any traces of these remote ancestors remain, and their magic practices, they should be looked for among the Chinese and the closely guarded secrets in the Lhamasseries of Thibet.

It is certain that these ancient people fell into monstrous evils, and became the first earthly masters of the black art, bestowing upon an unfortunate world the earliest vibrations of sorcery. The material proof of the existence of Atlantis is slight, but is an accepted fact among most occultists. In a work of this description details cannot be entered into, but the seeker will find circumstantial evidence of its actual existence by comparing the habits, artifacts, architecture, and myths of widely separated peoples, who can only have acquired their characteristics from a common basis, now extinct.

We find material evidences of magical practices in the European caves of the Palæolithic age; those belonging to the interglacial period, which is sometimes also called Aurignacian, after the cave dwellers of Aurignacia, whose remains and drawings link them with some of the primitive African tribes. In a cave near Bagnères de Luchon there are spirited drawings of masked men and animals; also, the impress of hands in a mutilated condition, some of which appear to have been dipped in a sticky fluid, while others have been outlined with black or yellow pigments.

Authorities on the subject do not consider that they are the imprints of lepers, but all have fingers torn or cut away at the first joint, and it is not unreasonable to suppose that the cause of this dismemberment was for sacrificial purposes. Many primitive peoples do the same thing even to-day. In the case of epidemics it is quite usual to offer a finger or two for the magical purpose of "cutting off" the deaths. Some savage tribes maim themselves as a mark of grief or mourning. Quite recently an educated Englishman, whose wife had left him, consulted the author on the advisability of sacrificing the first finger of his right hand in order to force her to return ; needless to say, he was advised to do nothing so drastic.

There is another cave in France with a drawing on the rock surface of a masked man with antlers. It is found on the walls of a little room at the end of a long passage, and evidently represents a primitive sorcerer masquerading as an animal. Nearby is a sort of altar, where this prehistoric magician probably made sacrifices. Antlers and horns have been the insignia of devils and black magicians from time immemorial, and are worn by present-day witch doctors. The carving in question is a particularly lively illustration of this early wizard, prancing and bedecked.

Further east, and coming to a different period, we find the great Zoroaster, the founder of the Magian religion, who is thought to have lived about 1000 B.C. or even earlier. Originally the aim of his teaching was the distinction between good and evil, with good triumphant, but as the years rolled on it degenerated into an idolatrous form of fire worship and its priests were certainly black magicians, judging by the methods they employed for divination and the like.

The Magi flourished when Cyrus founded the New Empire. They sacrificed to the sun, moon, earth, water, and winds, with many revolting rites performed with the blood and bodies of children and animals. In many countries witchcraft is found blended with religion. Every early religion has the characteristic of blood sacrifice, particularly of children and the first-born. The Jews are only typical of many in this respect. In fact, it was so common a practice that many may contest the theory that it was in any material sense black magic, even though all blood sacrifice is sorcery.

In India all kinds of magic are found blended with the holy Vedic rites, and the Samaridham Brahmna is composed largely of sorcery and incantations. In early Egypt the worshipper could only approach his gods through the media of magic rites. In following early evidences of sorcery and incantations we must not overlook the Jewish Kabala, nor the various forms of phallic worship which were a feature of the very earliest religions. Phallic worship, however, was not so much connected with black magic until its revival in later times. It continued, nevertheless, to run, as a disguised and unacknowledged thread, through all beliefs, and is clearly interwoven with the various Serpent religions, wherever found. It also leaves its traces in the formation of the Cromlechs and Dolmins of the Celtic peoples.

A great Sicilian traveller of Julius Cæsar's day discovered a Chaldean tribe composed entirely of a sacred caste, which devoted the whole of its time to the culture of occult science, and was eternally occupied in discovering secrets of the future and the spirit world by means of astrology and every kind of magic. The same historian tells us that the Assyrians practised divination and auguries, and undoubtedly handed down their methods to the Romans, whose customs regarding sorcery and the consultation of oracles show evidences of this origin. We know that in Homeric times black magic was extensively used, and there are still traces of it among the Etruscans. It is recorded that Menelaus, detained in Egypt, sacrificed children so that he might divine the future by their entrails ; a practice which he acquired from Egyptian sorcerers. Julian the Apostate is well known to have practised the black art at the Temple of the Moon, built at Carra in Mesopotomia, and after his death in battle an unfortunate woman was found there, hanging by her hair with her liver torn out.

Of Babylonian magic there is comparatively little data ; only the records of possession by demons, and various forms of exorcism found in cuneiform, on tablets of Assyrian and Babylonian origin, together with little figures and amulets used for working magic, and as protection against sorcery. Among the North American Indians, the Aztecs, and other native dwellers of America, black magic flourished as far back as we can trace. Many of these records, however, are based on the discoveries of early missionaries and are correspondingly scant. None the less, although so widely separated from other races of the world until comparatively recent times, their myths and legends prove in word and carving and architecture that their main ideas and practices ran parallel with those of better known peoples and lands.

Sympathetic magic acted between persons and some material object—such as a wax figure, and in a different instance between a wound and the weapon that caused it. Such was all very simple and elementary, but there were and are far deadlier forms. The non-Aryan nations of Europe carried on a procedure which was practically the same as the modern savage's demonism, and their religions sank into pure sorcery. Some people do not agree with this theory; claiming that there is too big a gap between Druidism and the earliest mention of witchcraft. Yet Druidism, in a bastard form, continued to exist long after it was officially supposed to be extinct. British magic and witchcraft was its successor. Britain was a centre of Druidism even for continental Celts, who sent men over to become Druid priests. There was, too, a school of this order in France, or Gaul, and Julius Cæsar mentions that their training was arduous. This training was chiefly in astrology and magic. The Druids were Magi, priests and hierophants, and also medicine-men. They deviated to the left-hand path; to use their powers for personal ends, to become invisible, to cause enchanted sleep, and in preparing spells to produce lunacy, disease and death.

From the earliest days, the Deity worshipped in black magic was the source and creator of evil, the rival of goodness. Various forms were the Egyptian god Set, the Persian Ahriman, the Python of the Greeks, the Jewish Serpent, Satanas, Balial the Devil, and later Baphomet of the Templars, the Goat Deity of the witches Sabbath. In the ancient Kabala Satan's name was that of Jehovah reversed, and he was not actually a devil but the negation of light and truth. In the Roman Saturnalia we find one of the earliest forerunners of black magic festivals. In this ceremony slaves reversed places with their masters, and there was general feasting and abandoned behaviour. There followed, all over Europe, festivals of a semi-religious nature, in which those taking part adorned themselves with hideous masks and gave themselves up to wild dancing, licentiousness and sacrifices.

As we shall see, a time came when black magic rose like a hideous psychic wave, swamping Europe and permeating all daily life. So widespread became the belief in the spirit of evil that it may be truly said that the devil reigned supreme. Black magicians flourished everywhere, and the world was a nightmare place of terror. Whenever the rays of the sun began to fade, and the twilight hours of evening and dawn appeared, the legions of evil were abroad to work their destruction upon mankind. The simplest action was fraught with danger, and could only be accomplished with the aid of talismans and counter-spells, and people lived in constant dread of the unknown.

This state of affairs gave the evil intentioned limitless scope to trick and mock, to gratify base and licentious appetites, to indulge in lust of every description, and unbelievable cruelty and sadism. Black magic sowed and reaped its horrible harvest of evil persecution, obscenity, madness, torture and death. Until, in course of time, black magic became organised to work against established religions and societies, and was practised in dark and secret places with the object of overthrowing established powers.

CHAPTER II

THE ANCIENT MAGIC OF THE EAST

Deals with Oriental magic of all kinds, divinations, auguries, beliefs regarding witchcraft and black magic, and accounts of various practices including those of China and Japan, etc.

IN dealing with the history of black magic it is extremely difficult to unravel the evidences of the black art from merely magical practices of a beneficent or protective nature. On the other hand, nearly all magic tends in time to the left-hand path; as being a devious means of attaining desires unobtainable by ordinary methods.

A good example of left-handed magic may be seen in the use of love charms and spells. They appear on the surface harmless and romantic enough, but they only too frequently degenerate into use in cases where some legitimate barrier exists between the two people. They may often be resorted to by women desiring to entice the husband of another, or vice versa. In cases where no material or moral difficulty was to be overcome, the magic of nature was quite sufficient, as it is to-day. However, that is a digression. As we delve into the mysteries of the past we find a mass of evidence of magic in mythology, folk-lore, history and religion, and gradually from among these records we are able to distinguish black magic, but even then it is hard to say where ordinary magic ends and sorcery begins.

In ancient Babylon, Assyria and Chaldea, magic was a prerogative of the priest, and in very early times there was in Mesopotamia a sect of priests set apart for magical practices. Their work seems to have largely consisted in exorcising troublesome spirits, suppressing demons, and probably practising hypnotism, which was a very usual art among the Egyptians and adjacent peoples.

In Babylonia such priests were called Asipu, and were pre-eminently exorcists, and probably necromancers as well. There were also the Barû, who were Augurs divining the future by the entrails of birds and animals; the livers of sheep being a very favourite means.

There was evidently warfare between the priest-magicians and avowed wizards and sorcerers, and even in those times there existed a very stringent law against black magic. The means of testing whether or no a man was a sorcerer was the very favourite one, employed in all eras, of trial by water. This took the form of flinging the accused into a river, and, if he were able by any means to save himself, he was considered innocent and his accuser drowned forcibly in his place; if he sank, however, it proved that he was guilty. The method must have caused some excruciatingly anxious moments for both the parties concerned. In later times European witches were subjected to similar trials in village ponds.

Tablets cast in the days of ancient Babylon and Chaldea relate how black magicians and witches roamed the streets of cities, ready to seize on any evil to be performed. Exorcists made images of witches, and called upon the fire-gods to burn them. Indicating the eyes, tongue, hands, feet and reproductive organs of the witch, the exorcist prayed that sin itself might cast her into a hell of fire and water. So that the witch should not, in turn, direct her sorcery to him, he fastened upon her the counter-spell of the Haltapper plant and Sesame, to make her undo her work and force back her own words upon her.

These Babylonian and Chaldean tablets abound in magical matters, and date back at least to the seventh century B.C. They are largely concerned with exorcism, the common method of dealing with sorcery and evil beings, and the inconsistency of the fact that the counter-spells involved were in themselves forms of black magic does not seem to have been noticed by the Babylonians; unless they believed in working on the similar rates of vibration and casting out evil by evil—as unsatisfactory a method in occultism as it is materially.

In both Assyria and Babylon, disease was looked upon as the work of evil spirits or sorcerers. Yet though many potions and herbs of a curative nature must have been taken, they were supplied by a magician and not by anyone corresponding to our idea of a physician, although the tablets mention a distinct body of surgeons and give some accounts of their work. These men are much to be commended, as the punishment for causing injury or death during an operation was to have both hands cut off.

In still later times, when physicians of a kind had been evolved, they were also practitioners of magic, and were called Asû ; the exorcists still existing as a separate branch. In those days it was fairly common for these doctors-cum-magicians to be sent from one country to another at the instance of royalty as a mark of favour to illustrious neighbours who were sick. They came chiefly from Egypt and Babylonia, as these countries were then the most important seats of science and learning. There is a tale recorded of how one of the Rameses, being married to the daughter of a Hittite King, Khattushil, sent his physician to heal his sister-in-law in an illness. This man failed to do any good, and Pharaoh next despatched a holy image of the Egyptian Moon-God, Khona, in order to cure her. The god at length arrived and according to legend wrought mightily with the evil spirit, while the Hittite King stood without with his soldiers and feared greatly. Happily the god was victorious.

Astrology does not appear to have dominated Assyrian and Babylonian magic as much as has been popularly supposed ; not, for instance, to the extent that it influenced the Egyptian magic.

The Egyptians had a great interest in astronomy, and in a kind of astral mythology closely linked with their discoveries in that direction. They were also great believers in the occult significance of numbers. Seven was thought to have power both for good and evil, and we find this number occurring again and again in magic incantations and for use in exorcism.

Although there were in Egypt many male practitioners of sorcery, there seem to have been as many women engaged upon the black art. The tablets upon which the events of the day were recorded refer to enchantresses, and we can conclude that they were by no means restricted to ancient beldames. Black magicians themselves have left very little trace of their doings, and our knowledge of them is chiefly gained through the records of the priest-magicians and exorcists of the measures employed against them.

Three things were considered necessary in exorcism. First, the word of power, by which the magician called upon the aid of gods or spirits. Secondly, the name and description of the demon or person being worked against.

Thirdly, charms, amulets, the inevitable figure of wax, and sometimes hair or nail-parings taken from the object of the ceremony.

Many tablets are inscribed with long lists of known demons to be exorcised. As these entities must therefore have been exorcised and removed from their human habitation many times over, we can only suppose that casting a demon out of one body certainly did not prevent him seizing on another, until he and the professional exorcist must have become quite old acquaintances. A great deal of ritual and ceremony was observed, such as sprinkling the room and person of the subject with water and massaging the body with special herbal ointment. But a very great part was played by the patient himself, who had to throw himself upon the ground, kneel, recite incantations, and so forth.

Ea and Marduk appear as the chief gods of the exorcising priests. The sun, moon and stars entered largely into their religion, but with scarcely the same astrological significance that they had in other countries.

There is little direct evidence of black magic, although we know it was very extensively practised by both the Assyrians and Babylonians. We know of their sorceries almost entirely through tablets dealing with exorcism, and we are told the results of their activities but comparatively little of their methods. Magicians of both countries used clay or wax figures for "working upon" their objects, and one formula tells us to choose mud from the banks of two rivers and form a clay image with it, inscribing upon this image the names of the persons concerned. We next require seven stalks from seven date trees (note the occult significance of seven), and, having made a bow from horses' hair, the image must be set up and the stalks shot at it from the bow with the words: "Destroyed be so-and-so."

The Tamerisk was used in black magic rituals, and cut with great ceremony with a silver knife or a golden axe. Nearly all Eastern peoples believe that Tamerisk possesses magical properties; some Egyptians hold it sacred, and it was used for good and bad magic by them as well as by the Chaldeans, Assyrians and Babylonians.

A common dread was the evil eye, and the chief charm against it was in the form of a knotted cord woven by a "wise woman." Assyrian magicians were in the habit of tying knots, while repeating incantations. One inscription bears a charm containing the phrase (presumably about a witch) "her knot is loosed, her works are brought to naught." In quite recent times the Russian peasantry believed that a bewitched person must have no knots or fastenings in a garment worn for exorcism ; it must be all in one piece, so that the witch or evil spirit would have no place to hide.

The endless verses describing various spells that had been put upon people must have been the work of the lesser magicians, and as such it is quite understandable that they left no first-hand record behind them.

The ear-rings and bracelets, that form such a striking feature of nearly all Assyrian drawings and carvings of both men and women, were originally worn for protection as amulets, and were frequently inscribed with incantations.

They believed that newly shed blood was attractive to devils and elementals, and had a great horror of it accordingly. We can trace here one of the origins of the intense loathing of female blood evinced by Assyrians and Semites, which resulted in a taboo upon women during certain periods. The magic and beliefs of these peoples survived into later times and even penetrated into Europe, filtering down through the ages, partly by the instrumentality of the Romany peoples, and also through the Jews.

Divination and auguries, and the consulting of oracles, played a large part in all ancient magic, and in Egypt oracular dreams were sought in certain Temples. Devotees slept on the skins of sacrificed rams, and the priests interpreted the resulting dreams. If they were satisfied, they threw pieces of gold into the waters of a Holy Spring in the Temple precincts—one imagines it was very unlikely that anyone had the courage to deny the gods their offering. Religious dances, mutilations for sacrifice, and the magical impress of blood-stained hands as a protection against evil, are found among nearly every race, and the same beliefs and customs crop up time and again.

One of the commonest Assyrian forms of divination was by pouring oil on water, and calculating future events by the patterns it made. The building of temples and palaces was only undertaken after having consulted oracles, or omens, to discover a propitious time for their construction.

Another method was practised by the Barû, or Seer, by means of the liver of a sacrificial sheep. After the animal had been slaughtered with the usual rites, the liver was exposed and the future judged by its appearance and that of the accompanying glands. Thus a swollen gall bladder indicated an increase of power for a reigning king or individual. Unusual marks on the left of the liver were thought to indicate misfortune, those on the right foretold favourable events.

This form of consultation is called hepatoscopy. Many of the appeals to the oracle were on political affairs and those concerning warfare.

The gods were supposed to indicate the trend of the future in the liver, since the ancients supposed that organ to be the seat of life. An equally popular means of divination was the sun oracle, dedicated to Shamish the sun god, which Assyrian kings consulted before undertaking any enterprise, and especially on occasions of birth and marriage, etc.

The Chaldeans kept a close watch upon the heavens for any unusual manifestations among the planets, and comets or shooting stars were thought to be the omens of misfortune to royalty and nations. Even the radiance of the various stars and planets was carefully noted and deductions made from their appearance. The Chaldeans made such a fine art of their knowledge that to the Greeks their very name was synonymous with astrology.

In ancient India the practice of divination by horoscope was largely spread by the influence of Persian and Greek astrologers, but even earlier the power of the sun, moon and planets over man was recognised. The Indian diviner of omens regarded every event of nature, from the rising and setting of sun and moon to earthquakes, floods and tempests, as direct portents of the gods. The flight of birds and the movements of wild animals held a special meaning for him ; he not only presaged events from these things but interpreted dreams, every possible object encountered in life having a dream symbology unknown to the ignorant. Much Indian divination was performed through the fear of witchcraft, and anyone suspecting that a spell had been cast upon them frequently consulted an oracle to find the best means of dispelling the evil, or a means of avoiding it altogether. To the superstitious Indian of humble caste, every humdrum happening of existence had a portent; every bird he noticed upon a tree, every animal that crossed his path, held a particular significance and was either a good or evil omen. Omens were more or less casual affairs, coming man's way as though by accident; but oracles were deliberately consulted, either privately or professionally, by priests or seers.

The ancient Shinto documents give a clear idea of Japanese theories of magic and omens, and the consultation of oracles held as large a part in the magic ritual of Japan as in that of other nations. The Japanese, too, believed in oracular dreams. There is an old tale of the Emperor Suinin, who had a dumb son, and in a dream he was told that if he built a temple to a certain god, whose name was withheld, the child would gain his speech. On awakening the Emperor anxiously consulted an oracle, and discovered the god's name by this means. He triumphantly built the temple, and on its completion the boy received the use of his tongue.

Like the Indians, the Japanese consulted oracles and omens in connection with the simplest affairs, and the most trivial events wore the aspect of omens to him. Even his gods were only "superior beings," just a little more intelligent and powerful than man, who needed even to consult oracles and practise divination themselves. A very favourite method borrowed from the Chinese was that of consulting the formation of the carapace of a tortoise, while another was divination at the cross-roads under the auspices of Funado, the road god. In the latter case one had to cut a special stake of bamboo, and going to a cross-roads at dusk to fix it in the centre. The diviner then stood aside, and made his prognostications from the remarks of the passers-by. The idea of the staff was to represent the stick or wand used by Izangi on leaving Hades, pursued by evil gods. He placed his wand upright in the sand, and malevolent spirits were unable to pass it and overtake him.

The Japanese believed firmly in the protective qualities of rice against witchcraft, and for that reason sprinkled it upon the floors in houses of pregnant women. It was also used at cross-roads, since for centuries back the place where roads met was regarded as having a sinister influence.

Every nation had its methods of "trial by ordeal" for witchcraft and sorcery, and one very much in favour in old

Japan was by boiling water and mud. When a cauldron of this mixture was seething, the suspect was required to plunge his or her hand and arm in and stir it round ; if the hand remained unscalded, innocence was proved. Still another means was to place the hand in a bottle or basket containing poisonous snakes, and extricate it without being bitten.

We have already touched upon the importance of cross-roads in Japanese divination, and such spots were prominent in many kinds of Japanese sorcery. Witches were thought to work their spells at the cross-roads, which were also regarded as of sinister danger to travellers. In consequence phallic symbols were erected there, as a protection to way-farers and to ward off witchcraft. Phallic emblems nearly always stood for preservation and good fortune, the generative organs representing life and abundance. And often special festivals were held, with great ceremony, in places where several roads met.

Strangely enough Japanese ghosts and demons were usually thought to be female. They haunted wells, forests and dark places generally, seeking to terrify and seize upon the unwary. Their strangest feature was an absence of legs !

To both the Japanese and Chinese, spirits and the spiritual world were, and are, very real, and play a large part in the lives of the people. The reverence of the Chinese for the spirits of their ancestors is well known, but quite apart from them there were ghosts of demons and goblins who had to be guarded against.

One spirit is largely responsible for the unique structure of Chinese buildings and bridges, with their strange angles and turns. He is called Sha, and as he could only move in straight lines, architecture took twists and bends to confuse him, and thwart his malevolent influence. For the same reason earthenware lions were placed on the roofs of houses.

The fox and serpent were specially connected with witch-craft, but almost any animal was thought to become a malevolent spirit in its old age. A Japanese belief was that the souls of those about to depart this life went to the Temple to announce their approaching death, and then either rapped, or rang the " spirit " bells, as a sign to the priest.

Some demon beings, called Oni, were exceedingly dreaded. They were believed to be hideously ugly, and were possessed of immense strength. Another, called Tenga, obsessed men and caused frenzy and disease. Japanese witches and sorcerers were thought to have the power of assuming gigantic size, and of travelling long distances by merely taking a stride. Their feats have formed the basis of many legends and tales for children, but they were nevertheless taken seriously enough by the people of the times, who were incessantly preoccupied in finding means of exorcising them and preventing their spells from working.

The Persian of ancient times personified every imaginable evil or ill attribute as a devil, and pictured them living in foul surroundings, the companions of the wicked and ignorant ; which shows that the Avestan beliefs of elemental evil were not far from the truth. They believed in an arch-fiend called Ahriman, who lived surrounded by malevolent followers, one of the chief being Jāhi (the harlot) embodying the spirit of sexual lust and destructiveness. All their magic was steeped in astrology, and sorcery was worked under the influence of the planets, while the propitious times for counter-spells and exorcisms was discovered by the same.

Nowhere in the East had demons and sorcerers more influence than in Tibet. The lives of the inhabitants were passed in an atmosphere literally charged with magic, and sorcery had there one of its firmest strongholds. There was a special fiend, named Pe-Kar, who was the guardian of the monasteries of the "yellow-hats" sect. To him human sacrifices were offered up, and rites of black magic performed for the discovery of gold, and many other reasons. The propitiating of this demon, and the activities of the "yellow-hats," are not entirely things of the past ; but Pe-Kar has now to be more often content with offerings of the blood and brains of slaughtered animals offered in bowls made of human skulls. These sorcerers summoned the spirits with whom they worked, by blowing on horns made from human thigh bones and beating on skull drums and gongs.

An especially interesting part of the sorcerer's paraphernalia was the three-cornered dagger, with which he stabbed or drove off the demons that he dispelled from other people.

A strange feature of Eastern magic has always been the

mixture of sorcery and the worship of gods; often, it is true, with the idea more or less of "holding the candle to the devil." Thus, in Burma, when temples and pagodas were built to the honour of Budda, living men were walled in at the four corners, as a sacrifice to the powers of evil.

A method of consulting oracles, which dates back to the remotest periods but is still to be found among primitive peoples, was that of placing a skull close by the head while sleeping. During the night the skull was expected to talk, and predict forthcoming events. Sometimes rice and different varieties of food and fruit were offered to the skull first.

Indian magic was as much a matter of avoiding sorcery as invoking it, and a great deal of it was directed against human ghosts, who, on account of violent death or some similar reason, had become inimical to mankind. The Churel, or woman dying in child-birth, has been mentioned elsewhere.

Among all classes of Indians it was a terrible misfortune to die unmarried, and the spirit of such was greatly feared. In the Deccan, the ghost of a young bachelor is thought to waylay travellers and mislead them, to impersonate husbands who are absent, and to cause all manner of misfortune. This has led to many post-mortem rites of "marrying" both young men and girls who have met untimely deaths, in order to prevent their ghosts from haunting the district and becoming a demon. The K'Chins of Upper Burma used to celebrate the whole ceremony of marriage, in the case of the dead person having been betrothed to a man or girl, as if that person were still alive, in order to insure the security of the spirit.

There have been reports of cases where, in the event of a girl having died, a man was chosen to go through the marriage ceremony and even have intercourse with the body, before burial, so that she might not "walk."

All diseases were regarded as the work of demons, and there were hundreds of ways of attempting to dispel them. A very common one was to take an animal and, after various ceremonies, to sprinkle it with blood and let it loose as a scape-animal, carrying the disease away. Threads and nails were extensively used, too. In dealing with undesirable spirits, the exorcist sometimes bound threads about a house and fastened them to a near-by tree. This was for the spirit to hang itself on, while iron nails were also hammered into the ground at the four corners of the house.

Demonology had a powerful hold on the people, and still has in many districts. An example of this was Shamanism. By that sect the devils were thought to be cruel, revengeful, capricious, and only able to be appeased by blood sacrifices and devil-dancing. Thus, a sort of medium of low caste impersonated the demon Viravesin, as Buffalo king, and killed the sacrificial animal by tearing out its throat with his teeth. The Shamanist believed in the potency of blood, and consulted a sanguinary oracle as follows. Rice was placed before the sheep or ram to be killed, and the creature was then wounded and its blood sprinkled on the rice. If it ate the grains it was a favourable omen, but if it turned away it presaged disaster. In either case the poor creature was killed.

Evil spirits and demons played a large part in Indian black magic, too, and by their aid the sorcerer could either have power over others or retain the demon to protect him. Magicians claimed to sell demons, sealed in bottles or in hollow bamboo rods, to those desiring vengeance on other people. When a man died, it was commonly supposed in some parts of India that his soul had been stolen by someone else's devil. The only way to discover the guilty demon was by consulting an omen, having an augur to inspect the animal's or bird's entrails, or by rice grains. This done, the heir to the departed redeemed his relative's soul with gifts, and then secured it in a jar or pot for safety, making it offerings of food from time to time.

It is a platitude to speak of the unchanging East, but nothing exemplifies this attribute more than its magic customs and practices connected with sorcery. The witchcraft of Europe has become modified and altered, at least in some degree, by religious persecution and changing fashions and habits; but that of the East remains to-day exactly what it was hundreds and probably thousands of years ago, handed down from generation to generation—the oppressive legacy of fear.

CHAPTER III

EGYPTIAN RITES AND PRACTICES

Is concerned exclusively with black magic among the ancient Egyptians, and the methods they employed.

THE words mystery and magic are so interwoven with the atmosphere of Egypt that it is difficult to imagine a time when Egyptians were not past masters in the art, black and white. Records prove that by the IVth Dynasty magic was firmly established, and played a recognised part in the lives of the people, though its actual inception was as old, and possibly older, than the gods themselves.

Toth was regarded as a powerful magician, and from him was derived the fame of Hermes Trismegistus. Horus was credited with magical powers, while, according to at least one papyrus, Astarte was looked upon as being an evil and furious goddess lying in wait for man's destruction, particularly by sea.

Isis, the mother of Horus, was the supreme enchantress. In early Egypt itself she appears to have been a goddess of protection and power against evil, and was honoured as the mother and symbol of creation. In later times, though, in many lands her worship gradually became confused with sorcery, and she was regarded as the deity of witches and the genius of necromancers. In the Tarot cards the High Priestess was represented in the Egyptian pack by the figure of Isis, and this symbology is still noticeable in the modern European version, though not so clearly as it was in that of the Middle Ages. Thus, originally the enchantments and magic of Isis were beneficent, but these aspects became perverted to the darker side by certain groups of mystics and occultists, such as the Gnostics.

An early Egyptian invocation to Isis as the protectress ran like this: " O Isis, great enchantress, free me, release me from all evil red things, from the fever of the god, and the fever of the goddess. From death, and death from pain, and the pain comes over me as thou hast freed, as thou hast released thy son Horus, as I enter the fire, and go forth from the water." The exact meaning is somewhat obscure, but it may even have been the plea of one expecting to undergo the tests of fire and water. It is interesting to note the fear of "red things," and how this colour was so connected with evil that it even led to red-haired men being burnt alive.

The vision of the Egyptians was far from being merely a matter of mystic cultivation; they stood pre-eminent as masters of the arts and sciences of the day. They were marvellous metal workers, and from this purely practical knowledge they developed their skill in alchemy, whose very name is derived from a black powder evolved in the process of separating gold and silver from their native ore. This powder was described as "Kamt" or "Qemt," meaning dark or dusky. In later years the Coptic Christians transmitted the words to the Arabs, and other peoples, in the form of "Kheme." To the knowledge of metals and their chemistry the term "Khemia" was applied. To this the Arabs added the article "al," and thus the word became al-khemia or alchemy.

This knowledge, and the attempts involved to transmute metals, grew to have its mystic side, and the wonderful black powder became mysteriously identified with the body of Osiris in the Underworld. The whole came to be thought of as a source of life and power, and the Egyptian alchemists were regarded as magicians, just as others were in Europe in the Middle Ages.

The Egyptian people themselves do not appear to have made any very strong demarcation between black and white magic. Enchantments, exorcism, divination and all magic arts were so universally practised that sorcery crept in almost everywhere, and was in turn connected with the worship of the gods. However, when acts of a definitely harmful and evil nature were perpetrated by means of magic, they came within the jurisdiction of the law, and were heavily punished, usually by mutilation or death. A papyri of the IIIrd Dynasty records the case of two harem conspirators, "who made magical writings to lead astray, and work mischief, and made certain gods of wax, and medicine to weaken the limbs of man." Both were condemned to death.

The Egyptians had very definite ideas about possession by evil spirits and demons, and the work of an exorcist can have been no sinecure. They particularly believed in possession by the spirits of negro and Asiatic women, and thought that these ghosts came to claim their victims secretly by night, "arriving in darkness, gliding in with its nose backwards, and its face turned," though details of the exact methods employed by such beings are disappointingly vague.

One of the most dreaded sorceries was to deprive a man of his heart. An ancient record of a black magician casting a spell upon another, says: ". . . thou fallest upon the ground upon which thy loin-cloth is spread, and there thou gropest in quest of thy heart." There is a picture upon a tablet of Nefer-uber-f, a priest, guarding himself from the destroyer of hearts, who appears as a ferocious creature, something between a man and a baboon, holding in the right hand a long knife, and flourishing his tail, while the priest protectively clutches his heart in his left hand. There are many scenes depicted, also, of the priests and gods weighing the hearts of men.

In some respects magicians were regarded with rather less than the customary awe, in a country where magic was almost commonplace and their gifts were ascribed more to their own knowledge than to any supernatural source. The instructions accompanying magical inscriptions presupposed that the private individual could carry them out, and that the magician was not always essential to successful results. For the same reason, professional magic had to be more than ordinarily impressive and mysterious, and therefore "hike," or magic, gathered around it a wealth of ceremonies and elaborate detail. This was especially so when certain deficiencies and failures in results had to be covered up.

Magicians sought to impress the people not only with the powers of the gods and themselves, but by means of all the ideals of antiquity and established authority. Special rites were performed at nightfall by a lector of the fane in the fore court of the Temple of Coptus, for example, in the honour of Isis, and the eeriness of the scene, increased by the light of the moon shining upon the book (of Cheops ?) must have been immensely impressive. Egyptian sorcerers, and other practitioners of magic, rigorously tested their magical performances, and if they were successful the trap-

"In the mysteries of Isis, the neophyte had to undergo a rigorous probation."

pings and purely theatrical aspects of the rites tended to fall away, being unnecessary.

Human sacrifices of a definitely black magical order took place at the tomb of Osiris, while similar orgies with human victims were performed at Heliopolis. In the latter instance, however, King Amesis eventually substituted waxen images. The hands and sex organs were customarily cut off from those slain in battle, and were also sometimes converted to the uses of the black magician. Embalmers, preparing bodies for mummification, always preserved the hair that they had had to clip away in the course of their work. This hair was placed carefully wrapped up within the cavity of the abdomen, in company with certain organs, such as the heart and liver. For, if a sorcerer could procure the hair of a person, it was believed that he could attain almost limitless power over them, not only in this life but even within the tomb.

The Warren magical papyrus mentions a method of obtaining knowledge as to whether a certain person was alive or dead by means of the sorcery of numbers. Thus: make him (presumably the querent) reckon the quarter of the cup, let him fill this with water, add....the number 612....and let him subtract 353, which is Hermes. If pairs are found in the numbers, he (the person enquired of) lives; if not, death has come.

Hydromancy was extensively practised by the Egyptian priests and sorcerers, with a boy under puberty, a pregnant woman, or a black female slave, as the seer. The media was usually a bowl of clear water, but it was also sometimes a pool of ink, or even ink placed in the palm of the hand.

The Egyptian sorcerer is related to have been able to imbue wax figures of animals or reptiles with life, and in this form sent them out to destroy the intended victims. As an illustration of this, there is a story that the wife of an official at the Court of one of the Pharaohs fell in love with a soldier, and had an intrigue with him. She was in the habit of spending the day with the man, at one of her husband's houses near the Nile.

Now, the chief steward of this place thought it his duty to warn his master of what was occurring, and mentioned at the same time that the soldier went down to bathe in the river every evening. The husband, who was named Abā-aner, listened carefully, and proceeded to secretly fabricate a crocodile in wax, over which he said some magic words. This he gave to the chief steward, with instructions to cast it into the waters next time the soldier went down to bathe.

The same evening when the lover left the house, the steward followed him, and directly he entered the river threw the wax crocodile after him. Upon which, the simulacra instantly turned into a living crocodile, and carried the terrified man down into the depths.

Seven days passed and then Abā-aner came to the river bank, bringing Pharaoh with him. He called to the crocodile, which rose up, bringing its victim in its jaws, and laid him down at the feet of its master. Pharaoh remarked upon the reptile's repulsiveness and fierceness, but Abā-aner laughed and, stooping down, placed his hand beneath it. Instantly, then, the creature became nothing more than a small waxen image. Pharaoh was, of course, astounded, and Abā-aner explained the situation to him.

Finally, raising his hand aloft, Abā-aner threw the crocodile back in the water, saying: "Begone, and take that which is thine with thee." Once more the object became a living thing and, snapping up the unhappy soldier, disappeared with him in a swirl of blood-stained water. To complete the good day's work, Abā-aner with Pharaoh's permission set about burning his faithless wife to death. And as he watched her writhing in the flames, and heard her piercing shrieks, he contemplated his two-fold revenge with the utmost satisfaction.

The Egyptian sorcerers were also credited with the power to restore amputated limbs, and even to replace the heads of the slain without injury. They whispered their commands in the ears of the dead, so that they should carry out the magician's designs in the land of the spirits, and wove spells and enchantments that made a man's strength fall from him like a garment, and turned his blood to water.

The Book of the Dead—or *The Coming Forth by Day*—was an elaborate manual of instruction and guidance for the souls of the dead in the Underworld. It was full of magic, but not of sorcery. It was a common practice for whole chapters and leaves from this book to be entombed with mummies, so that the dead would know how to proceed. The work also contained instructions for embalmers, and many spells and incantations to prevent the mummy from decaying.

A great sorcerer and necromancer was the last native King of Egypt, Nectanebus, who lived about 358 B.C., and who was thought to rule and overcome his enemies by the exercise of his magic arts. Indeed, he became an almost legendary figure; credited with semi-divine powers, as one who had familiar intercourse with the gods themselves. He was an astrologer, also, and is supposed to have stood by the side of Olympias, scanning the heavens while she was giving birth to Alexander the Great. Nectanebus wished the child to be born at the exact moment when the planets were most propitious, and begged Olympias to withhold the birth until he perceived a certain radiance in the sky. At length the psychological moment arrived, and the sorcerer called upon her to deliver the child, saying when he was born that he would be a governor of the world.

During the reign of Rameses III there was a conspiracy to dethrone him. A sorcerer named Hui, taking a prominent part in the plot, worked black magic to bring destruction upon Rameses. Hui was the author of various works on the art of enchantment, and made a book that is related to have driven men mad. In the case of Rameses he sued wax effigies of the King and members of the Royal Household, but his sorceries proved of no avail and Hui met with the usual fate of workers of witchcraft who were discovered.

The Egyptians placed implicit faith in the power of words and names. To know the name of a spirit or demon was to have control of it, and so we find many of them are given secret names as well, which only the magician or adept could know. Thus, it was believed that no deity could withhold a favour from those who called upon them by name. Their magicians had numerous ways of divining the future, the most important being astrology, and horoscopes were cast for everyone and everything imaginable. They also made moving statues for the pronouncement of oracles, which answered some questions by gestures or an inclination of the head.

The most important of the oracular statues was that of Jupiter Ammon, situated in the great oasis. People travelled from every part of the kingdom to consult it, alike on weighty matters of State or on quite trivial affairs. It is, I believe, somewhat uncertain what form exactly the statue took; but if it was a copy of the earlier one at Thebes, it probably had a ram's head and was certainly clothed daily by the priests in magnificent garments and sandals, and ornamented with jewels.

Sorcerers, who wished to perpetuate a curse, or to guard a tomb, would have several slaves chosen and tortured to death. Before they lost their last spark of consciousness, the sorcerer would confront them, giving a hypnotic command that in the spirit life they should guard the spot in question and pursue any who desecrated it with misfortune and disaster, fastening upon them to haunt them to destruction. Curses were carried out in a like manner. It is probable that at the time of Tutenkhamon (his real name being Tutenkhaton, 1350 B.C.), when he was incarcerated in his famous tomb, Egyptian sorcerers set the souls of slaves to guard it by this method. And this may be said to account for the misfortune that overtook many of those concerned in the excavation under Lord Carnarvon and Mr. Harold Carter in 1932.

There are innumerable objects and treasures both in England and on the Continent that have been brought from Egypt, and which have proved to be disastrous to all who owned or came in contact with them. It is easy enough to pooh-pooh such things; but the fact remains that logical minded people, who were not in the least credulous or superstitious, have met with misfortune just as much as those who were possibly more impressionable.

The obelisk, erroneously called Cleopatra's Needle, now standing on the Embankment at Westminster, was brought to England only after great difficulty, loss of life and shipwreck. Coincidence might explain some of these occurrences, but when they happen with such regularity as to become almost a recognised sequence of events, then that theory is not entirely satisfactory.

The Egyptian Magi had long discovered the secret of perpetual fire, and many tombs which had not been entered by any human beings for an immense number of years still had their lamps steadily burning when at length men entered there again. Every true magician had power over the elements, but the power of commanding the appearance of fire or flame in a certain place, for an indefinite (and sometimes very lengthy) period, seems to have been limited in early times to the magicians of Persia, Babylonia, Chaldea and Egypt.

In the latter country, though native sorcerers abounded,

"The sorcerer would confront them, giving hypnotic command that in the spirit life they should guard the spot in question."

yet they were overrun with Chaldean astrologers, witches and fortune-tellers, who made a fine trade from the poorer people, though at the same time the Chaldean magical adepts were honoured and sought after by every country. Adepts can read the future in the heavens with ease, and their rites and formulas enable them to exert their powers in any place at all times. The Chaldeans, even more than the Egyptians, believed in and propitiated elemental spirits, who seemed to them monstrous beings of semi-human appearance, ruling the winds and waters. The demon (or elementary) of the South-West wind was particularly dreaded, as being the gini of fever and madness.

Among their lesser accomplishments the Egyptian sorcerers possessed the art of dividing water, so that it would stand aside and expose the beds of rivers, and enable things that had been lost to be discovered. This, of course, was not really sorcery at all, but white magic. If we are to believe Chapter XIV of Exodus, verse 21, Moses possessed the same power; in the capacity of a sort of medium of Jehovah. However, I do not think there is any record of an Egyptian adept parting the water on quite such a grand scale as the leader of the Israelites.

As the God of Darkness, and the Evil genius of the other deities, we should expect to find Set the particular guardian of the magicians and sorcerers. Yet, in point of fact, it is Isis who seems to have always been especially invoked for magic of all kinds both black and white.

In considering Egyptian (or any other) black magic as a whole, it is very necessary to discriminate between what is unintentional sorcery and that which is deliberate. Any rites which entailed living sacrifices, and offerings of blood, were definitely witchcraft in execution. Some of the Egyptian mysteries were certainly black magic, as far as their ritual was concerned; particularly those which were performed in honour of Osiris and Isis. On the other hand, there is no evidence that they were conducted with the express object of sorcery.

In the mysteries of Isis, the neophyte had to undergo a rigorous probation. This included baptism for purification, and an arduous system which reduced the body almost to death, during which the soul was believed to reach the confines of good and evil spirits alike. While it thus hovered in the realms of mystery the spirits of the blessed imparted their wisdom to it, and those of the dark regions on the other hand endeavoured to inculcate such madness and horror within the mind that the stricken soul would leave its body forever. The exact rites which took place have never been described, but it is certain that they included a living sacrifice, which was offered when the neophyte had successfully passed through his trials and become an initiate of Isis.

The mysteries of Osiris were celebrated as a passion play, the subject being the sufferings, passion, death and resurrection of Osiris. They took twenty-four hours to perform, from six in the evening until the same time on the following day, and we can imagine that their mode of presentation was exceedingly beautiful.

The Egyptians had a marvellous sense of the beauty of colour, and the beauty of line and formation, and in their dramatic productions these qualities were given the utmost expression. Linked with their love of clarity and precision, the result in the passion play of Osiris was a piece of exquisite pageantry that moved forward imperceptibly hour by hour towards the triumph of the god. Yet, so perfect was the formation, that each hour comprised in itself a separate poignant drama, through which the main theme ran as a golden thread, culminating in the victory of Osiris over Darkness and Death. Indeed, here we can see quite plainly the presence of the same verities that lie at the root of the Christian religion. Although expressed differently, they are none the less the same in inception hundreds of years before the advent of the Great Master.

CHAPTER IV

JEWISH NECROMANCY AND MAGIC

Gives a brief outline of the history of Jewish necromancy, and its symbols and practices—the use of the mystic Kabala.

IT is an accepted fact that the Jews acquired most of their knowledge of magic from the Egyptians, during their period of captivity, but they certainly had their own characteristic practices that can be clearly recognised.

Their first references to magic appear in the Pentateuch. The Jews themselves attributed the earliest knowledge of magic and sorcery to a book of magic that was supposed to have been given to Adam before he was cast out of Paradise, and which was called the Book of Rāziel. Another version relates that witchcraft and sorcery were imparted to woman by the fallen angels Uzza and Azail, and also the use of cosmetics, which were ranked as wicked enchantments.

Jewish magicians invoked spirits with fumigations, gifts and sacrifices. They agreed with all other sorcerers that the gift most acceptable to evil spirits was blood, of which the operator must also partake to gain the desired results and by so doing became the associate of demons. The baleful influence of blood being thus recognised, it is difficult to understand the free use of it for religious purposes by the Hebrews ; unless they believed that Jehovah was capable of taking pleasure in the same offerings as Satanic beings from the Pit of Hell. Certainly, the harsh imagination of the Jew seemed incapable of conceiving anything but a God of Wrath.

The typically Hebrew attitude to magic was that its accomplishments were at best only temporary ; that they could be undone by other magicians ; and that magic itself was independent of the operator, who relied upon *doing* something, some art, which would have certain results, and not upon his own innate power. Witchcraft and sorcery were looked upon with deep aversion, as being impure and lewd, and those who practised it depraved to the last degree.

This special attitude evidently arose from the fact that so many of the rites of sorcery were performed naked and involved gross sexual practices. Witches were classed with harlots, and their works pronounced an abomination. Nevertheless the Rabbis did not go out of their way to be unduly harsh towards sorcery, except in very flagrant instances, when the penalty was that of being stoned to death. As magic became identified with idolatry, the exercise of the laws against it became more stringent.

Even so, the Hebrews wavered between the two fires of orthodox religion on the one hand and the paganism of magic on the other; and with them, as with other nations, magical rites and beliefs were intermingled with religious ceremonies, and white magic was unofficially practised. To the strictly orthodox Jew, however, magic of any kind was abhorrent (apart from the rites of his faith); and the very word magician stood unequivocally for one who dealt with dark and evil forces. Young boys were used for the discerning of spirits in the following manner. A male child, seven years of age, having been chosen for the ceremony, his hand was anointed with olive oil and into it was placed a crystal. The magician then seated himself on a three-legged stool, drew the boy between his thighs with his back turned—so that the man's mouth could be close to the child's ear—and took his free hand. Then, facing the sun, the magician repeated in the child's ear: "Aungil, I adjure thee in the name of the Lord God, God of truth, God keeper of the hosts, Alpga, Aidu, that thou shalt send one from the three angels." The boy thereupon was supposed to see a figure like that of a man, and the charm was repeated twice more. After that, when the three figures had appeared, the boy said to them: "Your coming be in peace," and proceeded to ask the required questions. If there was no answer, the child was to address the figures as follows: "Kaspar, Kelei, Emar, the master and I adjure thee with a second adjunction, that thou wilt tell me that thing"—whatever the required knowledge might be.

Hundreds of years later we read of Benvenuto Cellini and a priest employing a small boy in their magic ritual. Cagliostro also used boys for divination.

The Jews believed that the true knowledge of magic was only available to the adepts, among whom they classed Solomon. Josephus mentions the works on magic that he left, the most famous of these being the *Clavicule* or *Key of Solomon*, which is believed to have been translated from the original Hebrew by the Archbishop of Arles. The manuscript fell into his hands following a massacre of the Jews of that City, and during the Middle Ages several copies were made.

The Hebrew magician used all the usual paraphernalia of magic-wands, candles, black-handled knives, circles, pentagrams and the like. In fact, mediæval sorcerers and necromancers were indebted to the Kabala for most of their evocations. The former also used bowls inscribed with the names of mighty spirits. These may have been employed as crystals ; the Talmud refers to " the Princes and rulers of all shining objects and crystals," which appears to indicate the spirits who manifested by such means.

Many famous children of Israel had the reputation of being magicians beside Moses. Manasseh was one who observed times and enchantments, practised witchcraft and dealt with familiar spirits and wizards. Balaam was numbered among them, and taught the daughters of Moab to be witches ; it is, therefore, somewhat surprising that he was so taken back by the eloquence of his ass, accustomed as he must have been to supernatural events.

The witch of Endor was, of course, the outstanding example of Jewish necromancy, and it is unnecessary to enter into details of how Saul consulted her in order to get in touch with the spirit of Samuel, the prophet, who had been the spiritual and political guide of Israel during his life-time.

A form of sorcery, called " Kischuph," was extensively practised. By its means witches and magicians changed themselves into animals, and were able to cover great distances in a short space of time. They caused disease, pain and death to attack men and women and animals. The women who indulged in it had " made a covenant unto the Schedim, and met them at certain times to dance with them, and visited the spirits that appear to them in the shape of goats." In many places such women were killed by stoning, when their activities were discovered.

Another and more " mental " kind of Kischuph was

exercised by means of evil sympathy and disturbing the harmony of the natural elements by exciting false "rapports" between various objects and substances.

There is a story of how three Rabbis overcame the work of a Kischuph sorcerer. In the course of a journey the Rabbis, named respectively Joshua, Eleazar and Gamalial, came across a young man who had been robbed of his manhood and made a eunuch by a certain witch. On learning the full circumstances, Rabbi Joshua undertook to make the witch undo her work and restore his functions.

The three Rabbis therefore held a ceremony, in the course of which Joshua sowed flax seed in a circle upon a table. Just as the little mango grows under the hand of Fakir or Yogi, so the flax grew and sprouted on the Rabbis' table. Suddenly a shadowy form appeared, which materialised into the witch herself. The Rabbis adjured her to endow the young man with his former virility, but she vehemently refused to do so. They then threatened to call the witch's name aloud, and thus divulge it to the world; whereupon she confessed that she had cast her victim's organs of generation into the sea.

Having obtained this knowledge, Joshua released the witch from the bondage of the spell and she vanished. Joshua and his companions next took the eunuch to the seashore, where the Rabbis commanded the waters to cast up his organs from their depths. This miracle occurred, and the man's strength and powers were restored to him, so that in due course he became the father of one named Judah.

Another tale relates how some witches enchanted the young pupils of a Rabbi, and having lured them to their house produced food and drink by magic means. During the revelry the young men seized the witches in their arms and lifted them from the ground. Immediately, the banquet and all the dazzling appointments vanished, which illustrates the Hebrew belief that a witch could only retain her power so long as her feet were on the ground.

The Jews feared the sorcery of binding or enclosing the soul or heart of a man, which was evidently a relic of Egyptian black magic, and many references are found regarding this form of witchcraft.

The favourite method of inviting intercourse with the dead was by spending the night in cemeteries, and there performing ceremonies of necromancy. A sorcerer of this description was referred to as "he who burns incense to the shādîn, and he who passes the night by the graves in order to enter into communication with unclean spirits." Their customs were condemned as leading to insanity. A "Kohen" and an Israelite possessed by demons once sought out a physician. The latter prescribed for the Israelite, because "he was of those who spent the night at graves," but declared that the Kohen should need no such assistance, being a man of spiritual learning.

Jewish magicians divined a man's prospects of life by his shadow, on the night of Hosh'anah Rabba, by the light of the moon. If a man "lost his shadow" on that particular occasion it was regarded as a sure indication that he would die within the year. Frequent reference is made to the misfortune of those whose shadow has departed from them. The jocular expression "may your shadow never grow less" has an ancient and far deeper significance than its casual good humour implies.

The performances of Moses and Aaron, before the departure of the children of Israel from Egyptian bondage, were just as much magic as that of Pharaoh's magicians, and from the spiritual standpoint of our day it is difficult to believe that God would really endow His Prophet with power to smite any of His creation. Moses and his brother, having sat at the feet of the Egyptian adepts, had become superior magicians themselves, who worked by control of the elementary forces of nature, and may or may not have attributed their powers to Jehovah in their own hearts.

Biblical magic has been glorified by the word "Miracle," but that does not change its intrinsic quality. Indeed, judging from the frequently cruel results it is not merely always "white" magic, though it was justified by the Israelites in the name of Jehovah.

The prophets Elijah and Elisha had power over the elements also, and the former was evidently regarded by Ahab as one who could make drought or cause rain to fall at will; Elijah having stated that "there shall not be dew or rain three years, but according to my word." They both recalled departing spirits to life when the body appeared already dead, and had they not been respectively the mouthpiece of the Hebrew deity, would certainly have been regarded as magicians. Elisha must rank with those who charmed wild animals and birds, as he was able to call upon two she-bears to come and eat up the children who had treated him irreverently—an unworthy proceeding on the part of Jehovah's representative.

It is evident that the Jewish necromancers, male and female, worked with familiar spirits, called Ôb. The witch of Endor conjured her own particular "familiar" with ceremonies and enchantments, and only then did she enquire whom Saul wished to have raised from the dead. It was also a custom of Hebrew necromancers to use mummified bodies for divinatory purposes, which was another practice learnt from the Egyptian sorcerers. Heads were consulted, too—first-born children being slain, and the heads cut off, salted and embalmed. Gold plates were prepared with invocations engraved around the edges, and the heads mounted upon them. Thereafter they were kept very carefully, and consulted upon special occasions.

Metal images and mummified bodies were kept as household gods, and fulfilled the part of oracles, to be questioned in times of difficulty, as were those made by Micah. Quite possibly, also, it was a mummy of this description that Michal placed in David's bed to impersonate him to Saul's messengers. The Ôb, or familiar spirit, was considered responsible for the manifestations of necromancy; Rabbinical magic manuscripts mention it as "that spirit which caused a man to speak from some part of his dead body." Necromancers were thought to have the power of restoring activity to the dead, either temporarily or permanently, and the Jewish belief in vampires was linked with the work of the necromancers.

Strangely enough the spirits of the departed, and of demons, were frequently invoked in the name of the angels, or sons of light—such as Michael, Gabriel, Uriel and Raphael. The name Elôhim appears, also, inscribed within the pentagrams which stood for the personified emanations from the Godhead, as well as that of Asmœdeas the guardian of demons. All these invocations were handed down to the European mediæval sorcerers, principally through the Kabala.

This Hebrew system of theosophy had a great deal more importance attached to it than possibly it deserved, but certainly mystics and magicians of early times owed a great deal of their knowledge to it. The first was devoted to a mixture of primitive science and mysticism, and the rest to a transcendental theory of the Cosmos, which was exceedingly comprehensive, including as it did the science of numbers and other occult matters. The origin of the work is obscure; many have credited Egypt with being its true source, while other accounts make it no older than the thirteenth century and the work of a succession of Rabbis. The oldest Kabalistic book was the Sefer YᵉSûā, which the Jews themselves attributed to Abraham, but the most important part, and the one most frequently referred to, was the Zôhar.

The whole of the Kabala was unknown to the majority of Jews in all lands, and the orthodox Hebrew looked upon it with suspicion and disfavour. Until well on in the Middle Ages it was kept as a closely guarded "secret doctrine" by the Rabbis, who handed it down from generation to generation among themselves.

The central feature of the Kabalistic teaching expounded the Deity as being the source of Ten Rays, or Sephiroth. Of these Rays the first was the desire to become manifest, and the nine others emanated one from another. The Tenth Sephiroth was the creator of man, or Adam. The Nine Rays corresponded to wisdom, intelligence, love; after which, came justice, beauty, fortitude and so on, in trinities.

It taught that the spirits animating the human race pre-exist in a spiritual world of Divine emanations, and that every soul has ten potencies. On this plane of existence, and before birth into the material world, the human spirit was composed of the two elements—male and female, dwelling as one, but at the time of their nativity they temporarily separated and dwelt in different bodies. The destiny of the soul was to obtain experience and purification and, this achieved, it returned to the source En Soph. If purification was not attained in one incarnation the Ego returned to earth three times, before being absorbed within the Divine Flame once more. The Kabala insisted upon the importance of numbers, and supplied many names of angels and spirits and systems of invocations. The Seraphim figured among the angels. These spirits were also referred to as "fiery serpents," and were identified as the guardians of tombs, who were synonymous with the "Threshold Dwellers" of other theologies.

Serpents, in one form or another, played a large part in

the idolatrous worship of the Jews ; as is shown by the brazen serpents made by the children of Israel during their sojourn in the wilderness, and those of terra-cotta and brass that have been found in Palestine, together with the preserved and mummified heads of snakes. A serpent was the "totem" of the house of David, but the fiery serpents of the Kabala were evil or awe-inspiring spirits who appeared in serpentine form.

The practical books of the Kabala were extensively occupied with talismanic and ceremonial magic, but like a great many other such works were confusingly interspersed with matter of no value and crude symbology, sometimes of the coarsest kind. That which is of value, and true, has to be weeded out from that which is merely ridiculous and worthless. The complete Kabala was probably the work of about twenty different authors, chiefly Rabbis, and was added to from time to time until as late as the end of the seventeeenth century.

With all its faults, the Kabala stands pre-eminent among works of transcendentalism and serious magic, and as previously mentioned formed the bed-rock of the learning of mediæval magicians. The so-called "secret Kabala" consisted of a doctrine and mystic instructions handed down among the Rabbis. It existed by word of mouth alone and was never written, and though many occultists have claimed acquaintance with it, it is almost impossible to know if any of its teaching exists to-day, except possibly among certain Rabbis.

Divination was practised by the Jews on almost identical lines with that used by the Egyptians. The Jews' most noted oracle, however, was not connected with unorthodox magic, but was that of the Urim and Thummim within the Tabernacle.

This mysterious source was consulted by the Jewish priests on matters referring to the judgment of accused persons, whether they were guilty or innocent, and on religious and political affairs. Only one wearing the breast-plate of the judgment might consult it to obtain an answer from Jehovah. According to the 28th chapter of Exodus, 30th verse, the Urim and Thummim were actually placed within the breast-plate of judgment and worn over Aaron's heart.

Some writers have attached a magical significance to

the Jewish custom of circumcision, and others have tried to identify ceremonial sucking of the blood from the wound with rites of sorcery. It is, however, probable that the custom of the relatives actually partaking of the circumcised flesh, existent among certain Jews, may have been used for evil purposes. Probably the Jews, as well as other peoples, originally regarded and intended circumcision as an act of sacrifice to invoke fertility; in which form it was practised for centuries before becoming a custom attaching to infancy. In the very earliest times circumcision was performed on attaining manhood, or at marriage. While, later, the age was reduced to puberty, about the thirteenth year, and finally to the eighth day after birth.

An important Jewish sorcerer was Simon Magus, who is mentioned in the New Testament and who was supposed to have bewitched the people of Samaria into thinking he possessed Divine attributes. He seems to have had a thirst for power over his fellows, and approached the disciples of Jesus with a view to joining them. As, however, the disciples repulsed him, he began to imitate their works and miracles and even permitted himself to be worshipped. Simon Magus declared that he was a manifestation of God, and claimed a Divine origin for his Greek medium Helen. He imitated Christianity in the reverse sense, affirming the eternal reign of evil. Travelling to Rome, he was called before Nero, who eventually made him a Court magician.

There is a story that Nero imagined St. Peter to be a sorcerer also, and thought it would be amusing to pit Simon and Peter against one another. When, accordingly, Nero called them together, they both displayed various powers and Simon flew gracefully out of the window. St. Peter thereupon prayed fervently, and the magician fell and broke his legs, so that the saint triumphed.

The Jews had many methods of purification and dispelling evil. The best known was that of the "scapegoat," which became incorporated in the orthodox religious rites, although the underlying belief was a purely magical one.

At the appointed time the High Priest would take two goats as a sacrifice for sin, and at the same time make burnt offerings of a ram and a bullock. The goats were placed at the entrance of the Temple and the High Priest cast lots. One goat was to be for Jahveh (Jehovah) and the other for a scapegoat, which was allotted to the demon, Azazel. The goat allotted to Jahveh was sacrificed with the other animals, but the High Priest placed his hands on the head of the scapegoat, and confessed over it all the sins of the children of Israel, which were then considered to have been transmitted to the beast. A man, after that, was chosen to lead the unfortunate animal away into the wilderness, where he abandoned it to the demon to whom it had been given over. When the man who had thus loosed the scape-goat returned, both he and the High Priest went through a ceremony of purification.

It is interesting to note that the Kabala upholds the theory of metempsychosis, and admits the reincarnation of souls at least three times on earth ; a doctrine not accepted by orthodox Jews. Nevertheless, reincarnation has probably played a very large part in maintaining the consolidation of this wonderful people, who through all vicissitudes have maintained their racial characteristics within the very heart of nearly every nation upon the earth. So that it is not unreasonable to suppose that their spirits have returned time and again to animate Jewish bodies, thus fortifying and strengthening both the people's mental attributes and customs.

CHAPTER V

MAGIC IN GREECE AND ROME

An account of black magic among the Greeks and Romans, with references to famous characters and legends of the times.

GREEK mythology abounds with tales of enchantment and magic, and it would be wearisome to recount here legends with which most people are familiar, and many of which are attributable to Homer.

About the fourth century B.C., Osthanes, who was thought to have recorded all the magic secrets of his time, is related to have initiated Democritus, the Greek alchemist, into his own arts, and the latter is said to have been the author of the first book on medical magic.

The Greeks regarded magic powers as a gift that was inborn, or as a special privilege of the gods. To them, such things were connected with any abnormality, such as a hunchback, an hypnotic eye, or being born with a caul, which latter condition was supposed to confer the gift of prophecy. Most of the troubles and ills of mankind were due to evil spirits of the dead, wandering over the earth, according to their beliefs.

Hecate was especially the goddess of magic, and in her honour many ceremonies were performed. The white magician practised extreme chastity, and while preparing for his rites rigorously fasted, taking frequent baths and anointing his body with especially prepared oils.

For the actual ceremony the white magician wore a flowing white robe, without knot or fastening and adorned with purple streamers, and it was essential that he should have complete faith in his own powers. The time chosen does not seem to have been of great importance; astrological calculations not entering into the proceedings until a later date. However, certain hours were reserved for the performance of the rites of particular dieties, those of the magic Hecate being celebrated at sunrise or sunset.

The favourite places for performing sorcery and magic were graveyards and cross-roads, and the participants employed the usual wand, lamps, symbolical keys, portions of the human body, bones and the like. The Greeks also used an instrument called the rhombus, or witches' wheel. As the wheel spun round, it was thought that influence was gained over certain people or circumstances.

Greek sorcerers cast spells from a distance ; chiefly by means of wax figures, which were often made hollow, so that written incantations could be placed within them. Images of Hecate were used for the same purpose, made from the powdered bodies of lizards and roots of rue ; also, the bodies of birds with sprigs of myrtle and rue, with the name of the object of the sorcery written on the bird's body.

The Greeks had a magical alphabet, to be written in sacred ink and with endless incantations, which they considered gained power by constant repetition. They believed in the magic of numbers, especially odd ones, and made feasts and libations to the gods and demons. In the latter case the remains were disposed of at cross-roads.

If a demon were thought to have taken possession of a person, the sufferer was held down while the exorcist called the name of the Evil Spirit in a loud voice three times, and fumigated the nostrils of the sufferer with bitumen and sulphur.

Sorcery was especially resorted to in order to incite love. A famous love charm was the ceremony known as " Drawing down the Moon," in the process of which Hecate was invoked, and an image of clay imbued with a spirit which was bidden to go forth and fetch the desired man or woman.

Lovers made figures of dogs in wax, upon the sides of which words of power were written. The dog was fixed to a magic tablet, and placed over a tripod. The words written on the animal were next repeated impressively, and if the dog began to bark, it was a sign that the lover would gain his objective ; if, on the contrary, the image snarled and snapped, the supplicant's suit would fail.

Another powerful love sorcery was to make two figures of wax or clay—that of Ares, and another of a woman. The male figure was to stand upright, pointing a sword at the throat of a woman, who knelt with her hands tied behind her back. On the limbs of the woman were to be written the names of demons, and thirteen bronze needles stuck into the image. The lover meanwhile recited : " I pierce her heart " (or whatever part of the body was being stuck) " that she may think of me." Magic words were then inscribed upon a metal plate, and tied to the wax figures, together with a string knotted three hundred and sixty-five times. After which both figures were buried in the grave of a person who had died young, or who had met a violent death; the accompanying rites concluding with invocations to the demons and infernal gods.

Belief in werewolves and vampires was very strong in Greece from the earliest times, and has survived to the present day.

There is an account of how Apollonius of Tyana defeated a female vampire or "lamia," which in the guise of a beautiful woman had enticed one of his pupils named Menippus with the enchantments of love. The Philosopher-magician warned Menippus carefully to discover the origin of his beloved, but the young man replied that everything was prepared for the wedding on the morrow. Apollonius, therefore, attended the nuptial feast, and found displayed a luxury which could never have been provided by the humble Menippus. Accordingly the master rebuked the bride, declaring all the lavish appointments to be a magic illusion. At first the bride braved him out, but gradually under the power of the other's words she gave way, the attendants vanished and the riches disappeared. Before she also departed the Philosopher forced her to confess that she was a vampire, who had been nourishing Menippus with luxury, in order eventually to tear him to pieces and eat his living flesh.

This special kind of female ghoul, or lamia, was thought to roam about enticing men in the shape of beautiful courtesans, only to turn into the most hideous shapes and rend them to pieces when once the unhappy men were securely in their clutches.

Another story concerns the sorcerer Polycrites. It relates his marriage with a woman, and how, after only four days of matrimony, he died. In due course his widow bore a child, which was an hermaphrodite, and this abnormality was looked upon by the people as being a terrible ill omen, portending war between the Ætolians and Locri. In consequence, it was decided to burn the unfortunate widow and the monstrous child. Everything was prepared, and they were about to set light to the pyre, when Polycrites himself appeared from the grave—a dreadful sight, with mould and blood adhering to his shroud. In a terrible voice he bade the crowd desist from burning his wife and child, but they took no heed of him and proceeded with their preparations. Thereupon the living corpse seized on its own child and, tearing it to pieces, ravenously ate the body until nothing but the head remained, after which it disappeared in the direction whence it came. In the midst of the subsequent uproar (for none had dared disturb the ghoul), the leaders decided hastily to send an emissary to the Delphic oracle to enquire the reason for this disturbing event. They were checked, however, by a Voice emanating from the still bleeding head of the child on the ground. This Voice foretold many misfortunes and catastrophes in store for the Ætolians. The head was eventually placed on a pillar in the market place, and caused great consternation some days later by suddenly opening its eyes, which shone with baleful gleams, and announcing in a hoarse voice that the Ætolian armies had been cut to pieces in a battle with the Acarnanians. And this prophecy proved to be true.

There was a general belief in Corinth that the children of Media became vampires after their death, and were in the habit of prowling at night-time for the purpose of destroying infants. The Corinthians consulted an oracle to learn what they could do to stop these depredations, and were told to make a yearly sacrifice before the statue of a hideous woman in the form of a lamia, which was to be erected over the tomb of Media's children.

In the early spring, towards the end of February or the beginning of March, the Greeks held a three-day festival in honour of the spirits of the dead, called the Anthesteria. It was somewhat analogous to the " All Saints " celebration of later times ; the Greeks believing that on those days the souls of the departed returned from Hades and went " to and fro in the city." The new birth of nature, blossoming forth in all her beauty—and how beautiful she can be in Greece—typified the resurrection of the spirit from the bondage of Earth ; it was, in fact, an early prototype of Easter, before the birth even of the Nazarene.

At this feast honour was paid to Dionysius, and garlands of flowers decorated homes, where abundant food and wine was sent out to welcome the return of the dead. Good and happy spirits were thought to come first, but in their train followed those who were miserable and evil, and these last were accompanied by the very demons themselves. The Athenians also tied knotted ropes around their temples and sacred places, to keep evil spirits out at these times, while sprigs of the bush thorn (or Christ thorn) were placed in windows to keep vampires and witches away. Happy spirits were thought to return serenely whence they came, after this brief visit to the scenes and people they loved on earth, but the evil ones had a tendency to linger behind, and had to be driven away with the words: "Out of the house with you, out of doors, ye ghosts! The Anthesteria is over and done."

Strangely enough, the Greeks thought that the spirits of their heroes returned to be enriched by the blood of the living, as well as did the dreaded vampires. It was, therefore, possibly this idea which gave rise to the human sacrifices, which they made from time to time, believing that the blood of the victim contained magical properties, and that ghosts who tasted it received enchanted life.

The most famous of the forms of divination practised by the Greeks was that of the Delphic Oracle, which was held in a temple built over a volcanic chasm, on the southern slopes of Mount Parnassus. The wild and impressive scenery surrounding the temple was itself enough to imbue the minds of consultants with awe, as they wended their way to the Oracle. Soldiers, statesmen, philosophers, and men of every imaginable status in Greece, went there for advice and prophecies.

The Oracle spoke through the mouth of a priestess, called the Pythia after the serpent Pytho whom Apollo slew. She was seated upon a tripod, placed over the gaseous vapours arising from the chasm, and as the fumes encircled her the priestess became stimulated into a state, half trance, half frenzy. Foam covered her lips, as with glazed and staring eyes she uttered disjointed phrases, which were translated into clearer meaning by the attendant priests. Meanwhile the querent stood before the Altar, crowned with laurel, while powdered laurel leaves were burnt as incense. No woman might consult the Delphic Oracle.

Also famous was the Oracle of Trophonius; but there the consultant passed the night in the temple and experienced prophetic dreams, or at least dreams whose symbology was interpreted by the priests next morning. These dreams were frequently of a disturbing, not to say terrifying nature, and were probably considerably assisted by the fumigations and incense used.

Reference has already been made to the sorcery known as "Drawing down the Moon"; which was one of the major sorceries of Greece, and is even secretly practised to-day. The preliminaries included burning vervain and frankincense, followed by a solemn chant whose cadences were so potent that they were believed capable of calling down the moon or "making the cold-blooded snake burst in the field." An image of the beloved was bound round three times with fillets of three colours, while the words "Thus I bind the fillets of Venus" were recited, and the figure was then carried round an altar. Another wax image and one of clay were placed in the same fire, and as the figure of clay hardened so did the heart that was sought, or as the wax softened so was the heart of the beloved made tender. The goddess Hecate was invoked to possess the first image, and to go forth to entice the desired woman, and a sacred cake was broken over it, and laurels burnt before it.

Circe was also worshipped as a dark goddess of wrath and destruction, many sorceries being performed in her name and horrible sacrifices made in her honour.

The Harpies were feared, and propitiated as furious female demons of death. The earliest conception of them appears to have been a more or less symbolical one, identified with the pestilential winds of the sirocco that brought fevers and disease in their wake. However, the Harpies gradually became personified, and found a place among the malevolent gods and demons of Greece.

Death magic was a common form of sorcery, and in its pursuance tablets inscribed with the names of enemies and victims were buried in tombs, after being pierced with nails. Images, again, were made; having their limbs twisted and their bodies hammered to cause tortures and disease.

Witchcraft and black magic do not seem in Ancient Greece to have had many material penalties for a very lengthy period. But we read of the witch Theoris being burnt by an outraged populace, and eventually various other punishments for sorcery are mentioned.

The famous Elusinion mysteries contained elements that strongly linked them with sorcery, and also intermingled Greek and Roman ceremonies. People of the latter nationality were eligible to take part in them, but no other foreigners were allowed to participate. Both Greek and Roman priests made offerings and sacrifices of flesh and blood, often human, before rude altars erected in open spaces or dark woods. A trench was dug around the sacrificial stone into which the blood of the victims overflowed, and there the spirits were believed to come and feed upon it.

The Roman imagination was a remarkably sanguinary one. Ceremonies involving blood were used in the worship of the gods and at public and private feasts and festivals. For instance, after the chariot races in the Field of Mars, a sacrifice was made of the right-hand horse of the victorious team, and the tail of the animal dripping with blood was carried to the Altar of the Regia. The blood was subsequently stored in the Temple of Vesta till the following spring, when it was used at the festival of Parilia, where the citizens of Rome believed that they were purified by the lustral bonfire and magical rites of blood sprinkling. This was known as the sacrifice of the October Horse.

Most Roman magic had a Greek origin, and no mention of its official recognition is found before the "Twelve Tables," in which it was forbidden to change crops from one field to another by magic. Presumably enterprising farmers attempted to annex neighbours' property in this way.

The Etruscans and Sabines were especially considered to be possessed of magic powers; probably a large number of them were psychic and mediumistic, and thereby gained a reputation for power over the elements and were sought after as necromancers.

The Romans dreaded the "Evil Eye" even more than most peoples, and guarded against it by modelled amulets of the phallus that were worn alike by every one. Like the Greeks they celebrated the return of the spirits of the departed on certain days of the year, but their festivals wore a darker aspect and lacked the joyous and welcoming characteristics of the Anthesteria. Three times annually the Romans set apart days for the return of their dead, on which no work had to be done, no battles fought and no marriages took place. On those occasions the stone covering the entrance to the Underworld was ceremoniously removed, and the spirits who issued forth were placated with offerings. From the nature of the ceremony evidently only those of malevolence or gloom were expected. A depressing atmosphere reigned at those times, and the Romans turned with relief to their ordinary days and festivals; with the possible exception of witches and sorcerers, for whom passed exceptional opportunities of getting in touch with evil and earth-bound spirits.

There is a tale, probably familiar to many, of how Candidia, having fallen in love with the handsome and youthful Varus, decided to arouse his passion and obtain his love by sorcery. At dead of night, therefore, she repaired to a graveyard with three assistants, and, standing in the fitful moonlight with venomous snakes entwining her hair, she gave them orders to tear the young fig trees and cypresses from their roots among the graves. With wild incantations a fire was made of the wood, and to it was added herbs gathered in Thessaly, toads' eggs sprinkled with blood, the feathers of screech owls and bones torn from the jaws of a hungry dog. Perfumes of Colchis were then cast upon the blaze, so that the mounting flames might gleam blood-red upon the gloomy scene. Drops of water were next sprinkled on the ground by one assistant, while another performed the lengthy rite of "Calling down the Moon"; which we can only presume was successful in its object of drawing Varus to the scene, as the ceremony concluded by the third assistant digging a pit and burying the unfortunate lover naked, up to his chin. As Candidia certainly had him at a disadvantage in that position, we are left to suppose that she then dictated her own terms.

Roman sorcerers dug pits by night, into which they poured the blood of slaughtered animals and sometimes human beings. Holding aloft a lighted torch, they cried loudly upon demons, avengers and furies to come and partake of the ghoulish feast. They were invoked in the names of Hecate and Prosperine, and were thus enticed to do the magicians' bidding.

Human sacrifices for sorcery were by no means rare. In the time of Cicero and Horace boys were sacrificed for the purpose of black magic, and everywhere blood was thought to possess a magic virtue. At certain ceremonies the statue of Jupiter was smeared with blood, the officiating priests making incisions in their veins and cutting themselves with knives.

MAGIC IN GREECE AND ROME

The Romans loved to foresee the future. Every imaginable form of augury and divination was practised among them, and both Chaldeans and Egyptians were popular as astrologers, casters of horoscopes and interpreters of dreams. Old witches in the cities and country-side throve upon the sale of death spells and love philtres. They also made a trade of abortificants, and frequently practised the whiles of the procuress. Evil and depraved, they worked these spells among the dregs of the populace, until the time came when the Roman law took a very firm hand with witchcraft, and severe punishments were meted out, not only to those who practised it but to those who consulted the sorcerers. Love philtres were deemed poison, and the selling and buying of them became a criminal offence. Chaldean astrologers were banished from Rome in 139 B.C.

One has a dreadful picture conjured up of hag-like witches roaming the cemeteries by night, in search of poisonous herbs and bones for their nauseating mixtures. They rifled unprotected graves of their poor human relics, and by the light of the moon made dreadful fires, the while calling upon serpents and the hounds of Hell to come to their horrible banquet. Tearing a black lamb to pieces with their teeth, they offered dripping portions to the infernal creatures, which glided and prowled around. While they melted waxen images of their victims over the fire, the moon is reputed to have turned to blood, and as the images liquefied, the lives they represented expired in torture.

Belief in the vampires was equally strong among the Romans as the Greeks, and they were so similar in the general characteristics that it would be wearisome to repeat examples. Witches were thought frequently to turn into vampires after death, and in some instances to act as ghouls in the form of bats and reptiles during their earth life.

An outbreak of the birth of monsters, half-animal and half-human, following the reign of Nero, was believed to foreshadow disaster and to be the result of unions between vampires and women. Nero and his mother Agrippina both had the reputation of resorting to sorcery.

Sextus, the decadent son of Pompey, consulted the terrible sorceress Erichto, in order to learn the secrets of the future by necromancy.

On the occasion of Sextus' visit, the witch, having magically made the night pitch dark and caused the moon to hide its face, led her consultant with some of his friends to a battlefield, where she groped among the slain for a corpse that would serve her purpose. At length she found one with lungs and larynx intact, and together they bore it away to a gloomy cavern dedicated to the infernal gods.

The body was placed upon the ground, a ghastly sight with gaping wounds and limbs caked with coagulated blood, while Erichto wreathed her head with vipers and proceeded to make a terrible brew with poisonous herbs.

They next infused new blood into the corpse, and prepared it for the return of the spirit. This being done, the witch invoked the denizens of Hell, calling upon them with a loud unearthly voice and reminding them that she always came to them replenished with human blood, and had offered them many a sacrifice of unborn babes, torn from the mother's womb.

Before the startled gaze of Sextus and his friends Erichto then demanded of her familiars the spirit of the soldier which was still close to earth, and suddenly it appeared standing above the body. But the poor ghost shrank from returning to its mangled earthly form, and Erichto only persuaded it to do so by the promise that she would free it for ever from the powers of magicians and that it should never again be recalled to earth.

Painfully the soldier's spirit retook possession of its body, and stood erect to answer the questions put to it by the sorceress. Still bearing the imprint of death, the ghost foretold the coming fortunes of Pompey and his armies through its old form's cracked and purple lips.

The work at length over, the sorceress made a funeral pyre, upon which the corpse lay down, and she then repeated a spell releasing it from earth and the enchantments of magicians for ever. After which the pyre was ignited and, as the flames mounted and destroyed the remains, the whole ceremony was at an end.

Roman magicians used to bind departing spirits with spells upon their death-beds—a sorcery possibly learnt from the Egyptians ; and they visited the dying, to whisper to them commands that were to be carried out in the infernal regions. If a particularly revengeful and malevolent spirit was required, they did not hesitate to commit murder themselves, so that such a being might be at hand, previously bound to them by incantations and enchantments.

Nevertheless, when all is said and done, Greek and Roman sorcery leave an impression of grandeur on the mind. Blood-stained and hideous that impression may be, yet about the whole there is something of Olympian proportions and a certain dark magnificence.

CHAPTER VI

THE DARK AGES, MEDIÆVAL SORCERY AND BLACK MAGIC

Shows how a Satanic wave flooded the whole of Europe during the Dark Ages. Famous practitioners of the black art and their methods. Brief account of the punishments meted out to witches and sorcerers of the Middle Ages.

MAGIC held a potent influence upon the imagination and lives of all peoples from the earliest times, but in the Dark Ages it assumed gigantic proportions and the practice of Satanism became rife in every country. During this era the minds of men as a whole appear to have become clouded and debased, so that all cruelty and wickedness held an incredible sway, life was of no account, torture a joy to inflict, power was to the strong and the rich, and lust and violence went unchecked. No man could look with certainty for charity and humanity from his fellows, and a woman still less.

The few people born with a finer intelligence and sensitiveness, and blessed with a love of art, beauty and learning generally, found refuge from the coarse world in the religious orders of the day. Thus, the best brains and finest characters remained sterile, and the hapless children of the period were bred from ruthless cruelty, gross stupidity and brute force. It is a wonder, indeed, that the nations of the earth gradually struggled out of the mental and moral morass, and helps to prove that heredity, although an important factor, does not claim the last word. History shows that even in the convents and monasteries of that earlier day life was far from pure. Many dignitaries of the Church were lustful and luxury loving men, greedy of temporal power, and many an abbess was a very unworthy follower of the Virgin Mary. Nevertheless, the Church garnered in her religious houses the learning, art and wisdom of the Dark Ages, and conserved them to be handed down to more enlightened times.

It is open to question whether mediæval brutality and treachery were the direct results of the drawing down to earth of the lowest elements of the spirit planes, through sorcery and black magic, or whether the gross minds and crude life of the people provided a good soil for the seeds of Demonism and Evil.

In dealing with this period, the influence of the Crusades cannot be ignored, because they had a profound effect upon the religious outlook and psychology of the times.

In one aspect they were probably the salvation of all that was best and ennobling among the European nations, calling forth the spirit of chivalry and idealism. Men who otherwise might have scorned religion, welcomed her when she came to them sword in hand. The simple-minded people were stirred by the idea of their Lord's shrine in the hands of the infidel, and they flocked to the banner of His Church. In the midst of political intrigue, jealousy, greed, ambition and brutality, the underlying idealism remained unscathed and exerted a leavening influence through the spiritual darkness.

THE DARK AGES, MEDIÆVAL SORCERY AND BLACK MAGIC

Side by side with evil and sorcery, existed a penitential spirit, which was probably more a matter of "fleeing the wrath to come" than true repentance, for no one wished to ultimately go to Hell, however friendly they may have been with the Devil in this life. This is exemplified in the pilgrimages made to the Holy Land, which led eventually to the wars known as the Crusades. The same desire to run with the hare and hunt with the hounds can be seen in many of the pacts with the Devil, participants frequently making conditions of allegiance for a certain period only, thinking to outwit his Satanic majesty when they had secured sufficient of the world's goods.

Another effect of the Crusades was the mingling of Eastern and Western ideas and beliefs ; men who had been prisoners of the Saracens in particular, bringing back theories and practices of Oriental magic, upon which much of the current witchcraft came to be based. The Devil was already accepted as a personified reality, but the Infidels believed even more strongly, if anything, in the opposing forces of Darkness and Light, and their faith in demons very subtly strengthened the Satanic beliefs of their opponents also. The Knights Templars, especially, are reputed to have had a great deal to do with the Saracens, and to have become imbued with their faiths ; the very name of their supposed diety, Baphomet, being a corruption of that of Mohammed.

The Goat Baphomet of the Knights Templars.

The Crusades led, also, to the foundation of the various orders of Military Monks; with the possible exception of that of St. John of Jerusalem, which probably existed earlier in connection with the Hospital of that name, for the protection and welfare of pilgrims. Thus, the very attack upon Christianity was probably the means of preserving its existence through a long period of darkness and chaos.

At home, the Jews were taking advantage of the poverty caused by the wars, and extorting heavy usury from those who resorted to them for funds, and who were forced to sell their lands in order to finance the armies that travelled to the Holy Land. In consequence, everywhere Jews who were not too powerful were seriously persecuted and forced back upon themselves, which resulted in endless antagonism and enmity between them and the Gentiles of the countries they inhabited. They were accused of sorcery, witchcraft, unheard-of cruelties to children and others who fell into their hands, and were believed to practise black magic with the bodies of Christians.

Such, then, were the conditions under which sorcery obtained the greatest sway that it ever possessed over European peoples. It was the day of fierce emotions, intense hatreds and biased judgments. Warfare, famine and disease were men's constant companions, and Death awaited upon every hand.

In such an atmosphere men's minds were intensely susceptible to the lower astral impulses, and found expression in their faith in the activities of the Devil and his hosts of demons, and in the readiness with which they either gave themselves up to Satanic practices or else fortified themselves against them with exorcisms and counter-spells. Hundreds of men and women indulged in sorcery. They exercised their mediumistic gifts for evil, and were swept into an incredible vortex of bestial deeds and cruelty in their pursuit of the black art. They dedicated their children to the Devil, and from an early age inaugurated them into the abominable ceremonies of sorcery.

Those who followed the Devil's path lived in a grotesque world of gruesome imaginings and hallucinations surrounded by demons; they sank into the very quagmires of a mental Hell—and revelled in it. They became pitiable and disgusting wrecks, half-demented sadists and workers of evil for the love of it. Small wonder that the general terror of the supernatural and unseen was augmented by the fear of sorcerers and witches; though it is quite certain that many of their fears were unfounded, and centred upon perfectly innocent people—especially those who were what we now call "mediumistic" or "sensitives." It is interesting to speculate whether some of those supposed to be in league with demons, and who were the centre of malevolent manifestations, were not in reality mediums for spirit disturbances of the "Poltergeist" order; but this is merely by the way.

All over Europe people of every grade of society flocked to the gatherings of the witches' Sabbaths, there to give themselves up to debauchery and cruelty. Every action of life was governed by spells, the consultation of oracles and divination of all descriptions. Works called *Grimories*, or the *Black Books*, were eagerly consulted by the few who could read, in order to obtain information for calling up the dead, casting spells and exorcising demons, and the like. The inhabitants of the convents and monasteries were not exempt from an interest in witchcraft and sorcery, and most probably the *Grimories* were consulted even more assiduously within their walls than outside, as those who followed the religious life were almost the only ones possessed of the necessary education. There were three chief varieties of these textbooks of black magic, the *Grimorium Verium*, the *Grand Grimorie*, and that attributed to Pope Honorius, himself a sorcerer by reputation.

The true black magician, however, probably worked more or less in secret. He did not trouble about petty sorcery, or the casting of mediocre spells; his ambitions were higher, and he worked for power both on the material and spiritual planes. Such a one, possibly, was the extraordinary man known as "the Old Man of the Mountains" and the Prince Alamond or Alaodin.

Marco Polo relates that the Prince lived in an impregnable mountain fastness upon the borders of Persia.

There, in a fertile valley situated high up among the mountain peaks, the Old Man had made a veritable paradise. He called himself the companion of Mohammed, and everything was created to give the illusion of living in the Prophet's Paradise of Houris. It was a little kingdom of luxury and riches; flowers and fruit abounded in the lovely gardens, the women were clothed in the costliest silks and jewels, and music, feasting and material joys were the order of the day.

The entrance to the valley was guarded by a mighty fortress, manned with soldiers recruited from the surrounding districts and who were captured from time to time to serve the sorcerer. The method the latter employed was to send his envoys into nearby towns and villages, and the men chosen were drugged, and only awoke to find themselves in the Old Man's kingdom. Once there, they dared not leave; but there is every reason to suppose that they were more than well treated, unless they violated the wishes and rules of the Prince, whereupon they mysteriously disappeared.

Despite the joys of his earthly Eden, or perhaps because of them, the Old Man was at constant warfare with the neighbouring sultans and emirs. He made depredations upon the caravans of merchants, whose families had to pay out large sums in ransom if they did not wish to incur the enmity of Alamond. When the Crusades began, however, the Prince armed himself against the Christians with the rest, and his assassins, who asked nothing better than to die in his service, were sent into every country in Europe secretly to kill outstanding leaders. It is an interesting fact that the word "assassin" was first applied to these envoys of the Old Man of the Mountains, and was originally derived from that of the drug hashish, with which they were stimulated before attempting the murders for which they became notorious.

The Old Man's emissaries were responsible for the death of Augustus Conrad, Marquis de Montferrat; while Richard Cœur de Lion and Philippe Augustus are supposed to have been marked out for a sudden end by him. Hearing of the immense preparations that Louis IX of France was making for the conquest of the Holy Land, Alamond attempted to have him killed, but for once the plot failed. He then sent spies to the very Court of Paris for the same purpose, but is supposed to have so greatly admired the reports that he received regarding the King's courage and fine character that he altered his intentions, and made overtures of friendship instead, sending impressive gifts to the French monarch, including a magic ring. It was always thought that once the Old Man had decided upon an assassination the victim was as good as dead, and indeed it was rarely that he met with failure.

Every imaginable magic art was attributed to the

companion of Mohammed, including the power of fascination and the evil eye and the ability to render himself invisible. It is certain that he possessed the gift of arousing intense loyalty in his followers, and that once he had determined upon a given object it was almost invariably attained. The murders committed at his instigation, however, were brought about by the usual methods ; the only unusual feature being that the actual perpetrators were either drugged or hypnotised. At the same time, if the accounts of the conditions in the Old Man's little kingdom, and of the Old Man's activities, are not wild exaggerations, it is almost certain that he did indeed work with a profound knowledge of elementary spirits, and possessed the magician's ability to turn to his own use and advantage Nature's forces.

Every sorcerer was reputed to have a familiar spirit, which usually attached itself to the owner on his making a pact with the Devil, or at the Initiation of a Witches Sabbaths. The familiars of the magicians, on the other hand, were not in all cases evil, and often may have approximated the " guides " with whom present-day spiritualists are well acquainted. The famous Cornelius Agrippa was the possessor of an immense black dog that followed him everywhere. When the great magician found death approaching, it is related that he called the Satanic animal to him and, removing a collar studded with iron nails from its neck, upon which was written a magical inscription, he exclaimed : " Away, accursed beast, through whose agency I must now sink to perdition ! " The dog then dashed away, and threw itself into a foaming river, disappearing for ever. Faust, in later times, was also supposed to have a black dog as a familiar.

The toads, snakes, cats, owls, and other creatures thought to be the familiars of witches, are known to everyone, and even in children's stories, magic boxes, rings and boots used to figure largely. Though we consider these things entirely fanciful to-day, they were in reality but simple tales of events that were taken for granted as actual facts in the days of the far past. Thus, it was popularly supposed that familiar spirits could be enclosed in rings, or confined in bottles and boxes, just as the Persians thought that djinns could be kept in jars and flasks.

Johann Rosa confessed to having a spirit within a magic ring, which he consulted on certain days every week. By this means he was acquainted with everything that was going on, not only in his own home and town but abroad as well. This obliging sprite also gave such excellent prescriptions for curing all manner of complaints that Johann earned a great reputation for healing diseases. In the end, he was accused of sortilege, or enchantments, and the ring was publicly destroyed upon a blacksmith's anvil in the market place. Paracelsus was another owner of a familiar spirit, which he kept in the hilt of his sword.

Mandrakes were sometimes considered in the light of familiars. Witches kept both male and female specimens of the magic root in bottles, and there are accounts of persons who visited sorcerers having seen mandrakes, thus secured, jumping up and down, shrieking with protest apparently at their confinement. Very occasionally it would seem that entities of this description attached themselves to persons uninvited, and performed many services for those whom they singled out. But these attentions were not always welcome, and some people were ungrateful enough to have their voluntary familiars exorcised!

In the most primitive ages men attached a magic importance to bones, and to-day bones play a large part in the black magic rites of savage tribes. I have myself seen South American Indians point a bone at persons over whom they wished to cast a spell. Even the Church reverenced the supposed bones of saints, and attributed magical or miraculous powers to them. In the Dark Ages and mediæval times witches performed every variety of socery by this means. The bones and skulls of criminals were greatly in request, and skulls were used particularly as drinking vessels for the Black Mass, and in other magical ceremonies. The dust of bones was used in concocting potions to prolong life, and also for causing death.

There was a superstition that any woman at enmity with another who was pregnant could delay the birth of her child indefinitely by obtaining the bones of a criminal or sorcerer and performing certain magic rites with them. This method was much sought after by women whose husbands had been unfaithful to them, in an attempt to prevent another woman successfully bearing him a child, and there were many accusations against witches and those who consulted them, that women and girls had been killed by thus interfering with the proper birth of their infants.

There are legends, as old as Merlin himself, that bones or their dust had the power of impregnating women under certain conditions, and the following tale is found in various European countries under different guises.

A mountain chieftan wed a young bride on the eve of battle, and, the enemy surprising a band of his men sooner than expected, he was forced to ride away and leave her without consummating the marriage. The chieftan was killed, and his wife's grief was bitterly increased by the knowledge that he could leave no son to succeed him. The husband's followers implored her to resort to a witch, who dwelt in the mountains, to see if by magical means she could restore the dead chief.

The bride accordingly visited the ancient sorceress, but the witch was unable to overcome death in one aspect. She told the girl, however, to have her husband's body removed from the field where it lay and to wash and purify it. She must then get his followers to carry the corpse to a lonely spot upon the mountain-top, where it must be completely burnt at night in her presence alone. When nothing was left but the ashes of the bones, she must sit down and arrange her clothing around her waist, leaving the lower part of her body uncovered. She had then to repeat a formula given to her by the witch, whereupon a wind would arise and blow the ashes of the dead about her body, and she would conceive a child from them and in due course bear her husband a son. This rite was faithfully carried out by the bride, and she eventually bore a posthumous child, who grew to be the leader of his father's people.

Fascination was as potent an agency of black magic as the evil eye, and somewhat similar in its method of operation. The object of fascination, however, was to attract and enchant people, usually with the motive of making them fall in love against their will, or yield to unlawful passions. On the other hand, it was also exercised over animals, and in some cases over even material possessions. The Romans had believed in it so implicitly that they even created a god Fascinus in honour of this power, and vestal virgins rather strangely were mentioned in connection with the celebrations of the god's rites. He was represented by phallic symbols, which were hung round the necks of children and upon the triumphal chariot.

Varius, Prior of the Benedictine Convent of St. Sophia in

Beneventua, wrote a treatise called *De Fascino* ; in which he refers to " Hamaxobi and Biarbi " being deeply versed in the art of fascinating and enchanting men, so that they became enslaved and lost their reason. The old legend of Medusa's head, too, is familiar to everyone ; one glare from the terrible eyes being sufficient to turn a man to stone or strike him dead. And the Basilisk of Narcissas is equally notorious.

Some sorcerers were reputed to be able to appropriate gems or money, by casting their eyes upon them ; others were thought to have the power of splitting jewels in two with a glance, so that goldsmiths and those who dealt in precious stones particularly feared them. Wolves were accredited with the power of depriving men of speech, should they unfortunately gaze into the animal's eyes, and there was a peculiar belief that if one of these creatures attacked a man from the left-hand side it could be easily beaten off, but if from the right he was almost certainly doomed.

There was a deeply seated belief in the fascination or enchantment of shadows ; so that the witch, or magician, could use them either to produce sickness and death or to inspire love. This fear of the shadow is common in many parts of the world to-day ; the Slavs, particularly, shun the shadow of a red-headed man or woman, who are considered malevolent and unlucky. Wolves, also, were universally believed to enchant sleeping men and dogs by casting their shadow over them in the moonlight. In rather later times the shadow of the priest's fingers raised in blessing was considered to have an evil significance.

The position of the hand, with the second and third fingers raised, symbolises God and Perfected Man pouring out their blessing. Yet, like all forces manifesting in the physical world, this blessing may become a curse—according to the desire and the will of the Pontiff. A remarkable thing in connection with the hand so lifted, is that its shadow resembles the head and horns of the Goat Baphomet, the symbol of black magic. The use of the " shadow of the blessing " was regarded as the legitimate prerogative of the Pope, and was most terribly exercised during the Dark Ages and at the times of the Inquisition. The fate of the man or woman upon whom the shadow fell was terrible, indeed. Pictures representing the blessing were inscribed " Benedictionem," while upon the shadow appeared the word " Maledictus."

While those in high places were engaged in discovering secret poisons, and resorting to sorcery to rid the world of their enemies, the common people of all nations dabbled in witchcraft, if they did not actually participate in Satanic gatherings and revels.

On moonlit nights, lonely moorlands and wooded glades were the scenes of strange masquerades. Prancing figures, surrounded by terrible heads of beasts and reptiles, whirled round in a mad dance with naked women, their backs turned upon the rude altars on which lay the mangled figure of the human sacrifice, bathed in its own blood.

The witches made a thriving trade of spells and potions, and concocted the most extraordinary mixtures to produce disaster or love, as the case might be.

Scent was a most important item in dealing with the unseen world, and in necromancy, particularly, the odours arising from burnt substances had a powerful influence upon the spirits. From time immemorial, and especially in the East, the value and potency of incense and perfumes in all magic has been fully recognised, but the fearful smells that must have arisen from the revolting substances that the ancient sorcerers burned and boiled must have been calculated to drive away any but the most perverted beings, whether in the flesh or out of it.

Astrology was inextricably interwoven with all practices of sorcery, and the suitable days and times for performing the rites of black magic were calculated by this means. Each planet had its particular scent, or rather odour, by which its peculiar attributes could be invoked. Thus, to the Sun, a mixture of saffron, amber, musk, incense and the blood of a cock was offered; and to the Moon, camphor, boiled with the eyes of a bull, the blood of a lark and a frog's head. Mars was invoked with a heterogeneous mixture of magic herbs, saffron, the blood of a black cat, and so on.

The most nauseating compounds were used as love philtres, and anyone responding to the treatment meted out must indeed have been under a spell. The only wonder is that they survived. However, the prescriptions of the physicians of the Middle Ages are very little better, and many of them read so exactly like a witch's potion that if we were asked which was the magical formula and which the doctor's compound it would be impossible to tell.

The consecrated or unconsecrated host was used for many

purposes in connection with the black art and, stamped with invocations in letters of blood, it was considered the most potent means of operating malevolent influences. Apart from this sacrilegious usage, all potions or philtres employed in sorcery had to contain portions of three necessary ingredients—the scales of a fish, the intestines of animals and birds' feathers. These substances were augmented by nail parings, human hair, powdered bones, blood and the like. Crystals, and crystal gazing, were of course unknown ; but magic mirrors were used for reflecting the images of the departed and those who were absent, and for invoking visions of their conditions and circumstances.

The French placed great faith in the qualities of the "chémise de nécessité," which was much sought after by soldiers and others whose lives entailed danger. This famous vest had to be woven by a virgin during a night of Christmas week, to the accompaniment of evocations and incantations.

Over the heart, or in the centre, was embroidered the head of a two-faced man, surmounted by the crown of Beelzebub, and the garment's property was to render the wearer invisible.

Continental sorcerers caused death at a distance by means of magical arrows, invisibly directed to their mark by demons or elementals. These Satanic archers were called the "Sagittarians," and were greatly feared. At Lautenbourg, in Prussia, a sorcerer by the name of Pumbert was in the habit of daily shooting off three of these murderous missiles, but the inhabitants of the district became incensed against him and at a prearranged time they fell upon him in a body and literally tore the man to pieces. The same form of witchcraft was to be found among the Lapps and Finns.

Everything pertaining to the human body was used for magical formulas, as we have seen, and without having recourse to witches and sorcerers, the fluids and substances of the body were often privately employed for the making of spells to influence others. Indeed, nearly all ordinary people dabbled in sorcery in the Dark or Middle Ages. Women, in particular, believed that the substances mixed with emanations and secretions from their own bodies had power over those they wished to enchant. Thus, they would make dough of flour and, having heated themselves by some means, would remove their clothes and rub themselves with the dough in order to impregnate it with their sweat. This done, they would bake little cakes from the same mixture and give them to any man whom they wished to entice for base desires. A similar little sorcery is still performed by the peasant women of Hungary, who bake cakes and take them to bed with them, before giving them to the men they desire as sweethearts. A means of dispelling an enchantment of this description was for a man to walk a good distance in new shoes until his feet perspired. If he removed the shoes immediately he returned home, and drank wine from the right shoe at once, he would be free from the spell.

In magic most revolting compounds were often made, to be taken or burnt, involving the use of urine, sweat, and other human fluids, and the pubic hair and other matters too gross to mention, and which would be unthinkable to all but the most depraved.

The belief in Satan, as an actual personality, was so strong that he was accredited with performing the most amazing feats, such as building bridges, removing churches from their original foundations, and so on. And there are several legends of the Devil having constructed bridges, in exchange for a Christian soul. The first creature to set foot upon the bridge must become the slave of the demon; but Satan seems to have been very easily cheated, as on the famous occasion when the inhabitants of St. Cloud fobbed him off with a black cat!

This spirit of poking fun at the Devil, and making him ridiculous, is a noteworthy point of many ancient myths. And, while demons and the Satanic powers and influence were universally dreaded, at the same time there existed an impish glee and lack of awe at the idea of a human getting the better of the Prince of Darkness, which is reminiscent of unruly schoolboys setting up against an overbearing and irate schoolmaster.

One of the mythical figures of these times was the Wandering Jew, who was doomed to roam the world until Christ came again. It was believed that he had offered some insult to the Master as He staggered beneath the weight of the Cross to Calvary, and therefore wandered without rest until the Judgment or, according to some accounts, until his sufferings and repentance earned pardon and release. Various people of standing claimed to have seen and known him, but he was popularly feared and dreaded, and strangers were often treated with suspicion as possibly being the Wandering Jew himself.

Prester John was another legendary figure, but this supposed European priest and ruler of a distant Asiatic kingdom scarcely belongs to the realms of sorcery, although magical powers were attributed to him. During these eras, there were literally hundreds of people who had established reputations as witches and sorcerers, and among the plethora of outstanding names in this respect it is difficult to isolate the most important.

A certain Peter of Apono was famous as having power over materials, and was also a water and mineral diviner. His chief feat, however, was to cause money to return to his pocket, and he even supplied coins that possessed this property of always returning to the owners. He was in the habit of using a well belonging to a neighbour to obtain the water he needed for his household, but for some reason or other the permission to continue doing so was withdrawn, Peter thereupon, with the assistance of the Devil, caused the water to overflow and flood his neighbour's land.

In the British Isles Thomas the Rhymer was a famous seer, who predicted events many years ahead of his time and was commonly supposed to be a sorcerer. Merlin was probably the most ancient of the British sorcerers of whom there is any record, but he is almost a mythical figure. Merlin is, in fact, a link with the Druids, and most probably belonged to that Order or to one of its surviving branches.

A sorcerer, Gerald Desmond, lived in a castle situated in the middle of Lough Gur, and there he brought his young bride at her marriage. In course of time, the bride became very inquisitive about her husband's practices in black magic and, seeking him out one day in his secret chamber, desired him to reveal to her the mystery of the Black Cat.

After much argument, Desmond agreed that she should witness some of his sorceries, but on the condition that she uttered no sound, since otherwise the castle would fall in ruins and sink beneath the lake.

Her promise given, his wife thereupon witnessed such terrible and horrifying sights that it seemed as if the room had been transported to some corner of Hell itself. The brave lady stood her ground, however, until, when all seemed quiet, her husband lay down at her feet and stretched literally, from wall to wall. This was too much for her and, uttering shriek upon shriek, she was crushed by the ruins of the castle, as its walls caved in upon herself and her husband, and at the same moment the little island was engulfed within the lake. Every seven years Gerald Desmond is reported to rise from the waters, and, riding upon a white horse, shod with silver, to circle the lake three times before returning to its depths.

In the twelth century there was a black magician named Artephius, who claimed to have lived more than a thousand years by magic means, and who was identified by some alchemists with Apollonius of Tyana. He was the author of some very extravagant works on magic, which however were not of any great value.

Berthomine de Gert, a sorceress of Gascony, specialised in love philtres. She also ultimately made some extraordinary statements about the witches' gatherings in her confessions, relating that, if anyone murdered a witch on her way back from the Sabbath, the Devil would temporarily impersonate her at home, so that none should know where she had been.

One love potion was composed of the powdered navel string of a new-born baby boy. Another, reputed to be very efficient, was the tongue of a sparrow enclosed in a wax wafer, and was to be kept upon the body for four days, after which an opportunity must be made to see the desired woman and, placing the wafer under the tongue, kiss her while the charm was still in the mouth.

Wax figures were as much used for creating love as for working death spells. In order to entice a woman, an image must be made of her in virgin wax, with her name written on the forehead. The name of the admirer must be imprinted on the figure's breast, with blood taken from the third finger of the left hand. Four new needles had to be selected, and one placed in the back, one in the head, one in the heart and one in the pelvis. A fire was then made, in the woman's name, which must afterwards be written in the ashes. Salt and mustard-seed must be sprinkled on the image, which had finally to be placed in the heart of the fire, and as the flames leapt up so would the woman's passion be kindled.

The Rabbi Jachiel, a Jewish sorcerer in France, was reputed to have marvellous powers over the elements, by means of which he lighted his house ; but it is now thought he may have had some advance knowledge of electricity.

" Her husband . . . stretched literally from wall to wall."

At night the windows of his home blazed out with a strange light, and if unwelcome and inquisitive neighbours knocked too frequently at his door, he caused blue sparks to be emitted from the door-knocker by pressing a button in his laboratory.

At some time during the Middle Ages there existed a Witches' Tower at Lindheim, prints of which were made as recently as the eighteenth century. It was a strong castellated tower, in which sorcerers and witches were supposed to assemble at night to perform black magic, and no one dared go near it either by day or night. This tower was the centre of countless rumours and legends, and human sacrifices were supposed to be made within its walls, particularly upon the fifteenth day of the month. The number fifteen had a Satanic significance, and came to be regarded as an evil number of bad omen on account of its use by Black Magicians.

Nearly all the alchemists were popularly supposed to be sorcerers, but in all probability very few of them actually were ; with the exception of men like Paracelsus, and later Michael Nostradamus, who in the sixteenth century was astrologer to Charles IX.

The famous Nicholas Flamel, and his wife Perenelle, were considered sorcerers of the deepest dye, and even after their death the house they occupied was avoided as a centre of Satanic influences. In passing the place, wayfarers crossed themselves and hurried to the opposite side of the street.

Poor Jacques Dulet, savant and alchemist, was imprisoned for sorcery in the reign of Philippe le Bel, and committed suicide after his wife had been burned alive as a witch.

Those who did not engage in sorcery were overcome by an almost hysterical fear of it, and the most fantastic construction was placed upon matters of natural phenomena. Thus, nearly every storm was thought to be the work of some wizard, and at one period strange and alarming visions were seen in the sky almost universally, but especially in France. Demons, dragons, skeletons, and all manner of dreadful and horrifying shapes appeared in the clouds and struck terror into the hearts of those who beheld them.

After the Inquisition had been established by Papal authority, and had taken into its hands the punishment of witchcraft and sorcery, various "secret" societies arose. These were ostensibly for the furtherance of Justice, but more often they were conspicuous for what would nowadays be called "lynch law," particularly when their power had consolidated.

Such was the society which was founded in Westphalia and called the Vehmgericht (in France, the Saint Vehme). Originally this terrible and mysterious band of men was established as an improvement on the existing system of justice, and sought to administer equity by their own hands. Men of power and position belonged to it, and their "free judges" sat in various towns, covering a wide area known as the Red Territory. The function of the "franc-judges" was to travel about the country looking for crime, and on the discovery of criminals to denounce the latter immediately and administer summary justice. Very little imagination is needed to perceive the abuses this system lent itself to, and eventually the Saint Vehme became so blinded by its own power, and the terror it inspired, that it scarcely troubled to offer even a pretence of justice. Finally, the people gathered sufficient courage to protest against its iniquities, and it was disbanded, but not before it had tortured and executed many innocent people.

There was also the Inquisitorial society of the "Council of Ten," which was inaugurated in Venice in 1310. Originally, it was called into being as a sort of emergency council, and was only supposed to exist for two months, but later it was reassembled and lasted five years. Its members worked in secret, and could not be distinguished from ordinary people by their dress. It was noted for the harshness and cruelty of its judgments, even in that age, and those it condemned to death were poisoned. When meeting in council, the members of this sinister body wore black robes, with a square black cloth covering the face, the eyes only being visible. On one side of the garments was incongruously embroidered a medallion of the Prince of Peace, and in their hands they carried a stout bar to the end of which was attached a short iron chain—presumably for the purpose of flagellation.

Nearly all the various bodies of Monastic Knights fell under suspicion of sorcery even as the alchemists did, and also the famous Order of Rosicrucians. This latter mystical society, which was founded on the Continent and has survived in various forms to the present day, was introduced into England by Fludd, the alchemist and astrologer, in the reign of Queen Elizabeth. Some accounts give an even earlier date, but though the Rosicrucians were undoubtedly known before Fludd's day, they seem to have had no authorised branch established in Britain. Various men who earned the reputation of being sorcerers were also Rosicrucians, such as Friar Bacon, but it definitely was not a Black Magic society.

The Knights Templars, originally founded to protect the Holy Sepulchre in the wars with the Saracens, became a very rich and powerful society, having members in nearly every country in Europe. Indeed, so overbearing and arrogant did they become, that "the pride of a Templar" became a by-word. In course of time, however, rumours began to be whispered about the infamous blasphemies of the Templars; that they were heretics, and worse. It was reported that they worshipped a huge idol in the form of a goat, which was called Baphomet, and before which they performed revolting ceremonies.

Templars themselves had hinted at horrifying experiences in connection with their initiations, and at last the King of France, Philippe le Bel, and the Pope turned their attention to the sect. The King was actuated by jealousy of their riches and was badly in need of money, while the Pope quite possibly feared their spiritual influence. The Templars were undoubtedly heretics, in so far as they had acquired some of the Gnostic principles and probably did not believe in the Divinity of Jesus the Christ although honouring Him as a Master. On the other hand, they had mixed considerably with the Saracens in the East, and some of the beliefs that they adhered to had an unmistakably Mohammedan flavour and very likely followed the doctrine of the Gnostic Ophites of Islam.

The Church accused the Templars upon their initiation of spitting upon, and trampling under foot, the Cross, at the same time crying three times, "*Je renonce Jesu.*" They were also supposed to be stripped naked and kissed upon various parts of the body, before being led into the presence of Baphomet, whom they greeted with cries of "*Yalla!*" There are various accounts of their ceremonies, all of which differ. Some accounts relate that homage was paid to a dog or a cat, and remains of the idol known as the Goat (Baphomet) have been discovered as definite evidence that they employed such effigies. The idol form was, however, probably regarded as a pantheistic and magical figure of the Absolute. The animal head (usually that of a goat, with a torch between the horns) represented the responsibility of matter and the expiation of physical sins in the body; the human hands of the figure, betokening the sanctity of labour, were pointed above and below to two crescents, the upper white and the lower black, corresponding to good and evil, mercy and justice; the organs of generation were veiled, symbolising the mystery of creation; the belly was green in colour, and scaled as a fish or reptile, its female breasts were blue; on the forehead, beneath the torch, appeared the sign of the pentagram, with one beam in the ascendant. The whole image was seated upon a cube, the symbol of four, the square and foundation of all things, the feet being placed upon a sphere representing the world.

Whatever may have been the true nature of the ceremonies of the Templars, their downfall occurred when Philippe le Bel arranged to trap Jacques de Molay and the principal Templars at a royal ceremony in Paris. The Knights were graciously received and entertained by the Court, but were subsequently suddenly arrested by the King's soldiers and hailed before the Inquisition. Under torture the Knights confessed to many dark practices and were condemned to various fates, their Order being disbanded. Their various trials spread over a number of years, and they received very different sentences and punishments in different countries.

A number of civilian people in Germany, called Stedingers, had very similiar accusations made against them by the Holy Inquisition; their real crime in the eyes of the Church being heresy. It was related that they, too, had terrible ceremonies of initiation and horrible rituals, but there seems to have been little real evidence of these things. So much of the Inquisition's proof of its accusations rested upon the infirm basis of confessions extracted under terrible torture, that the just and reasonable mind cannot accept them as authentic.

The Papal authorities had issued a remarkable work called the "Malleus Maleficarum," by two Inquisitors, Jacob Sprenger and Henricus Institor. This was nothing more nor less than a treatise on black magic and the practice of witchcraft in general, although it was written with the intention of acting as a warning against such things. It revealed how sorcerers were able to rouse storms and cause thunder, earthquakes and shipwreck; to turn themselves into animals and become the companions of demons, after having made pacts with the Devil; and much other information of a similiar nature.

We have seen that every sorcerer was thought to have inevitably bound himself to Satan in return for some favour; like the famous Dr. Faustus who gave himself to the demon Mephistopheles, but was eventually found dead and terribly mutilated—a very usual fate of black magicians. The legend of Faust or Faustus, in fact, became so popular in different versions, that it is unnecessary to enter into the details. There can be little doubt that such a person at some time existed, and was a dabbler in the Black Art.

The Inquisition destroyed many works on sorcery, but the *Clavicule de Solomon* and the *Sword of Moses* escaped this fate, and remained unscathed to hand on magic formulas, rules of exorcism and necromancy, details of the processes for casting spells, and so on. The *Sword of Moses* was the work of a magician named Abraham, who lived in Germany probably during the fourteenth century. He was trained in occultism from an early age, and later journeyed to the East to continue his studies. Eventually he settled in Prague, where he met a man by name Anthony who initiated him into further mysteries. We gather from his writings that he was attracted by black magic for a time, but grew weary and disgusted with it and turned his attention to the higher aspects of magic. The *Sword of Moses* was an elaborate work on magic and sorcery, giving very complete details of the requirements and methods of the magical adept.

Abraham's friend Anthony apparently had made a pact with the Evil One for forty years in return for his wisdom; but before this time had expired he was found dead with his tongue torn out, possibly as a retribution for having revealed some of his magic secrets. This idea of the Devil claiming his own was found everywhere, and it was even thought that he came and carried witches off bodily to their particular little corner of Hell at the end of the time that they had promised to serve him. Many people even declared that they had seen the Evil One doing it!

The punishment that the early Church inflicted upon sorcerers and witches was not nearly so drastic as that later meted out by the Inquisition. Thus, the first Ecclesiastical

Councils, such as that of Laodicea in 363, contented themselves by merely driving sorcerers from the Church and fining them. It was not until the Middle Ages that the persecution became so bitter, and the methods employed so cruel.

The "Holy" Inquisition became the most pitiless and ferocious institution the world has ever known; condemning men, women and even children to the flames, and submitting them to ghastly tortures, in the name of God and the Saviour of Mankind. The atrocities the Inquisition committed constituted the most blasphemous irony in religious history; defiling the Catholic Church with the deaths of innocent victims who were burnt to avoid breaking the maxim "Ecclesia non novit sanguinem."

It was believed that the Devil left his mark on all those who were pledged to him, and that this spot was perfectly insensible, no matter what part of the body it occurred on. Suspected witches or sorcerers were, therefore, pricked with pins, needles and knives from head to foot in order to discover this mark. If the unfortunate person did not react to every prick or stab, it was counted as absolute proof of guilt. They were then thrown into rivers and ponds, to see if they would sink or float.

Suspects were put to the ordeal by fire, and forced to drink boiling oil. Another torture was to strap the victims down and constantly pour water down their throats, until the body could hold no more. The Inquisitors, again, used a dreadful ceremony called "the Question." In the process of this, the accused person was torn with red-hot iron pincers furnished with iron spikes, which made it scarcely surprising that such startling confessions were obtained from them. Another torture was "the Collar." This instrument was also fitted with spikes, and was held fast by cords fixed to the corners of the room. The sufferer was placed in such a position that the soles of his feet roasted slowly, and was eventually handed over to the executioners to be burnt, if there was a spark of life left in his wretched body. Flagellation, thumb-screws, the rack, all entered into the agonising and shameful programme of the Inquisition.

Long lists of persons convicted of witchcraft contained the names of little children (from about six years of age, and of both sexes—but more generally girls), who were spared none of the horrors of the dreadful executioners. They were committed to the flames in the name of the Master who had said, "Suffer little children to come unto Me." Moreover, the accusations of sorcery often became as ridiculous as they were cruel and unjust; even leading in France to the burning of a poor horse, which had been trained to recognise figures and make divinations by indicating numbers with its hoof.

Again, religious persecution was not confined to the destruction of those who were believed to be practitioners of witchcraft and black magic; the arts of divination were equally punished. Thus, the wandering Bohemians, or gipsies, often suffered on the simple score of palmistry, soothsaying and clairvoyance. These travelling magicians were seldom sorcerers like the occultists who were settled in villages and towns, and, though renowned for the evil eye and other psychic gifts, they rarely penetrated more deeply into magic than cartomancy, palmistry and the like.

The children who were burnt at the stake were probably mostly ones who had been dedicated to Satan by their parents, but there are accounts of some having actually asserted that they had seen the Devil. In Spain and Italy sorcerers who appeared before the Court of the Inquisition were grotesquely dressed in a special costume, consisting of a Dalmatic and a Mitre, called the Carocha. These robes were beautifully designed, and of a special variety according to the fate of the wearer. Thus, a witch who was condemned to be burnt wore a mitre covered with the figures of demons in the act of poking the fires of Hell, in the midst of which a woman's head appeared on burning coals. In some rare instances the victim avoided the stake by confession, and if she had obtained this mercy she performed a public penance in a dalmatic ornamented with tongues of fire representing the Holy Ghost, symbolical of her reconciliation with God and her renunciation of witchcraft.

The method of burning witches varied somewhat, but it must have been an equally painful process however inflicted. The stake to which the victims were bound was usually surrounded by a very high pyre of faggots, to the top of which they had to climb. It is possible that some of these unfortunate people were suffocated by the smoke before feeling the pangs of burning, but there are accounts of life having lingered until the body was merely a charred mass. In the case of sufferers possessed of true occult powers, the pain may to some extent have been a withdrawal into the

Etheric Body ; in other words, some may have been able to exercise a form of self-hypnosis to overcome their agonies. It is, for instance, recorded of many saints, and martyrs that, while they underwent their torture, they could withdraw themselves sufficiently by their ecstasy of mind to enable them to sing praises ; while it is related of Cranmer that he deliberately burnt his right hand in the flames, because with it he had once signed his renunciation of the Catholic Church.

In Holland a favourite method of burning under the cruel Duke of Alva and his "Council of Blood" was simply to make a large fire on the ground. The witch was then strapped to a ladder and, when the flames were burning fiercely, she was first propped upright by two men and afterwards flung face downwards in the heart of the fire. Sorcerers in some countries were forced into a hole just large enough to accommodate a bed composed of faggots, and when they had been lashed to this couch of torture, more faggots were mercilessly piled on top of them and set alight with torches.

Methods of extracting confessions included the "Boot" ; an iron contraption that fitted the leg with crushing force. When pressure was brought to bear on the victim, this "Boot" was caused to tighten so much that the flesh and blood were literally pulped and the bones crushed.

The Inquisitorial judges were more cruel in certain countries than others, and again in certain districts. Though France and Spain were notable for the hideous ferocity of their persecutions, even they revolted against the methods and sentences imposed by the judges of Arras in France, who cannot be exonerated from motives of personal gain. For there the sorcerers were accused of heresy as well, and by that means the Ecclesiastical Councils seized their property and extorted heavy fines from their relatives. And it is a notable fact that of the priests and monks burnt during these periods, few were openly accused of sorcery ; the charge of heresy being brought against them more frequently, except in flagrant cases.

The Papal authorities in those days made a scandalous trade out of selling Dispensations, so that people who were rich and influential enough escaped the flames and tortures of the Inquisition.

Somewhat later, in 1569, Jean Wier, a native of Brabart, who was a celebrated physician, did much to decrease the tortures of the witches by writing his *Cinq livres de l'imposture et tromperie des diables.* This book set out to prove that many of the accused were not sorcerers at all, and therefore did not in any way merit the punishments meted out to them. Joan of Arc, whom the English burnt as a witch and who was accused of sortilege, nowadays would merely have been called a " clairaudiante."

The district of Bambury in Germany was supposed to contain most witches, and as late as the seventeenth century this town went so far as to build the " Haxenhaus " or " Malefitzhaus " (" House of Witches "), where suspects were imprisoned and tried. The building was a triumph of architecture and accommodated about twenty-six women at a time, but it is to be regretted that so much skill and appreciation of beauty could not have been put to a better purpose.

Literally thousands of people of all ages and conditions were burnt in the course of a year under the worst period of the Inquisitorial persecutions, and at the time when the Knights Templars met their downfall fifty-nine of them were burnt in a single day, including their leader Jacques de Molay. Such executions pandered to all that was worst in human nature, and the crowds that attended these human sacrifices were maddened by a sadistic lust of bestial cruelty. The onlookers, indeed, thrilled and rejoiced in the sufferings of the victims, and displayed as devilish a spirit as any that could have been evoked by the vilest sorcerer. It was comparatively seldom that a Laval, or a Gaufridy, who alone could possibly have merited the fiendish torture employed, was brought to book.

For days and weeks the fires of persecution never went out, one victim after another being led to the stake. There is a record in Jersey of how a young woman accused as a witch was burnt in the Royal Square. The poor girl was pregnant and already in labour, and as the flames began to mount her child was born. By some means or other in her agony the wretched mother managed to kick the infant from the encroaching fire. But the inhuman bystanders cast the progeny back into the flames that were consuming its mother, crying that they desired no imp of Satan.

Although the extreme cruelty and enormous numbers of the accusations and persecutions for sorcery gradually diminished, they continued to exist until the eighteenth century.

CHAPTER VII

THE CHURCH AND MONASTIC BLACK MAGIC

Deals with black magic practised within the Church and furnishes instances when her dignitaries were accused of witchcraft, and the dealings of saints and ecclesiastics with demons and the black art.

DURING the Middle Ages the Church paid as much attention to Satan as she did to the Virgin and Son, and certainly fed the forces of darkness by increasing and trading upon the fear of the Devil and his attendant hosts of demons. She possessed also her trained band of exorcists, who practised as much magic as the professional caster of spells.

At a time when alchemy was preoccupying the minds of men, the clergy were no exception to the rule, and nearly every parish priest was engaged upon alchemical experiments and sorcery in a greater or lesser degree. The state of affairs in many monasteries all over Europe was even worse. It is not to be denied that many monks, friars, and priests led saintly lives, but there was another side to the picture. The confinement and unnatural conditions of life led to terrible states of mind among the inhabitants of monasteries and convents, and many abnormal practices were the result. Hysteria and sexual disturbances gave place to religious exaltation on the one hand, and to visions of Hell, Satan and myriads of demons on the other. No better breeding-ground for sorcery could be found.

Monks were not always men who had taken up the religious life from motives of piety, nor had many of them taken full vows; though all alike were enjoined to celibacy, and at least outward chastity. That this chastity was often a mockery there is abundant evidence, and the perversions they fell into were more revolting than a lapse from continence.

It is small wonder, therefore, that there are so many accounts of these men and noted "saints" being troubled with Satanic manifestations and demoniac visitations, Even making due allowance for credulity, superstition and a desire to impress the outer world, there is still ample ground for concluding that these people did, indeed, come into contact with the dark and malevolent forces of the spirit planes.

Many of the " saints " of the Dark and Middle Ages would not necessarily be considered holy nowadays, but, rather, fit cases for psycho-analysis and the mental specialist. Many of their " pious " actions betrayed an abnormal state of mind, inducing them to act under influences that, contrary to their own statements, must have come from a far from exalted origin. Many holy women meditated upon the crucified figure of Jesus with a love that was far more carnal than spiritual in its expression. Guichard, Bishop of Troyes, was accused in 1303 of being the son of a demon, and of calling up his father whenever he needed Satanic assistance. For which convenience the bishop suffered imprisonment.

Nowhere during the Middle Ages was sorcery more practised within the Church than in Spain and Portugal. These countries had already acquired a great knowledge of magic, sorcery and alchemy from the Moors, and those cults became grafted on to the esoteric knowledge of the monks and priesthood. The latter grew to find that their spiritual power became gratifyingly augmented by temporal power, when backed by a practice of the black art. In past eras the Church teemed with men who were intensely ambitious, and was the school for political supremacy. In that respect their secrets stood them in good stead, for by such means they influenced weak-minded royalty and women who held unacknowledged power.

On the other hand, the Church held the learning and culture of the times in her hands, and many men whose intellect and achievements were far beyond their age earned the reputation of being magicians and enchanters simply because the ordinary people of all classes could neither understand them nor their works. Thomas Aquinas, whose wonders were far-famed, may well have belonged to such a group, though he seems to have been the Master, or Instructor, of at least one sorcerer, Albertus Magnus, who became Bishop of Ratisbon in Bavaria.

The Church discouraged any occult knowledge or manifestation outside her own walls, but made ample use within of matters attributed to the Devil when performed by others. However, when magical practices, either among groups or individuals, became too blatant the Pope or his representatives were forced to denounce them openly. So it came about that a very favourite method of divination, used by all ranks of the clergy, was forbidden publicly. This was called the "Sortilegium," or divination by "sortes" or lots, which had even been used by St' Agustine himself.

The system was perfectly simple. Seven candles were lighted and placed upon the altar of church or chapel, and an invocation uttered in the name of the Trinity that light might be shed upon the immediate future or some particular problem. The Bible was then placed on the altar and opened at random, the first verse meeting the eyes being interpreted as having a bearing upon the case in point. I believe quite a number of people have engaged in this form of prediction for themselves, without knowing that they were practising sorcery in the eyes of the Church.

The accounts of saints, hermits, priests and monks who held converse with demons, are too numerous to mention, from the famous temptations of St. Anthony onwards. However, there is a flavour about many of them that make one think that they were either pure inventions for the glorification of the Church, or else that actual dealings with evil spirits were very much altered and glossed for the same reason. A case in point is the Golden Legend, in which may be read a description of conversations between St. Dominic and a devil. The answers of the demon to the Saint's questions very much support the interests of the clergy of the day.

At one period a perfect epidemic of demoniac obsession swept through the convents of Europe, accompanied by attacks by the Devil on the nuns and the practice of sorcery. This outbreak was particularly marked in Germany, Holland and Italy. The nuns declared that the Devil himself visited them, had carnal conversation with them, and in some cases actual intercourse. Their behaviour became extremely peculiar—they being impelled to sing and dance to the utterances of blasphemies; to climb trees in the convent gardens; to disarrange their clothing in a suggestive manner, or to abandon it altogether. The devils in them threw them on the ground, caused them to swell to abnormal sizes and to abandon all evidences of piety or sanity. During and after these attacks they vomited nails, pins, bits of iron and all manner of peculiar substances that they vowed had never been swallowed.

Sister Mary of the convent of St. Esprit, in France, caused

"The Church made ample use, within her walls, of matters attributed to the Devil."

a complete upheaval in that holy establishment, and gave a certain priest a great deal of trouble in his efforts to exorcise the obsessing demon. The nuns of the convent of Nazareth, in Cologne, also suffered from sexual manifestations, induced by attacks from the Devil and his followers Similar outbreaks occurred at the convent of Auxonnes, throwing the nuns into terrible convulsions, during which they emitted fearful shrieks and cries and went into all manner of unnatural contortions. The dignitaries of the Sorbonne investigated these cases, and apparently could only come to the conclusion of demoniac obsessions.

In the year 1633, the Bridget Nuns, near Xanthus, behaved like sheep, jumping about and bleating continuously. While, when the sisters of an Ursuline convent in France were seized by one of these Satanic onslaughts, their confessor, Urbain Grandier, was suspected of casting spells over them by sorcery and was accordingly arrested. No evidence of having made a pact with the Devil could be found against him, but it was alleged that his life was immoral and that his writings proved his beliefs and practices to be contrary to established religions. Nuns then came forward, admitting their complicity with demons and testifying against Grandier, so that he was accordingly burnt at the stake. The troubles at the convent continued, however, and it was a long time before the disturbance was finally quelled by the exorcisms of a certain Brother Surin.

Another strange manifestation of collective mental abnormality, though not directly connected with sorcery, was the Brotherhood of Flagellants. There had been several outbreaks of religious self-torture, but the worst occurred about the middle of the eleventh century; inaugurated first by a monk, Dominicus Loricutus, and later by Peter Damian, Cardinal of Ostia (1072).

These men lashed themselves and each other unmercifully with knotted leather scourges until the blood ran, two or three times daily. They gathered bands and, marching into towns and villages, called upon the inhabitants to come and be scourged for their sins. Men, women and even children joined the Flagellants, and threw themselves into orgies of self-torture, and sadism.

This sadistic practice swept over Europe, and became especially popular in certain districts, and it has been noted that an outbreak of religious flagellation frequently preceded an epidemic of the Plague, or Black Death. The fanatical Flagellants at length began to claim ability to cure disease and cast out devils, and the Papal authorities became disquieted by the abuses of the sect. Pope Clement VI and the Emperor Charles IV finally prohibited their practices, although they were by no means immediately stamped out.

These were the times when the Witches Sabbaths, and sorcery of all kinds, engaged the minds of the people. In many outlying villages and hamlets nearly all the inhabitants frequented Satanic meetings, where they could give unbridled rein to their passions and find an outlet for the dullness of their lives in the excitement of demonism. As a result the Church no doubt felt it must provide some counter-attraction, and the clergy introduced various feasts, moralities and miracle plays. These were certainly far from holy in their respective precedure and execution, and even if they succeeded in so far as they appealed to the populace, to a disinterested onlooker they might not have been found so very different from the influences they were designed to supersede.

One such performance was the Feast of Asses, celebrated publicly in churches or in the chapels of the monasteries. Readers will notice beneath the foolery a disquieting resemblance between some of the practices at this and similar feasts and those performed at the Sabbaths and celebrations of the Black Mass. In this particular ceremony an ass, covered with sacredotal robes, was led to the altar, where a priest conducted a service before it and hymns were chanted as discordantly as possible. Pails of dirty water were flung at the heads of the singers, and the ass provided with food and drink. The feast continued on and off for two days, the participants, both monks and laymen, drinking, dancing and braying like asses.

A variation of the Feast of Asses was for a " Pope of Fools " to be chosen, who burlesqued the divine service. During the service rubbish was burnt in the censers, and obscene singing and dancing took place. Sometimes the monks, priests and laity disguised themselves in the skins of animals and behaved with abominable depravity, the while ordure and filth were scattered among the audience and games of dice were played upon the altar.

The moralities and religious plays were full of " cross-talk " between saints and demons, very much to the latter's disadvantage, and the Devil himself always figured to receive ultimate defeat at the hands of the clergy. There were all kinds of religious representations of the life of Christ, but not all were remarkable for either beauty or art. Among them was a very naïve play based on the legend of the Garden of Eden, in which Adam and Eve appeared entirely naked! One of the charges brought against witches and the sabbath gatherings by the Church was the immorality of their nude dancing, but the inconsistency seems to have passed unnoticed at the time.

An enormous number of monks and priests gave themselves up to sorcery, and there was no lack of apostate priests to perform the ceremonies of the Black Mass. Some abandoned the Church, but many more continued their practices within the monasteries and convents, or became the private confessors of royalty and nobility, for whom they conducted their blasphemous sorceries. It was notorious that Catherine de Medici had such a priest at her beck and call, and Benvenuto Cellini secured the assistance of one who performed necromancy and sorcery to restore Cellini's mistress at the Coliseum in Rome. It is recorded that even Cardinal Wolsey was in league with a monk who cast spells on his behalf, and manufactured for him a magic ring which had such power that when he wore it Henry VIII could deny him nothing.

Many charges of sorcery were brought against eminent and learned men within the Church; but it is not always easy to determine the truth of them, accusations of that description frequently being made by those jealous of their achievements or power.

For instance, Trithemius was an abbot of the Benedictine Monastery at Spanheim and also an exceedingly clever man. He had many abstruse works to his credit and was an advanced alchemist. The Emperor Maximilian, being terribly grieved at the early death of his first wife, Mary of Burgundy, in his distress sent to Trithemius for consolation. On the latter's arrival, the Emperor repeatedly said that he could be comforted if only he might see his wife again. Trithemius asked him if this was his earnest desire, and the Emperor having replied in the affirmative, the Abbot then and there proceeded to call up the spirit of his wife. The lady appeared before her astonished husband's eyes, as fresh and lively as in life, but the Emperor exclaimed that it could not really be her! Trithemius then asked Maxmilian to remember some particular mark on his wife's body by which he would know her, and Maxmilian recalled a small scar upon the back of her neck which no one knew but himself. The Abbot asked him to inspect the apparition for this mark, and sure enough it was there. Instead of being grateful for the manifestation, however, the Emperor was displeased and denounced Trithemius as a necromancer and banished him to the monastery. When eventually he died, Trithemius communicated to a monk a prescription for the elixir of life, although it seems scarcely an appropriate moment for recommending a method of securing comparative material immortality!

A very great number of the clergy made walking and talking statues, which were possibly not magic in intenton but early attempts to manufacture "robots." They also made brass heads, for the purpose of acting as oracles. One of these "talking heads" was the work of Robert Grossetête, Bishop of Lincoln (1235), and the friar, Roger Bacon, possessed one as well.

The priests of Rome certainly did not disdain temporal power, and it must often have been as much ambition as anything that impelled them to sorcery; the Jesuits, in particular, being lovers of power and deeply versed in occult matters. However, they did not employ their magic for this alone, but were in some instances noted for using sorcery for immoral purposes. This was the sorcery by breath, which is a well-known method in the East.

Breath is the very essence of life, and it can be used by the occultists for many other purposes than merely breathing. The effects of "insufflation" are well known; by this process prolonged warm breathing upon a person stimulates their magnetism, and operators, if good and without wrong intentions themselves, have been enabled to cure diseases by such means. On the other hand, there is a similar method that is used in sorcery. This last is cold breathing and has a repellent effect; animals, particularly, can be warded off by a steady cold breath, which they greatly fear.

The priests in question breathed upon the women whom they desired, and thereby aroused in them insatiable sexual passion for the breather. So many scandals had arisen in the Church on that account that Augustine, Jerome and Gregory denounced this form of sorcery, while the Emperor

Constantine forcibly proscribed against "sorcery by the breath to arouse lustful passions."

Several priests met their death at the stake. One of them being the Curé of Peifane, who seduced a well-born and virtuous woman, the Dame du Lieu. Another was a priest named Gaufridy, who breathed upon a penitent at the confessional and had intercourse with her, for which he was burnt by the Parliament of Provence

Père Girard, again, a Jesuit priest, was accused at Aix in 1731 of seducing a certain Mlle Catherine Cadiere by the same means, and of other revolting offences in connection with her. The lady in question was young and pure and lived with her parents, but her confessor became enflamed with a passion for her. One day Girard found an excuse to blow away something from the lady's gown, and from that moment she fell under his spell and became infatuated with him. Her religious ecstasies increased, and she even displayed the Christ stigmata of wounded hands and feet and bleeding forehead! It was not long before the priest found an opportunity to see her alone, whereupon he breathed on her again and placed her in such a delirium of passion that she realised nothing until his purpose was accomplished. For some time their relations continued; the priest trading upon his charge's simplicity and religious fervour, to induce her to believe that she had done nothing wrong. At length doubts arise in Mlle Cadiere's mind, and she told her parents all that had occurred. In consequence Père Girard was arrested, and accounts relate that he was acquitted of the charges, while others state that he was burnt at the stake.

A marked feature of these ecclesiastical sorceries was that the victims nearly all experienced visions and ecstasies, and received these stigmata already referred to; although in the circumstances they could not possibly have contracted anything but the worst and lowest spiritual influences. It will thus be seen that the ecstatic and exalted frame of mind peculiar to religious fanatics is largely due to physiological and psychological causes, allied with unwise opening up of the personality to astral influences.

Even the Popes were not exempt from charges of sorcery. Silvester II, among others, was believed to have attained his position by making a pact with the Devil, and to have obtained much of his wealth from buried treasure discovered by sorcery. However that may be, he was one of the most brilliant and learned men of his day, although he is supposed to have confessed his complicity with Satan to his Cardinals before his death. His very tomb was regarded with awe and considered to have magical properties, one of them being that his effigy wept tears before the accession of subsequent Popes.

Pope Leo the Great wrote a collection of charms and incorporated them with a magical work called the *Enchiridion of Pope Leo,* but it was on the whole a very inferior production. Notwithstanding this, it found favour with the Emperor Charlemagne, who is reported to have written to Leo expressing his pleasure in it and remarking on his good fortune since possessing it.

Benedict IX came from a noble and ambitious family who secured the Papal throne for him, and was noted for his evil life and debauchery. He was also a past master of sorcery, and among other things made the matrons and maidens of Rome follow him up on the hills and groves, though what transpired after that history does not relate.

Boniface VIII was thought to be an exponent of the black art. When arrested and charged with witchcraft, he refused to recognise a council not called by himself. He was eventually released, but the anxieties and troubles which he had experienced conduced to his death. He was believed to have power over the elements, and to be able to produce thunder and lightning at will.

The magical achievements of the Bishop of Ratisbon caused quite a stir in his day, the well-known Catholic bishop having the power to bring about changes of temperature and to produce fruits and flowers out of their season. He was considered a sorcerer, but he himself claimed that he had no assistance from either God or Devil, relying entirely upon the achievements of his own power.

In the reign of Louis XVI the infamous Abbé Guibourg was associated with a notorious woman named Catherine Deshayes (La voisine), who practised sorcery and was involved in cases of poisoning. They celebrated the Black Mass in cellars, and sacrificed young children for their abominable purposes. Lemignan, vicar of St. Eustace in Paris, was also convicted of having dedicated and sacrificed children to Satan.

In England the magical adventures of a monk called William Stapleton, in the reign of Henry VIII, were recorded at the Rolls House. In 1527 he was living in the monastery of St. Benet at Holm in Norfolk, and was set upon the road of sorcery by certain works on black magic lent to him by a parish priest. He began after six months study to practise sorcery, and obtained a magic ring, a plate, a cup, a sword and a circle. Eventually he secured leave from the monastery, and set about discovering buried treasure. However, he failed in his first tests to discover gold at Calkett Hall, by means of a book to which another monk was said to have bound a spirit by necromantic methods. Having taken up sorcery in good faith, Stapleton was obliged to fall back upon common fraud in order to substantiate his claims. In the end he was imprisoned ; probably at the instigation of Cardinal Wolsey, whom he had accused of sorcery in the course of some investigations.

Nor was sorcery confined to the male orders of the Church. A Spanish nun, named Magdalen of the Cross, was Abbess of a convent at Cordova. The nuns strongly suspected her of black magic and, knowing this, in hope of obtaining the Pope's pardon, she confessed that from an early age she had had almost nightly intercourse with the Devil in the shape of a Moor. The demon, as a recompense for her favours, was said to help her to perform seeming miracles, such as levitation, and at certain celebrations of the Holy Eucharist the Host was conveyed to her through the air in the presence of the congregation of nuns.

Pope Joan, who once occupied the throne of the Vatican, was reputed to be the blackest sorcerer of them all. A certain work on magic has been attributed to her, and the female Pope or Priestess on the Tarot cards was said to represent her ; but, on the other hand, this figure is certainly symbolical of Isis. It is possible, however, that at one time a set of cards was made with the High Priestess of the Major Arcana, resembling Pope Joan, in the aspect of a Priestess of Isis.

There are endless accounts of pacts made with the Devil. One actually exists in writing, made by the monk Louis Gaufridi already referred to ; although Satan would appear to have failed his partner, in view of the monk's ultimate fate. The Inquisition with all its attendant horrors does not enter here ; but who knows if the Church's ferocity towards witchcraft and sorcery may not have been all the greater in its attempt to cover the corruption within ?

CHAPTER VIII

WITCHCRAFT, VAMPIRISM AND WEREWOLVES IN EUROPE

Deals with witchcraft on the Continent, and relates various beliefs in vampires and werewolves, with accounts of instances of Lycanthropy, etc.

AS we have seen, witchcraft—whether real or imaginary—flourished everywhere in Europe during the Middle Ages. It continued to be common, in spite of suppression, until fairly recent times, and even to-day is by no means dead as so many people imagine. Witches were persons of both sexes, who were able to perform acts beyond the scope of ordinary folk by means of help from evil spirits and by the casting of spells.

However, the word "witch" came to be applied almost exclusively to women who were believed to achieve their power by making a blood pact with the Devil, sealed with their blood. They were usually old and ugly, and for this reason many unfortunate old ladies, whose only crimes were loneliness and a lack of beauty, went to the stake. There are many accounts of spritely and seductive young witches, who by "sex-appeal" lured men to destruction or introduced them to their own evil ways. They were supposed regularly to attend witches' meetings or Sabbaths; these ceremonies being terrible orgies where the participants indulged in drinking blood and urine, kissing the posterior of the materialised devil—usually in the form of a goat, and trampling upon the Host in the ceremony of the Black Mass. Promiscuous sexual indulgence took place, and every filthy act the human mind can conceive was performed accompanied by gluttony and drunkenness.

Witches of all ages attended these lively gatherings by flying away on their broomsticks, or else being taken by a spirit in the form of a wild animal, who also thoughtfully conducted them back before sunrise. It was not so simple a matter for a witch to handle her broomstick, and there are amusing accounts of mischievous demons tipping them up and upsetting them in the branches of trees, where they were subsequently found woefully entangled. Sometimes the witches conducted friends to these gatherings, and then accidents were more than ever apt to happen *en route*, presumably owing to the disapproval of Satan, who was quite particular in his own way about whom he accepted. Priests, however, were especially welcome.

Before starting out, it was the custom to anoint the body with certain ointments, which in authentic cases undoubtedly helped by their drug-like qualities to produce physical excitement, hysteria and hallucinations.

Every witch had her familiar, an animal, reptile or bird, which was her constant companion and was believed to be an evil spirit taking that form. On their first initiation at their Sabbaths these women were often presented with a toad, which they were strictly enjoined to take great care of. The witches dressed these engaging pets in a sort of crimson velvet sack, with a little hood like a monk's cowl, and tied around the middle. Milk formed their chief diet, and this they were supposed to imbibe from the witch herself, from a third " teat " which had been made beneath the arm by a nip from the Devil's pincers. Cats, owls and snakes were also used as familiars. The neophyte was given a new name in place of the baptismal one, usually of an evil and revolting character, and this was written in blood in the Devil's book, the covers of which were bound in the skin of unbaptised infants.

There is a great gulf between the majestic witch of classic antiquity, such as the Witch of Endor and of the Norse Sagas, and the witches of Europe in the Middle Ages. The latter had degenerated into commonplace practitioners of petty evil for the most part, and had lost the grandeur of earlier times. They were, on the whole, women of the peasant class ; ignorant, crude and themselves credulous, although there were instances even then of ladies of high rank having given themselves up to the black art. Sometimes the alliance was forever, sometimes only for a term of years ; but in our experience it is easier to ally oneself with evil than to turn from it, and, once having set dark forces into operation, it is to be expected that the majority became the helpless servants of the powers invoked. The evil one set his seal upon his followers once they had vowed themselves to him by [illegible] k with his hoof, a nip with pincers or some other implement, all of which had the same property of being insensible forever after. This insensible spot was always searched for with pins by the examiners in trials of witchcraft.

The worst kinds of sorcery, witchcraft and black magic were practised in France, Spain and Italy, and although the folklore and history of Germany teemed with accounts of witches and so forth, they do not take on the degraded aspects of French and Italian magic until the fourteenth century. The Black Forest, the Harz Mountains, and particularly the Brocken Peak, were the home of every possible form of magic and wizardry in Germany. In Teutonic legends the beautiful witch is often a feature; for example, there is the Lorelei, who by her glorious hair and marvellous singing lured enchanted voyagers and fishermen to destruction on the rocks of the Rhine, and Wagner has immortalised the symbolically glorious witch of the Venusberg in *Tannhäuser*.

In the British Isles the meeting-places and the meetings of witches and warlocks were called "covens." The relation between this word and the word convent is interesting, as betraying its religious connection. A coven grew to mean a meeting-place for twelve witches and the Devil. Now, this Devil may indeed have appeared as a materialisation of evil in assemblies of intensely Satanic power, as most occultists will agree, but more often than not the Chief or Leader of the coven, personally known only to a few, impersonated the Prince of Darkness.

The Chief of the coven arrived quietly and inconspicuously and, divesting himself of his garments, donned a mask with horns or antlers, and had another fixed to the lower part of the spine for the assembly to kiss. This posterior mask was nearly always used, particularly in early times. A French witch, accused of kissing the posterior of Satan, indignantly refuted the idea of obscenity exclaiming, "It is indeed another face that he bears beneath his tail!" However, sometimes the votaries were not even helped by this illusion of covering when the Goat offered its buttocks to receive the affectionate kiss of the neophyte.

The actual Sabbath occurred only once in seven years, and the other meetings were merely "covens." At the Sabbaths the Black Mass was practised, but this we will deal with separately in a later chapter. A dreadful feature of meetings was the presence of little children, who were

"The actual Sabbath occurred only once in seven years."

brought to be sealed to the Devil and were only too frequently the votive offering or human sacrifice. Stillborn babies and unbaptised infants were especially sought after for cannibalistic purposes. All over Europe many witches were midwives, who dedicated babies to Satan the instant they were born. The Church became alarmed by this wholesale incursion upon its future members, and a society of male midwives was formed under the auspices of the priests and Church, to counteract the activities of the Satanic nurses and to baptise infants even before the severance of the umbilical cord.

Children were so greatly in request by the Devil that if the witches were unable to produce a child of their own in the ordinary course of events, they had to procure one by some means or other, and many unfortunate little ones were kidnapped, or in some cases kept by the witches until the time for sacrifice arrived. We can thus see where the foundation of many of childhood's fairy stories arose, particularly those of Grimm and Hans Andersen. In Germany St. Walpurgis night was the great event in the witches' calendar, and an eyewitness of one of these hellish gatherings is related to have seen a ring of children seated beyond giant toads, the witches' familiars, being yet too young to take part in the rituals and orgies. There are, however, many accounts and old engravings extant of children being presented to the Devil to receive his mark. Witches also used the corpses of children extensively in making fat for their ointments and candles.

The Sabbaths and covens were only witches' high-days and holidays, and the greater part of their work was carried on from their own little huts and hovels. Most witches were women who lived alone, in part, because like most occultists they chose to do so, in part because the general community feared and shunned them.

In their dwellings witches concocted love philtres and potions, and worked their spells and enchantments. For the most part such were composed of herbs like Artemisia, Hemp, Camphire, Flax, Coiander, Anise, Cardamom, Aloeswood and Chicory. The purpose of the mixtures was to make apparitions appear. A concoction founded on a basis of animal matter consisted of a Lapwing, Lion's Gall, Bull's Gall, the Fat of a White Hen, Eyes of a Black Cat, and Ant's Eggs. All had to be boiled together according to the ancient manuscript in which the charm was found. The sorcerer does not tell us where to obtain the Lion's Gall, but perhaps an obliging demon provided that! Aromatics were used, too, especially in necromancy, and an old recipe of that sort comprises Musk, Myrrh, Frankincense, Red Storax, Mastick, Olibanum, Saffron, Benzoin and Labdanum. In the event of anyone wishing to invoke the very Prince of Spirits, the following ingredients were prescribed to be burnt—Juice of Hypericon, Saffron, Artemisia, and the root of Valerian. Witches always anointed themselves with ointments before departing up the chimney to their Sabbaths. One such ointment was composed of Aconite, Belladonna, Water Parsley, Cinquefoil and Babies' Fat. The property of some of those ingredients was to produce various states of excitement or numbness, and they undoubtedly not only spurred the witches on to their wild doings but produced hallucinations as well. The Mandrake, which was extensively used in black magic of all kinds, is the plant that is supposed to utter a terrible cry like a human being on being plucked. It is of two varieties, the male and female, and witches often kept both specimens in bottles for magic purposes. From the Mandrake, mandragonia is obtained—a powerful narcotic used by the old Greeks as an anæsthetic.

Although tradition portrays the witch as ancient and hag-like, many young women indulged in sorcery as well. Some were even married, and their husbands unaware of their true nature until some accident betrayed them. Such often escaped from their homes at night by placing their husbands in an enchanted sleep, or by leaving an image resembling themselves in the bed. There are many accounts of husbands denouncing their wives for witchcraft on discovering their activities, and one cannot but wonder how often this was found an easy way of getting rid of an unwanted wife!

No one has reasonably explained why witches always departed up the chimney, although many theories have been advanced. There are a number of engravings and pictures depicting them about to ascend in that manner, some of them intensely interesting. Goya has given us two of the best pictures on the subject; one representing a materialisation of the Goat Baphomet surrounded by a few followers, the other depicting three male sorcerers about to depart for a Sabbath up the chimney. The atmosphere of the second picture is very grim and macabre, the sorcerers being in the process of changing into animals.

Much of the practice of witchcraft depended on the possession of the Evil Eye. This was sometimes believed to be an involuntary gift, often accompanying a squint, and proved to be an even more unfortunate matter for the possessor than other people, sometimes even leading them to the stake. Upon other practitioners of witchcraft this baleful glance was said to be bestowed as a reward by the Evil One, and by it were enchanted children, lovers, animals, crops and cattle, and a host of different things. If a crop failed, a cow fell sick, or an accident happened, everyone began to look around for the possessor of the blighting Evil Eye.

Witches were kept quite busy, causing all manner of sickness and harm at the behest of those who consulted them. Even to-day in rural districts the Evil Eye is dreaded. In old times, if the possession was only acquired and not a natural attribute, it was thought that its power could be warded off by saying something disgustingly rude, or by displaying some atrociously vulgar gesture accompanied by loud laughter. Which custom led to some very Rabelaisian performances, as may be imagined. Another method of neutralising the influence was by extending the first and little fingers of the right hand, representing the horns of the Moon. It is recounted that the Devil had told his followers: "If you bear anyone ill will, look at them full and wish them every evil in my name, and you will get your heart's desire."

During these times compacts with the Devil were very common, and were made for apparently trifling objects. There were three methods. The first was a solemn ceremony, complete with circles, burning herbs and so on, in the midst of which the Prince of Darkness himself would appear. The second was a simple request in writing, signed by the one who requested his favours. The last took the form of merely a tacit understanding. All engagements taken on by the Devil were of criminal or impious nature, and if the human covenanter failed to keep his word, or wished to withdraw, the punishment was instant death.

At all times and in all places a favourite form of witchcraft was to cause illness or death by means of a wax figure. A small image was made representing the victim, and this was subjected to all kinds of adverse treatment; pins being stuck through the eyes, heart, bowels, and so forth. Such treatment was accompanied by burning herbs and various incantations, with the object of causing agony and death. Sometimes a human heart and long needles were used in the ceremony.

As it was the custom to leave the bodies of malefactors hanging in chains on public gibbets until they literally fell to pieces, it was not difficult to obtain human remains for the practice of black magic. Sorcerers and other practitioners of witchcraft used to make a variety of candlestick called the Hand of Glory, chiefly from the flesh of criminals obtained in this manner. Sometimes a whole hand was dried and used, and sometimes a variety of stands were made in the shape of the crescent moon. These human candleholders were said to have the power of making everyone who saw them unable to move. Thieves confessed to having obtained such magical articles, which also had the property of opening any lock to which they were held.

No sorcerer or witch could have communion with the dead or with demons without first making a circle. And modern occultists also recognise the importance of circles. There are many forms of circles and pentacles ; they are a feature of what may be called good magic as well as black, and form a very important part of all exorcism. For instance, there was an evil spirit named Lilas, who was supposed to be the wife of Satan. Her particular activity was to enter the room of a confined woman and kill the newly born child. In order to exorcise this she-devil, the attendants made circles on the walls with charcoal, within each was written : " Adam, Eve, Lilas, avaunt ! "

A great deal of the literature of witchcraft has been attributed to Solomon. One such book was banned by Pope Innocent VI, because it was filled with evocations and rules for communicating with Devils. Another, *La Claveicule de Salomon,* is full of interest to the sorcerer, and would-be necromancer and student of the occult.

By the third century the Church had found that, in order to cope with witchcraft, they needed a band of special exorcists. Demons and devils were almost as common as witches, often appearing in the most grotesque forms. Sometimes they were shapeless trunks, with no heads, but immense bellies with faces upon them, the arms and legs stuck out at extraordinary angles. Sometimes a face replaced the genital organs, or, again, those appeared in an exaggerated form upon unlikely parts of the body. It is enough to say that the creatures presented every possible nightmare conception. Incidentally, such beings may be said to have an existence of a sort upon the lower astral planes; they are the elementals created by man's evil desires and unclean thoughts. When the occult truth is recognised that every thought makes a definite creation, then foul shapes of an elemental kind will be disintegrated and cease to wield their influence upon this plane of existence. The sufferer from "delirium tremens" is not deluded; he is simply all at once conscious of the devils his habit had created, and finds himself surrounded by the vile shapes of his passion for drink with all its attendant vices and horrors.

It would almost seem that the people of earlier times were scarcely astonished or perturbed by the most amazing manifestations, judging by the very old engravings which show quite comfortable and even friendly relations between demons and ordinary people. Monks and saints, presumably backed by the moral support of the Church, are to be seen complacently surrounded by every variety of loathsome and grotesque creature.

Many people famous in history are mentioned as having had dealings with witchcraft, either being themselves sorcerers or having had dealings with them for various reasons. Benvenuto Cellini gives a most interesting account of resorting to sorcery, in order to get in touch with his mistress, Angelica. The poet Virgil undoubtedly practised witchcraft, and is supposed to have had remarkable adventures with a Princess of Babylon by means of sorcery. The history of witchcraft in Italy is closely interwoven with the Church, even some of the Popes not being exempted from accusation of practising the black art.

Italy was, also, the home of astrology in Europe. It is very interesting to note how Italian witchcraft appears to-day as the survival of the pagan religions of Rome. Even now there are old people, in out-of-the-way places, who know the Etruscan names of the twelve gods; while sorcery is known there as "La Vecchia Religione"—the old religion. In these parts a magic rite is sometimes carried on by the young people. A feast, composed of meal, salt, honey and water, among other things, is placed upon a table and a special conjuration said over it. The conjuration is fourfold—one being to the meal, one to the salt, one to Cain, one to Diana the Moon Goddess. After that, naked men and women sit down to eat, and later dance, sing and make love in the darkness.

In speaking of the black magic of the past we cannot ignore Gilles de Laval, Lord of Raiz, Marshal of France. He was a native of Brittany, and fought against the English under Joan of Arc. On his retirement from the strenuous life of a soldier, he married and kept up an immense estate of great luxury. In course of time his need of money caused him to investigate alchemy, and finally to ally himself with a sorcerer named Prelati. In the pursuit of their ends the two men took to the most hideous practices of the black art imaginable, in which the mutilation, torture, rape and murder of little children of both sexes played a very large part. At length, while the Lord of Raiz was away on a pretended visit to the Holy Land (but in reality was only on a short journey to consult his sorcerer), his wife, who had had her suspicions aroused, investigated and discovered the most gruesome and terrible relics of her husband's guilt. Laval returned suddenly, having been told that he must now go to the length of sacrificing his unborn child to the Devil. He discovered that his wife knew everything, and proceeded to take her to his chapel reserved for the Black Mass, where his priests and accomplice presided. There Laval announced his intention of literally disembowelling the wretched woman in order to make a cannibalistic sacrifice of the child she was carrying. At that point, however, there mercifully occurred the unexpected arrival of the lady's brothers to visit her. The Lord of Raiz was compelled to release his victim, but under the threat of immediately carrying out his dreadful purpose if she hinted at any trouble to her brothers. The lady managed to face the visitors with outward serenity, but she and her sister were at length able to convey the facts of their terrible position. After a fierce struggle between his own retainers and those of his wife's brothers, Laval and his sorcerer Prelati were captured. Accused of sodomy, rape, murder and sorcery, they were finally tried by the Bishop of Nantes, and executed by being hanged and burnt somewhere about the year 1440. The beautiful castle of Champtoce, the scene of innumerable horrors, still stands in a lovely valley; but the peasants say that the ghost of Laval, accompanied by some of his tiny victims, haunts the castle walls in wailing and great misery.

The practice of witchcraft and sorcery eventually became so rife that the Church set up an Inquisition to deal with it, when literally thousands of people, including small children, were sent to the stake. Indeed, such an hysterical fear seized everyone that all accused of sorcery had little chance of reprieve. The authorities lost all judgment between true evil-doers and the innocent (there were probably far more of the latter), and the mildest mediumistic gift was supposed to manifest witchcraft. Joan of Arc, whom the English burnt as a witch at Rouen, was an outstanding example. In a word, the hideous cruelties inflicted upon these poor creatures were as terrible as the crimes of which they were accused, and so a vicious circle of horror and bloodshed was caused.

Many of the accusations included that of turning into an animal, or of forcing others to do so. The commonest form of this was transformation into a wolf, which gave rise to the universal European legend of werewolves. Nearly every country in the world has records of similar creatures; only sometimes it is the changing of men into tigers, hyenas, leopards and, in colder lands, bears, foxes, dogs and cats. I have heard of seal-men in Iceland and the Esquimo lands of the far north.

I have seen myself many strange transformations in this connection in my own country. The accounts of enchantment by which people were turned, either permanently or for a time, into animals seem to have very slight foundation, although they are as numerous as the legends of the werewolves themselves. Closely bound up with this subject is that of Lycanthropy, and it is possible that people suffering from this horrible mania, which is very rare now, formed a basis for many of the so-called enchantments. Now and again, particularly among the peasantry of France and the peoples of Austria, Russia and the Balkan States, instances do crop up where the individual is seized with a desire to violate graves and devour corpses.

A famous case in point was that of a French soldier, Sergeant Bretrand, as recently as 1849. The authorities of the great cemetery of Père la Chaise in Paris were puzzled and horrified by the wholesale desecration of graves and the mutilation of corpses that took place in July of that year. Attendants had noticed a shadowy form flitting about the graveyard, and had imagined it to be a ghost. Many rumours were rife, and the cemetery more rigidly guarded. The horrible activities were then transferred to more out-of-the-way cemeteries. At last the ghastly visitant was shot at, and left behind in his hurried escape the portion of a military tunic. Late that same night soldiers in a barracks discovered a sergeant so badly wounded by bullets that he had to be removed to a military hospital. The unhappy man thereupon confessed that an overwhelming impulse would seize him to tear open graves and violate and feed upon the corpses they contained. If the bodies were newly dead, so much the better. The full details of the sergeant's admissions are too horrible to relate. After his nauseating orgies, Bretrand would be overcome by a coma and not impelled to his horrible lust for many days.

Gilles de Laval, already mentioned, became a victim of this same mania through his practice of black magic. Laval admitted that while tearing open his living victims it gave him the most exquisite pleasure to behold their sufferings and torture, and that tears, cries and supplications only enhanced his terrible joy. He was also overcome with coma after his holocausts.

In recent years the murderer of Dusseldorf, Peter Kurten, who was executed in July, 1931, destroyed many women and children and a man, after violating them and literally feeding upon their quivering flesh and drinking their blood. Kurten was, moreover, possessed by the rage for blood (hæmatomania); being called the vampire of Dusseldorf, as most of my readers will remember. His known victims numbered over a score, but there were probably many undiscovered; besides women who had been attacked but had been fortunate enough to escape.

There was also a case in America in 1935 of an old man who was sentenced to the electric chair for sacrificing and eating many children for the purposes of black magic. At his trial the old man confessed to his misdeeds in this respect.

Returning to far earlier times, in 1521, a Frenchman admitted that he was a werewolf and had become so after making a pact with the Devil at the witches' Sabbath. By anointing himself with a certain ointment, he could turn

" A young woman was pointed out . . . as one who turned into a wolf at night."

into a wolf during the hours of night till dawn, and in that form he had killed and mauled many people, besides having sexual intercourse with wolves. A peculiarity of were-animals is the sympathy that exists between their animal form and that of the human with whom it is connected. Most werewolves left their own bodies during their excursions, and if anyone were able to kill or injure these creatures the witch or the sorcerer would be found dead or wounded in a similar portion of the body. Hunters in many lands had tales to relate of having shot an animal—wolf, bear, or tiger—only to find in its place the body of a man. The legends and instances of this kind are too numerous to recount.

Hundreds of German, Scandinavian and Slavonic stories for children are based on the subject of witchcraft and were-wolves; not really the most suitable subject for them, to our modern minds.

As night fell over the little villages of Europe, so many of them situated on the outskirts of forests, in deep valleys or stowed away high up among the mountain peaks of Italy, Switzerland or Germany, or surrounded by the frozen wastes and sinister forests of Russia, the peasantry hurried back to their cottages and feared to brave the uncanny dangers and horrors of darkness except in numbers. A lone wolf, slinking through the trees to prowl around the deserted little tracks and humble homes, on the outlook for an opportunity to seize upon a woman drawing water at a late hour from the village well, might only too likely be the dread werewolf lusting after human flesh and thirsting for human blood. Hearts throbbed and blood froze at an unexpected knock upon the door, which so often lured a peasant out to the waiting ghoul, or admitted the weary traveller who would later in the night assume his or her wolfish form, to ravish and rend the helpless family or depart with a cherished child.

The human being who was a werewolf was supposed to have the characteristics of glaring eyes (often with the pupil vertical instead of round), long front teeth and very long nails. The writer's wife, when visiting Germany as a child, remembers having a young woman pointed out to her in a Bavarian village as one who turned into a wolf at night, and would come and eat her up if she were not careful. This girl was a laundress, and on several occasions when bringing clean linen to the house tried to ingratiate herself with the children in the garden. The children, however, were repelled by the other's glassy eyes, cruel mouth and hands which, despite her occupation, had abnormally long nails. For the rest I believe the girl had golden hair and a fine complexion; nevertheless all the community feared and shunned her, if on no other grounds than purely instinctive ones.

The subject of werewolves is closely linked up with that of vampirism. The vampire is that terrible phenomenon, the living corpse. At night the vampire was supposed to rise from its grave and, gaining entrance to houses, to attack people in their sleep. The creature usually fixed its teeth in the veins of the neck, draining the victim of his or her blood. This performance was carried on nightly, the persons thus attacked becoming more and more weak and frequently dying of consumption if they did not succumb earlier. In past centuries the vampire was universally dreaded, and even to-day is still believed in and reported as existing all over Europe, particularly in the eastern portion of the Continent.

The vampire is also noted for its sexual activities, and its nocturnal visits are equally connected with lust as its thirst for blood. They are supposed to possess great strength when fully vitalised by their disgusting nourishment, even begetting children, who in their turn become living vampires. If any district was suffering from the depredations of these ghouls, an investigation was made of the local cemetery. There the coffin of the vampire, after being found and opened, was invariably discovered with its corpse fresh and full of blood—the eyes open, the lips full and red, the teeth and nails grown to an unusual length. The body was also flexible, and lacking the rigidity of death. The creature, however, was powerless during daylight hours, and, exorcising ceremonies having been performed in the cemetery, a stake was thrust through the corpse's heart. At that there would sound a terrible scream, while fresh blood spouted from the wound. As a rule, the body was then subsequently burnt.

Among many Russian tales of vampirism, there is an amusing one which runs as follows. A certain *mujik* was driving along a country road after nightfall, and paused to rest his tired horse by a cemetery. It was a bright moonlight night and, by that ghostly radiance, the *mujik* was horrified to see a nearby grave begin to heave, until by and by the

" At night the vampire was supposed to rise from its grave and to attack people."

earth fell away on either side and a coffin appeared. The lid burst open, and from the interior the corpse of a man dressed in his grave clothes emerged. The *mujik*, however, was not wanting in courage and, when this spectre had departed, he climbed over the low wall, went to the empty grave and removed the coffin-lid to the shelter of some nearby trees. There the man hid and awaited events. After an hour or so the vampire appeared, visibly refreshed and licking blood from its lips. When it reached the grave, it halted and gazed anxiously around, as though searching for the coffin-lid. Its glance then fell on the *mujik* and it fiercely demanded what he had done with the essential covering. "Not so fast, not so fast," said the *mujik*, "what have you been up to, I should like to know?" "It is none of your business," retorted the vampire. "Return my coffin-lid at once." "Not I," said the *mujik*. "Tell me first what you have been doing." "Don't waste time," shouted the ghoul, "the dawn is nearly here, and my time is getting short, and if you do not return it at once I shall attack you." "Pooh!" said the *mujik*, "you are full up already, and if you are in a hurry to return to your grave tell me whom you have killed." "Well, if you must know," said the vampire, "I have killed two little boys, and now where is the lid?" "Not yet," said the *mujik*. "Tell me how I can revive the children." "Fetch me the lid, and I will tell you," replied the ghoul. The *mujik* thereupon produced the top of the coffin and, seizing it, the vampire said: "Cut off a piece of my shroud and take it with you. Go to the boys' home and, shutting yourself in with their bodies, boil a pot of water. Put the live coals in the pot, and the piece of my shroud, and the steam that arises will revive them." So saying, the spectre hastily jammed itself into the coffin, which began to sink into the earth. Owing to the fact that the lid had not fitted properly in the creature's hurry, a piece of the shroud protruded. The *mujik* quickly cut this off and the coffin disappeared, the earth falling into place again just as dawn came. The *mujik* drove at once into the village, and was not long in finding the children's home. The parents were overcome with grief at the fate of their little sons, but the *mujik* assured them he could restore them to life. He set about carrying out the vampire's instructions, and sure enough as the steam arose from the live coals, the piece of shroud and the boiling water, the boys came to life again. The parents were overjoyed, but neighbours coming in to see the miracle suggested that the *mujik* must have caused the children's death in the first place. So everyone fell upon him and handled him very roughly, until he could make himself heard above the din, and was at length allowed to explain about the vampire. In the end they all adjourned to the cemetery with the priest, and, on opening the grave, the vampire was found fresh and warm, although he had been dead many months. Exorcism was performed, and an ash stake driven through the heart. The corpse at that uttered a fearful cry and, after an immense gush of blood, fell into decay and was burnt.

The grave of a vampire can usually be distinguished by several small holes appearing on the surface, about the size made by a man's finger.

In some countries it was the custom to decapitate the corpse, remove the heart, and impale the body with a stake of white thorn. As a precaution against vampires a wreath of garlic is sometimes worn around the neck while sleeping, or protection sought by using assafœtida on the body. In the West Indies great faith is put in this grass to ward off vampires and all occult evils. For many years a custom survived in England of piercing the hearts of suicides with a stake, which appeared to be a relic of belief in vampires; this custom was abolished by law in the year 1824.

In many parts of Europe people believed that so long as the body remained intact in the grave it drew vitality from the remaining members of the family. Not so long ago a Scotsman is reported to have exhumed the body of his daughter and burnt her heart, as he thought she was devitalising her remaining brother and sister and making them ill.

There were epidemics of vampirism in nearly all countries during the Middle Ages, which were assigned to witchcraft. There are immense numbers of accounts of vampires nightly visiting women, with amorous intentions, and sucking their blood as part of their lustful indulgence. Some even went so far as killing, or warding off, husbands who stood in the way. There were, however, also female vampires. Witches were said to practise vampirism, often sucking the blood of children and frail people. One quaint way of frustrating such women was to kill a dog or a cat, and place the body across the threshold. The witch would then have to stop and count every hair on the animal's body, for some obscure reason, and by that time dawn would have come and her power would be gone.

Bulgarian exorcists believed that they could imprison a vampire in a bottle. Their method was to present the ghoul with a picture of a saint, or an icon, whereupon it would retreat in fear and, if a bottle half-filled with blood were placed nearby, the vampire would vanish into it and it could be corked down and destroyed. Scandinavians believe extensively in vampirism, but consider it essential in destroying the creatures to pierce the heart of the vampire with a single blow from a maple stick ; if two blows were given, the creature would be revived.

Another belief is that the dead persons themselves are not always the vampires, but that an evil spirit animates the corpse for the satisfaction of its own foul desires. This is a far more reasonable theory, and the Hon. Ralph Shirley stated as recently as the year 1934 that he doubted whether vampirism is as absent from our midst as people think. However, it is difficult to obtain evidence in such cases ; the facts being usually concealed, in the same fashion as in the case of the birth of monsters.

CHAPTER IX

THE ALCHEMISTS AND SORCERERS OF THE THIRTEENTH TO EIGHTEENTH CENTURIES

Gives an account of the famous alchemists and sorcerers of the thirteenth and eighteenth centuries, and their pursuits of the elixir of life, etc. And the results of their practices ; the Mesmerists, etc.

THE art of alchemy first saw the light in the East, and was introduced into Europe by the Arabians through Spain. The great Arabian, Geber, called in his own country Bu-musa-Juba, the Azdite, was one of the greatest pioneers of true alchemy. These chemical philosophers claimed to be able to transmute base metals into pure gold or silver, and their two great quests were for the Philosopher's Stone and the Elixir of Life.

A perfect wave of alchemy swept over Europe during the Middle Ages, coinciding with the spread of witchcraft, and the mysterious activities and magical claims of the alchemists caused them to be looked upon as magicians by the majority of people. The true alchemists were serious scientific seekers, philosophers with vision and high ideals, and there are many illustrious names among them, covering several centuries. There were, however, men of a different calibre, who were simply charlatans mixing up their alchemy with inaccurate astrology, and practising fortune-telling and petty sorceries. They made large sums of money out of credulous people for their false experiments, and from fashionable women seeking perennial youth and rejuvenation. Many of these men turned to sorcery and black magic, hoping by their aid to discover an easy method of transmutation, and were willing to plunge themselves into any villany, in the hope of discovering the secret of fabricating gold and of the Elixir of Life.

Mention of the " Puffers " cannot be overlooked. This branch of alchemists did not attain the fame of their greater brethren, and were indeed looked upon by efficient workers as mere bunglers. They were derisively called " Puffers," being considered good for little more than puffing at their furnaces with bellows. However, though none of them rose to any great degree of alchemy, and expended their time and substance without achieving their goal, they, nevertheless, made accidental discoveries of great value to early chemistry; in fact, this science gained more from them than from the true alchemists. Thus, Kunckel accidentally isolated phosphorus, and Blaize de Vigenere stumbled upon the discovery of benzoic acid without knowing it, in the course of his experiments.

Alchemy had two aspects, the material and the mystic. The latter was expressed in the most elaborate symbology, which has been handed down, absolutely intact, from the earliest times. It was conveyed in exactly the same metaphorical language by alchemists of every age, without change or modification, since alchemy was held to be exact and perfect, and therefore did not admit of any change whatsoever, even through the passage of centuries.

Part of the use of symbolism was to ensure that the alchemists might at all times be understood by brother adepts, and at the same time it effectively cloaked their knowledge from the vulgar. They thought that by the true understanding of creation and the cosmos the secret of transmutation could be fathomed, and held that the first chapter of Genesis was the greatest page in alchemy. All calculations were based upon astrology, and number and colour played a very important part in their philosophy. Black was the paramount colour; next came ruby red, the hue of the fire of the sages; then perfect gold; then green—the "Green Lion" holding an important place, among others.

In alchemy of both the material and transcendental order the four elements were brought in, to assist in the completion of "the Great Work," as the search for the philosopher's stone was called. This stone was a mystery; a stone, yet not a stone. No one could hope to discover it, or to effect transmutations, who was not pure in heart and of single purpose. Only he who was noble, patient, just and pure, could attain the goal and initiation of alchemy. The alchemists' watch-word was: "Pray theosophically, and work psycho-chemically."

The Great Work took anything from a year to complete, the time of its commencement being calculated astrologically. The sun should be in the sign of the Ram, and the moon in that of the Bull. The vessel used for containing the necessary substances was egg-shaped; the matrix, or Orphic egg, which is found at the base of all initiations. This was called the Aludel, the furnace being an Athenor. This furnace had, also, a particular significance. The primitive substance of alchemy was mercury, but alchemists insisted that it was not ordinary mercury but that of the philosophers, which is purified and quickened by a secret process involving sulphur and mercury. All these, then, must be of the special variety of the sages, and not the ordinary and common substances. "Sulphur," it was said, "is everything that burns. Mercury is that which goes into air and consumes itself in vapour, and the residue is pure salt." Fire was essential in completing the Great Work, but there again it was the mystic fire that vivifies and does not destroy, as ordinary fire does. Some alchemists claimed that it was necessary to know how metals grew in the earth; engendered, as they supposed, by sulphur (a male principle) with mercury (female), the test of alchemical power being to discover their seeds.

Materially, it is recorded that certain of the alchemists succeeded in the transmutation of mercury into silver or gold. But on the whole there were many more discouraged and disappointed seekers and experimenters, who, if they did not drift into sorcery and charlatanism, lost money and health in their pursuit of the unattainable.

During the period covering the time from the thirteenth to the eighteenth centuries, there were so many alchemists of renown, both in Britain and on the Continent, that it is only possible to mention a few.

In England Michael Scott, whose patron was Frederick II, Fludd, Roger Bacon, who joined the Franciscan Brotherhood, Norton, George Riply, Alexander Seton, a Scotsman, who studied alchemy on the Continent, and Ashmole, who founded a society of alchemists at Oxford, are among the most outstanding and noted of the philosophers. On the Continent Jacob Boheme and Van Helmont were brilliant exponents of alchemy. The famous Dr. John Dee and Edward Kelly were alchemists, but they were of course also sorcerers and practitioners of necromancy.

One, Nicholas Flamel, was a master alchemist in France during the fourteenth century. He wrote extensively on alchemy, and compiled a very valuable treatise on the subject adorned with mystical illustrations of a transcendental order, depicting among other matters the symbolical Hermetic Androgyne. There are, also, alchemical hieroglyphs in the Cathedral of Notre Dame attributed to Flamel. He recorded that on two occasions he was successful in the transmutation of mercury—the first time into silver, the second into gold, in the presence of his wife Perenelle. That was in the year 1382.

In the seventeenth century there was a band of men who called themselves the Brotherhood of Hermetic Philosophers, known also as Rosicrucians, who brought the occult mysticism of the alchemists into prominence. Robert Fludd became very interested in them, and introduced them to the notice of English doctors and philosophers. The Oxford alchemists were descended from this Rosicrucian society, the famous Ashmole being one of the last of them.

English alchemy finally became discredited through a certain Dr. Price, who had a prominent position and who claimed to have succeeded in making transmutations. Some gold that he was supposed to have obtained by this method was even presented to George III. However, on being pressed to give another demonstration before members of the Royal Society, of which he was a fellow, Price committed suicide on the appointed day in the presence of his audience.

Alchemy continued to exist in isolated societies, and among a few individuals, up to quite recent times, and there are still a small number of transcendental alchemists. There was an association of alchemists in Westphalia, which continued until the year 1819 under the name of the Hermetic Society, and in 1830 there existed two well-known alchemists, Cyliani and Cambriel.

Paracelsus is a prominent link between alchemy and sorcery. This remarkable man was born in Germany during the fifteenth century, his grandfather being an illegitimate son of royalty. His father was interested in medicine, and at an early age Paracelsus began to study both chemistry and medicine. He very soon decided for himself that the doctors of his time knew nothing of any worth, and that the only way to knowledge was to study nature for himself. With that end in view he started on his travels, which took him into nearly every country of the known world. In Egypt and Arabia he received occult instructions from the magicians and alchemists there, and became versed in the science of metallurgy.

Eventually he returned, and lived for a time at Basle, attracting great attention by his theories and magical pretensions, and also by his flamboyant personality and eccentric behaviour. He wrote extensively on occult subjects, and attracted the attention of many men of learning as well as merely credulous people. In many ways Paracelsus appears to have been a charlatan, but he was nevertheless an extraordinary and in some ways a great personality. He brought disfavour upon himself by publically burning the works of Galen and Aricenna, and was forced to leave Basle on account of a conflict with the law.

After that he wandered from one place to another, living by his wits and applying his occult knowledge to gain his own ends by sorcery and other means. There are various accounts as to his death, some relating that he was poisoned and others that his own profligacy and excesses killed him. However that may be, Paracelsus left to posterity some of the greatest works on magic in existence, and as a figure is so well known that it is scarcely necessary to enlarge upon him or his work.

The alchemists John Dee and Edward Kelly made themselves famous both in England and on the Continent. Of the two, John Dee was a man of learning, and was genuinely attached to his investigations for the love of wisdom alone. In the course of time, however, he became hopelessly credulous, and after he had taken Kelly into partnership he allowed himself to be involved in various nefarious schemes, completely under the domination of the other.

Dee originally was well-born, and after completing his education travelled on the Continent studying astronomy and alchemy. He returned home after a time, and then once more crossed to France. When he settled in England again he had the misfortune to be imprisoned at Hampton Court for alleged sorcery against Queen Mary, daughter of Henry VIII, but was released.

Dee then settled down to his favourite study of alchemy, and became interested in the Rosicrucians theories, being very ambitious of discovering the Elixir of Life and the Philosopher's Stone. He became utterly lost in his alchemical dreams, and worked himself into a highly impressionable state of mind. As a result, it is not surprising that he was suddenly visited by the Angel Uriel in his laboratory one day, and advised to take up crystal gazing. This he did with great zest, receiving the most remarkable impressions and visions, though he probably used what was known as a "Magic Mirror" for the purpose.

However that may be, Dee appears to have been quite overcome with the manifestations he was receiving, which did not confine themselves to the crystal as time went on. Accordingly he looked about for an assistant, or neophyte, who might record his remarkable experiences; he himself having become quite bewildered by his conversations and intercourse with the spirit beings. He found the man he sought in Edward Kelly, who at this time was a druggist in Worcester. Kelly's past did not bear a very close inspection, and among other misdeeds he had been convicted of coining, for which he had had his ears cut off. He was in the habit of wearing a black skull cap, well pulled down, to hide this defect. He was also an alchemist in some degree, and a practitioner of necromancy.

Kelly soon saw in Dee an easy tool, to be used for personal gain and social advancement. He probably had genuine mediumistic gifts, but in any case the visions as interpreted by him became more and more marvellous, and increasingly concerned with the affairs and movements of the famous pair. At the same time the visions lost some of their celestial aspect, and Kelly began to impart his fears to Dee that it was not always pure spirits they were contacting but "Goblins Damned." By this means Kelly began to secure the hold over Dee that lasted nearly all their lives.

Kelly is believed to have practised necromancy on many occasions, both before he met Dee and later. On one occasion he is recorded to have exhumed a body from the grave and forced it to speak and disclose certain information, although there are varying accounts of this episode. Mention of a well-known illustration of Dr. Dee and Kelly calling up a spirit in a churchyard has been made in another chapter.

Dee, continuing his investigations in alchemy, and patiently searching for the secret of transmutation, suddenly announced that he had discovered the Elixir of Life. This was Kelly's opportunity, and money poured into their coffers from wealthy men and women seeking rejuvenation.

About this time a distinguished Pole, named Laski, visited the Court of Queen Elizabeth and was very much disappointed not to find Dee there ; Laski having heard of his fame as an astrologer and alchemist on the Continent. However, it so happened one day that, while waiting with the Earl of Leicester for an interview with the Queen, Dr. Dee also appeared. An introduction took place, and it was not long before Laski, dazzled by Dee's learning and Kelly's plausible personality, was financing their alchemical activities and being duped by their false or misleading visions.

The worthy pair then went to Poland with Laski, in order to make transmutations of iron into gold. The alleged object of the expedition was the founding a kingdom predicted by the "spirits," with Laski as ruler and Dee and Kelly as his principal advisers. But, alas, time went on and nothing of any moment occurred, except that Laski was losing all his money. At length he appears to have lost faith in the couple, and have financed them to depart elsewhere.

They next wended their way with sundry adventures to the Court of the Emperor Rudolf, where they were received guardedly. Dee's learning and fundamental honesty created respect wherever he went, but Kelly was frequently "seen through" and treated with corresponding caution. However, even in this case they became very popular, and were widely consulted in their capacity of astrologers and magicians. So much so, indeed, that at last the Papal Nuncio complained of the favour shown to heretical sorcerers, and the Emperor ordered Dee and Kelly to leave without delay.

We next find them in Cracow, suffering an eclipse in their fortunes and in fact living on the meagre proceeds of divination and sorceries. Kelly had Dee completely under his influence by this time and, having fallen deeply in love with the latter's young wife, the "spirits" began to expound a doctrine of community in all things, including wives, between the two men. This idea did not at all appeal to the doctor, but the "spirits," as represented by Kelly, showed him that sin was only relative and that it was God's will that both men should share each other's wives. Kelly knew Dee was dependant upon him as his "skryer," and, in order to get his way, left the doctor for a time, only consenting to return if this communal arrangement were established. Dee gave way and Kelly came back, but there was still trouble with the wives to be overcome, as they had no wish to be shared. However, Kelly and Dee signed a solemn pact, and the wives submitted unwillingly.

The new arrangement was not a great success, as the wives quarrelled and were bitterly jealous. None the less, the strange *ménage* persisted, though lack of money increased their difficulties. Finally, Dee and Kelly separated for good, after many and various adventures. Some accounts relate that Dee returned to England in poverty, others that his expenses were paid by a nobleman and that he travelled in luxury. But it is certain that he was no longer looked upon so favourably in England; many rumours of his dubious work with Kelly having reached the ears of the Queen. Her Majesty, even so, received Dee fairly graciously, possibly having a superstitious dread of the consequences of slighting the magician.

Meanwhile, Kelly descended upon Bavaria with his so-called elixir of life and was imprisoned as an impostor. In attempting to escape he had a fall, and sustained injuries from which he died. Dr. Dee held various posts of more or less importance, but finally retired to his home at Mortlake. After the parting with Kelly, he employed other "skryers," as they were called. But they all appear to have been charlatans, and in his old age he fell into poverty once more, becoming known purely as a sorcerer and magician and living by astrology and fortune-telling.

After the accession of James I, he appealed to the King for protection from the persecution which he suffered on account of his reputation. But the King having become tired of him, nothing appears to have been done, and Dee died in poor circumstances in his Mortlake home.

Besides the search for the Elixir of Life and the Philosopher's Stone, alchemists of all periods sought for a method of making living creatures apart from the usual process of procreation. Paracelsus, in particular, claimed to have made artificial men, called "Homonculas." The process was, roughly, as follows. The necessary spagyric substances having been obtained, they were shut up in a glass phial and left to incubate in horse dung for forty days. At the end of that time, something was found to be living in the phial, and that something was a man, but transparent and without a definite body. This creature consolidated and grew if fed with human blood consistently for forty weeks, by which time it would have developed into a child, but much smaller and needing more care than the usual human variety. Paracelsus was supposed to have manufactured many of these monstrosities, which never grew very large or showed particular intelligence. It is a definite fact that he spent much time experimenting in that direction, but his success is problematical.

Another alchemist, Albertus Magnus, worked for thirty years upon a " man of brass," and cast together his materials under certain astrological constellations which threw so much spirit into his brazen man that it was reported that he grew visibly. When this monstrous creature was full-grown he is stated to have been excessively talkative, and the inhabitants of Koln became quite worried about having such an unusual citizen in their midst. The great Thomas Aquinas was Magnus's master, and one day he became so tired of the brazen man's wagging tongue that he declared that it was possessed with a demon, and there and then dealt it a blow on the head, which silenced it for evermore.

Heads of brass were frequently made by sorcerers for the purpose of divination, and learned men disputed among themselves considerably as to whether they spoke of their own intelligence or were possessed by " demons." Buried treasure was another subject that engrossed the mind of the lesser alchemists, and they are recorded frequently to have practised black magic in the hope of discovering hoards of wealth. They made pacts with the Devil in order to secure knowledge of the whereabouts of treasure, or for the secret of transmutation, promising themselves to do good with the wealth once it was attained and to turn their backs upon evil. Very few, if any, of them appear to have succeeded in this venture, for in cases where sorcerers obtained large sums of money and lived in luxury, they all died in poverty with their money squandered or exhausted.

The most romantic figure of all in this respect was Cagliostro, who first appeared at Palermo in the eighteenth century. His origin is obscure, but he seems to have been a difficult boy whose mother, being a widow, placed him in the care of Benedictine monks at an early age. Under the apothecary of the monastery he learnt chemistry and medicine, but this life was altogether too dull for him and, having escaped, he took up a rough life among vagabonds. Now, there lived in Palermo a wealthy goldsmith named Marano, who was exceedingly credulous of everything magical, and the young Cagliostro, knowing this, made his acquaintance and posed to him as a veritable master of the occult.

Marano had already expended a good deal of money on false alchemists, but he placed faith in Cagliostro, who informed him that he knew of buried treasure in a field. It would, however, require the expenditure of a large quantity of gold to procure the necessary apparatus for the treasure's recovery. At length Marano reluctantly parted with the gold to Cagliostro, and a night was arranged to begin operations.

The two entered the field about midnight, and having first made a circle, Cagliostro began a series of the most terrible and blood-curdling incantations. The terrified Marano fell flat upon his face, and, while he lay upon the ground, a number of Cagliostro's ruffian friends rifled his pockets and then made off, the false magician accompanying them. Marano created an uproar about this escapade, and Cagliostro left hurriedly. Having now plenty of money, however, he began his travels, calling himself "Count."

About this time Cagliostro came in contact with the mysterious Althotas, whom he claimed was his master in occultism. On the other hand, so little is known of this individual, except through Cagliostro, that it is somewhat doubtful whether he had any existence outside the latter's vivid imagination. However that may be, it is certain that "They" travelled extensively in Egypt, Arabia and parts of Asia, gaining knowledge and instruction from the priests of ancient religions and occult societies. Until, in the course of time, their journeys brought them back to Malta, where Althotas suddenly disappears from the picture. Cagliostro simply stated that he had died there.

At about this period in his adventures the now famous occultist obtained large sums of money from a Sicilian Prince, and married a lady named Lorenza Felicini. It is usually agreed that she was a woman of great charm and honesty, and that though she and her husband had a deep devotion for one another, Cagliostro had the effect of undermining her integrity and persuading her to assist him in many nefarious schemes. Their home became the resort of gamblers and card sharpers, besides those in search for the marvellous.

The Cagliostros travelled about from place to place, and came over to London, where they lived in great style in Witcomb Street. There they left behind a reputation for honesty and fair dealing, and for being occultists of genuine powers. When they left on their journeys again they were accompanied by a Frenchman named Duplaisir, with whom Countess Cagliostro eloped. She is supposed to have been imprisoned at her husband's instigation for this little interlude, but upon her release they were permanently reunited.

Cagliostro himself was always in conflict with the law, suffered several imprisonments, and was more or less forced to keep moving from one country to another, either on account of his sorceries or other misdeeds. He and his wife lived for a time at Strasbourg, where they were fêted and treated with immense esteem; Cagliostro now undertaking to cure people of various diseases by magical means, which appear frequently to have succeeded. He had always been interested in freemasonry, and he evolved a masonic system of his own which he called "Egyptian Freemasonry." Both men and women were eligible for this society; Cagliostro styling himself "The Grand Copt" and his wife "The Grand Mistress."

The Cagliostros then settled in Paris, where people had a passion for the occult, and they made enormous sums of money from their masonic lodge. They lived in a house surrounded by large grounds, while to increase the mystery Countess Cagliostro could only be seen as a rare privilege, clad in diaphanous garments. They gave banquets at which the dead were the chief guests, and at which performances of necromancy supplied a sensational interest. The ceremonies of initiation to their lodge had many startling and somewhat grotesque features; the fair initiates especially having to undergo some very remarkable experiences of an enthralling and slightly ridiculous nature, after having sacrificed large sums of money on the altar to the Grand Copt.

Cagliostro and his wife visited the supposedly immortal Count de St. Germain, and he and Cagliostro had the whole of French Society at their feet at a time when people were harsh and practical, not to say cynical, in all other aspects of life, but intensely credulous of and attracted to the occult. People were caused by Cagliostro to see marvellous visions in his magic mirror, to become rejuvenated by his elixir, to receive cures and to fraternise with spirit beings. In some of the gatherings of his society his followers were called upon to cast away their clothes, when he himself would descend from the ceiling seated naked upon a golden ball with a star shining upon his forehead. Jaded Parisians rushed to Cagliostro's *salons*, finding a new thrill among his marvels and an outlet for their emotions, if nothing else, as members of his Egyptian Freemasonry.

At length, Cagliostro became involved in the affair of the Diamond Necklace, in company with Cardinal de Rohan, a Madame Lamotte, and other famous people. The necklace belonged to Marie Antoinette, and much intrigue centred around it. There was a trial at which Cagliostro acquitted himself splendidly, leaving him more popular with the people than ever. It was a gift with him, at all times, to touch the imagination and keep the friendship of the poor—probably on account of his generosity. This trial may well have been one of the causes which finally set light to the French Revolution, so much of the lives and habits of those who lived in careless ease and luxury being exposed.

Cagliostro left France with his wife and came to England once more, but a French newspaper called the *Courier de L'Europe* published an exposure of him and from that moment his descent began headlong. He wandered from place to place on the Continent, harassed everywhere; resting awhile in Italy, where he wrote a prophecy of the downfall of the French aristocracy. But the Pope, ever the enemy of freemasonry, denounced Cagliostro's Masonic Society and the Holy Inquisition arrested him in 1788. In the following year he was condemned to death, but the sentence was commuted to imprisonment for life, which the Inquisition intended should be tantamount to death owing to the terrible conditions under which he was confined. After endeavouring to escape from his first prison, Cagliostro was transferred to even worse surroundings in the Castle of San Leo, where he dragged out a terrible existence under slow torture until he died three years later. His wife was imprisoned in the Convent of St. Appolonia, where she was reported to have died in 1794.

The Pope ordered the destruction of Cagliostro's works,

but strangely enough an Inquisitor was appointed after his death to write an account of his life. This was done, although the result was largely coloured by Catholic prejudice.

The Elixir of Life, so anxiously sought by all alchemists, attracted Cagliostro among the others, and he claimed to have discovered it. Disappointed but not disillusioned, some of the philosophers foresaw in the discovery a means of prolonging life so that they might extend their studies and experiments, while others counted only on a means whereby they could charge heavy sums to the rich who desired to renew their youth.

The Count de St. Germain was rumoured to have lived for centuries, and to have known Solomon and the Queen of Sheba. He was in some respects a charlatan, but at the same time an adept at chemistry. At the Court of Louis XVI he was greatly in fashion, and maintained an atmosphere of grandiose mystery about all his magical performances. His apartments were furnished in a lavish style to create awe and mystification, visitors being admitted only with much theatrical display. As I have said, he and Cagliostro had the whole of the French Court at their feet, and sorcery and divination became the absorbing pastime of the aristocracy.

Cagliostro's treatment for rejuvenation was a complicated one. It was to be started on attaining fifty years of age, and necessitated retreat for forty days. It had to be begun in the month of May, with fasting ; the patient only partaking of early morning dew, gathered on clean linen from sprouting corn. The next step was to be bled, but not excessively, and after purging to remain in bed. Doses of "Universal Medicine" were next to be taken, which produced deep sleeps. On the thirty-sixth day followed a glass of Egyptian wine ; on the thirty-seventh the last grain of this medicine ; after which a profound sleep would ensue. During this sleep the hair, teeth, nails and skin should renew themselves. On awakening a bath of herbs was prescribed, and on the last day a dose of Elixir of Achrat taken in red wine.

Earlier philosophers believed that the precipitation of the Philosopher's Stone in mercurial water would restore youth and prolong life, and nearly all of them had their favourite concoctions for this purpose. The fact remains, however, that none of them attained to any unusual old age, let alone immortality, and so we must suppose that all failed in their quest. The Count de St. Germain alone may have possessed some secret of prolonging life, but his origin and birth are so obscure that it is impossible to tell with any accuracy how old he was. Some accounts give him a Semitic origin, and even identify him with the Wandering Jew.

The dust of mummies was also thought to have a powerfully revitalising effect, and formed a part of many of the prescriptions of Elixir of Life. Not only could some of the sorcerers prolong life (according to themselves), but they effected abnormal conditions in the climate. Thus Albertus Magnus, already mentioned, entertained a certain nobleman in Koln during a severe winter with a display of flowers, fruits and warm summer weather. The famous Baptista Porta is reported to have been able to produce wine to drink while his companions had only water, and on a hot summer's day, when others complained of the heat, he magically procured a cool breeze that almost froze them.

Before the days of Cagliostro (to be exact a century earlier), there was a noted Italian astrologer, Cosmo Ruggieri, who had already made death spells fashionable. And it is rather amusing, in the light of her own sorceries, that Catherine de Medici should have complained about him to the *Procureur-Général* by letter, stating that he had made a waxen image of Charles IX with intent to injure him. She had been told that Ruggieri had repeatedly struck this image on the head, and later enquired if the King were yet bleeding or if he had begun to vomit. The Italian was accordingly arrested, but Charles subsequently died of a mysterious consumption.

The English Queen Elizabeth, again, was very disturbed when a wax figure of her was found in Lincoln's Inn Fields, stuck full of pins. The Queen had Dr. John Dee brought hastily to her at Richmond, to explain the whole ritual of death spells, and it was some time before he could calm her fears in that respect.

During the seventeenth and eighteenth centuries methods for curing disease were as much sought after as favours to be attained by magic, and this led to many methods of healing and curing, quite apart from the strange medicine and surgery of the time. An illustration is furnished by Sir

Kenelm Digby and his famous "Sympathetic Powder." Sir Kenelm was banished from England (his grandfather having taken part in the Gunpowder Plot), and lived in Paris. His life was devoted to the natural sciences, and he gained many occult secrets from a Carmelite monk who had travelled in the East. About 1657 Sir Kenelm Digby introduced this sympathetic powder, or salve, which had the property of healing wounds, especially those made by firearms. Instead of applying the substance directly on the wound, bandages soaked in the wounded person's blood were steeped in the salve (which was largely composed of sulphuric acid powder) and these were placed not upon the injury at all, the cure working through the sympathetic action between the blood and its source. This system became the rage in France.

A hundred years or so later, Mesmer from Vienna discovered that a magnetic force similar to that possessed by iron was to be found in everything. Mesmer opened a consulting-room in Paris, whither people came to be cured of every sort and kind of illness. The chief feature of the mesmeric healing was the magnetic tub, a sort of vat with cords and iron bars to which the limbs of the patients were attached. After having remained seated by the tub for a time, the invalids (particularly women) fell into fits and convulsions, which are generally supposed to have cured them. Mesmer had about a hundred people whom he had instructed as magnetisers, some of whom belonged to the nobility, who also "mesmerised" people by making passes over the affected parts of the body. The term mesmerism is often used in connection with hypnotism, and the original mesmeric passes possibly had a soothing affect that produced a semi-hypnotic state; but originally it was confined to healing by magnetism alone.

People flocked to Mesmer's apartments, and the magnetic tub became quite a fashionable rendezvous. The spectacle of the convulsed invalids was very enthralling, even to those who required no cure. The tub itself was not a mystery. It was merely filled half-way with water and had bottles of water arranged around the sides, though Mesmer himself said that iron filings would have served the same purpose. Music from an orchestra was provided, and the most extraordinary scenes took place to its strains—some people ecstatically announcing their cure, others falling into convulsions, and still more rushing wildly about and embracing each other under the force of the magnetism. Naturally it was a very profitable craze for its inventor, but the magnetic tub was available to the poor on certain days.

Controversies raged about him ; his followers proclaiming his marvellous cures, and scientists denouncing him as a quack. The Church went further and accused him of dealings with the Devil, and Mesmer had a bitter enemy in a certain Abbé Fiard. However, it was not long before all the marvels and crazes and inventions of the French nobility were to be swallowed up in the horrors of the Revolution.

CHAPTER X

SYMBOLS AND ACCESSORIES OF MAGIC

Explains the symbols and material objects used in sorcery and necromancy, gives various incantations, etc.

ANCIENT magic, whether black or white, required the assistance of many accessories for its successful completion; modern magic, on the other hand, tends to be a matter of Desire, backed by Will. The Masters of the World have always been able to produce their miracles by the power of Will, operating in harmony with the forces of Nature, without any other adjuncts, whereas lesser magicians have been compelled to use symbols and material things to obtain their results. And this is particularly true of black magic. However, the accessories used by magicians of both kinds were very similar, and in some cases identical; the sorcerer merely perverting, or inverting, their original intention.

In the Middle Ages different days of the week were chosen for different magical performances, as exemplified in the writings of Abraham the Jew. White magic was to be enacted on Sunday, the magician wearing purple vestments ornamented with gold and jewels. The powers of the Moon were to be invoked on Monday, white vestments embroidered with silver being worn and the head crowned with a tiara of twisted golden silk. Pearls and crystals, again, were the chosen ornaments, and an incense compound of camphor, aloes, amber, sandalwood and cucumber seed was to be burnt. For evocations to acquire transcendental wisdom, the vestments had to be of a brilliant green ornamented with pearls, while hollow glass beads were worn containing mercury.

Magical ceremonies of a religious character, or for invoking material forces, were conducted in scarlet robes; a brass tablet with mystical inscriptions being worn round the neck or on the breast, and the head crowned with a garland of fig leaves, oak, poplar and pomegranate. If vengeance was desired, the magician must be clothed in robes of red, flame, or rust colour and wear a wreath of absinthe and rue. When death spells were to be cast, black must be worn; with a chain of lead around the magician's neck, an onyx ring upon his right hand, and a garland of cypress, ash and hellebore about his head. Sulphur, alum and assafœtida were burnt in the ceremony. In practices of black magic, the sorcerer wore scarlet or black robes, with a leaden cap on his head, inscribed with the symbols of the Moon, Venus and Saturn, and also a garland of vervain and cypress. Aloes, camphor and storax, were burnt.

The exorcist priests of the Church were no less specially robed for their task of dispelling evil spirits. At midnight they entered a circle, wearing a new surplice and with a tall pointed cap on their heads on which appeared the ineffable name Tetragrammerton, written in the blood of a white dove. The circle itself was sprinkled with the blood of a black lamb and a white pigeon. The use of blood made this rite one of black magic in itself, but with sublime inconsistency the priestly magician went on to abjure the spirits of Hell in the name of Adonai, Eloahin and Sabaioth. Such ecclesiastical exorcists seem to have been particularly anxious to get rid of spirits who were thought to be guarding buried treasures, which then would become the property of the Church.

This question of buried treasure exercised the minds of ancient occultists considerably, and in connection with it there was frequently employed the art of Rhabdomancy, which was similar to that of water divining or water "dousing." The operator used a forked stick of hazelwood or oak, and with this held between both hands walked over the ground where treasure or minerals were thought to lie. When he had arrived at a spot that covered such things, the stick would twist violently in his hands, as in the case with the water diviner. In the Middle Ages Rhabdomancers were employed to discover mines, and the whereabouts of precious stones.

During the seventeenth century there lived in France a man named Jacques Aymar, who was able to trace robbers and murderers with his rod. He was once called in to discover who killed a merchant and his wife, and after he had inspected the scene of the crime, and cut small pieces from their garments, the magnetic vibrations in the stick led him a considerable journey. When he turned from the path that the murderer had taken the rod became lifeless, but as soon as he picked up the trail again it became vibrant and difficult to hold. Eventually it brought him outside the prison of a town at some distance from the crime, and where there was a hunchback, undergoing a sentence of robbery. When taxed with the crime, the hunchback confessed that he had indeed murdered the merchant and his wife.

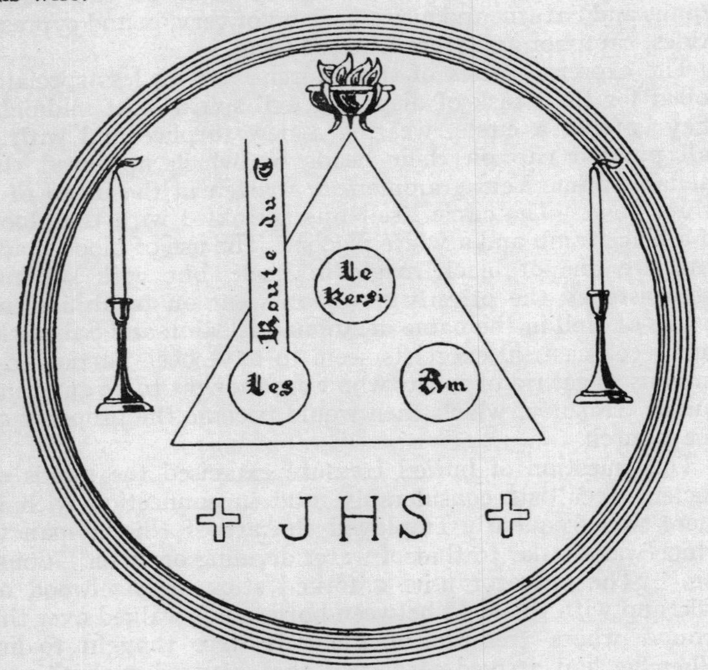

The Triangle of Pacts.

Circles were, and are, a necessary adjunct to any successful magic involving dealing with spirits. And there are literally hundreds of different varieties of circle mentioned in ancient magical manuscripts. One of these, called "Le Dragon Rouge," was professed to have been published at Avignon about 1522, but was more probably a production of the early nineteenth century. However, it gives many interesting accounts of magic rites, among them the correct formation of the mysterious "Triangle of Pacts."

In this the magician, or Karcist, traced the circle with an enamelled stone, and then outlined it with strips of the skin of a goat fastened down with four nails. Within the circle a triangle was drawn, at the apex of which was a brazier containing fire. Beneath this was an oval erection, in horizontal position, in which the sorcerer stood. On the sorcerer's left was another circle from which a pathway led, called " La Route du T," and on his right another plain circle. In these last two circles the assistants were placed. Outside the triangle two candles stood on either side, while beneath the letters J H S appeared with a cross before and after. The candlesticks were surrounded by wreaths of vervain, and the fire was composed of charcoal, willow, camphor and spirits, placed in a new receptacle. After having gone through the ceremony of invoking the spirits, the participants were supposed to follow the path from the triangle, which would then infallibly lead them to Satanic Treasure ; though how, and why, it is difficult to see.

Once the magic circle had been entered, the magician must not on any account leave it until all manifestations had ceased under the peril of his life. The circle usually contained one or more pentagrams and interlaced triangles, though a few were perfectly empty. Others, again, presented a most complicated arrangement of geometrical figures and pentacles. The size of the circle was exactly nine feet in diameter, by the most careful measurements, with a smaller one following it at a distance of six inches from the rim of the outer. Within this space was written the names of the Beings to be invoked, or the magical names of powerful spirits interspersed with crosses.

There is evidence that prehistoric man worked with circles, as did the ancient Druids of Europe. The Assyrian sorcerer made a circle sprinkled with lime, and set seven little winged figures within it before the image of a god. Hindu magicians made circles of black pebbles.

Properly speaking, the sorcerer was not one who had made a pact with the Devil, like the true necromancer. He was independent, and invoked the spirits for good or ill as Master. Although the term " sorcerer " has come to mean one who is a black magician, that is not necessarily the case. One who wished to invoke the Devil and make a pact with him had to perform a preliminary sacrifice on the third day of the moon, in a wild and desolate spot between twelve and one in the morning. The sacrifice consisted of a kid, dog, cat or a cock and hen; but the kid or goat seems to have been chosen for preference. A garland of vervain was placed around the victim's neck and tied with a green ribbon. With the right arm bare to the shoulder, the Karcist decapitated the animal or bird with a very sharp steel knife and, having made a wood fire, burnt the body.

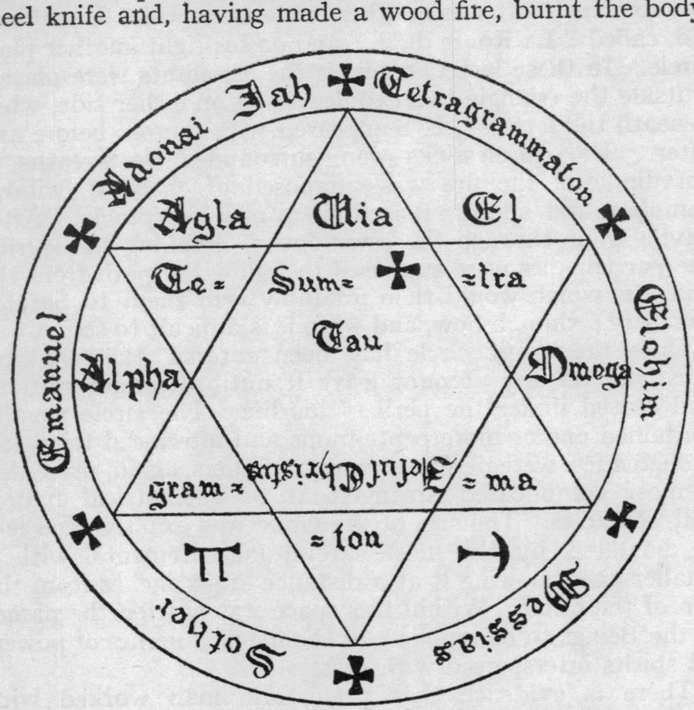

Circle for all Conjurations (sixteenth century).

When a goat or a kid were used, the skin was kept to form the circle for the final ceremony.

On another night, chosen by astrological calculations and usually at the full moon, the magician and an assistant returned to the scene, taking with them a rod, or wand, and two candlesticks, with candles of pure wax made by a virgin girl and two wreaths of vervain. The magician wore a blood-stone ring, and proceeded to make a circle with strips of the skin of a goat or kid. A fire was kindled with wood, incense that had been blessed by the Church, camphor and four nails from the coffin of a dead child. A bottle of brandy was taken, too, for replenishing the flames, and must on no account be drunk by the participants in the rite—which must have been a temptation to fall from strength for some would-be Satanists, having regard to the uncanny object of the excursion and the conditions under which the invitation to his Satanic majesty had to be made! If it were not convenient to wait for the full moon, a night of wind and rain had to be chosen, and if a thunderstorm could be thrown in, so much the better. Ruins of churches and monasteries were very favourite localities, as were also old Druid or Roman remains and churchyards.

If the Devil was summoned indoors, a disused cellar or vault was propitious, hung with black draperies. Some forms of black magic confined themselves to sacrificing a black cock, from which the eyes, heart and tongue had been removed.

Sometimes the assistance of the Devil or his demons was sought without the magician wishing to go so far as to give up his soul to the Evil One. Generally, however, once he had been invoked, the Devil refused to carry out any wishes without a pact having been made with him; which fact doubtless caused some moments of agonising indecision on the part of the reluctant necromancer. These strange pacts were simple statements of allegiance, signed in the blood of the person concerned.

Many pacts were made verbally, at witches' gatherings and the like. But in solitary cases the Devil, like other people, evidently preferred to "have it in writing." Nevertheless, there are very few of these documents still in existence; partly because when witches and sorcerers were burnt their pacts were burnt with them, and partly because they were dangerous things to let others see or to leave about. Warring against the Church as they did, they easily led the participants to the stake if discovered; as in the case of Urbain Grandier, who was accused of enchanting the nuns of a Ursuline convent. Grandier had made three pacts with the Devil, which were ordered to be burnt with him; but one must have been overlooked, as it is now preserved in the Bibliothèque Nationale, and was a singularly damning document from the point of view of the Church of the day.

Another, written in blood on virgin parchment, was much simpler. " I promise great Lucifer, to repay him in twenty years for all he shall give me, for witness whereof I have signed X. . . ."

Even after having made the unholy arrangement, amateur sorcerers were often anxious to evade payment and tried to rob the Devil of his dues. A humorous touch is given by a prayer made for use after a pact had been made, and

The Pentacle or Five-pointed Star.

by which it was hoped to escape the Evil One at the eleventh hour. The prayer runs thus : " Inspire me, O great God, with the sentiments necessary for enabling me to escape the claws of the Demons, and of all evil spirits."

Of almost equal importance with the circle were the pentacles or pentagrams, which were chiefly used in white magic and for protection and exorcism. They consisted of the names of spirits of superior power, with suitable accompanying symbols. They were also used for binding evil spirits, and reconciling beneficent beings. The interlaced triangle, called by the Hebrews the Shield of David, and also known incorrectly as the Seal of Solomon, was used within circles. With one beam in the ascendant it was used for white magic, but in the reversed position it was a potent sign of the black art. Mystics will understand

The Interlaced Triangle or Seal of Solomon.

the deep significance of this symbol, and therefore realise its potentialities for evil when reversed.

Another important symbol was that of the five-pointed star or pentacle, whose origin is lost in the mists of antiquity, but which is attributed to Solomon. It stands for the microcosm, and this too could be used in the inverted position.

According to Eliphas Levi the pentagram, or pentacle,

signifies the domination of the mind over the elements, and by this sign one enchained the demons of the air, the spirits of fire, the phantoms of the water and ghosts of earth.

No magician was complete without his wand, varieties of which are found in every quarter of the globe. They were, and are, always composed of wood; bamboo being very much in favour in the East, while in Europe hazel, elder, oak and cypress were chiefly used. This rod, or wand, measured anything from 1 foot to 19½ feet in length, and was cut from a tree that had never borne fruit. The two ends were cut to sharp points with a sacrificial steel knife, and sometimes steel caps were fitted made of metal that had previously composed a magician's knife. Magical inscriptions were cut or written upon the wand, through which ran a magnetic needle. For binding evil spirits and propitiating good ones, Peter de Abano calls the wand the "most priceless treasure of the light," and advises the magician to wear pure white linen woven by a virgin and a white leather cap and shoes. He must first, however, take a complete bath in exorcised water.

In addition to his wand, the paraphernalia of the magician included two or more candles; a crystal, or magic glass, set in pure gold, surmounted by the interlaced triangle and with the names of Michael, Gabriel, Uriel and Raphael written around it; a magic ring; a sword, or knife; and a torch-like receptacle for incense, which could be held in the hand or rammed into the ground. This last was sometimes replaced by a tripod.

There was a special rite for binding spirits that might appear in the crystal or magic mirror. Having become visible to the Karcist and his assistant, if they refused to speak they were to be conjured in names such as "Methralton, Raziel, Cassiel, Michael, Raphael and Gabriel," in the hope of compelling them to do so. In order to bind the spirit, the magician repeated: "I bind thee spirit that art appeared in the stone of crystal, that thou do not disobey my commandments, but do all things for me that to thy office pertaineth, and more also. I bind thee, not to go thy way from me, until I release thee. Here to remain until thou hast fulfilled all my commandments, for I will use art towards thee . . . and thou spirit, therefore herestand, I charge thee, in the crystal stone." The formula concludes with a general curse on all evil spirits, to be used for stone, glass or circle. A fire was next to be made of such abominable substances as dry cow's dung, brimstone, sulphur, and having written the spirit's name upon a piece of parchment, it was to be burnt with a curse.

Magicians' knives and swords were made after a variety of styles, and were used both for sacrifice and for marking out circles and symbols upon the ground. The sword had, also, a higher significance of power on the spirits.

Paracelsus' sword was famous and takes a prominent place in the portraits of the great mediæval sorcerer and occultist, in which he appears holding the hilt between his hands. This hilt was made in the formation of a crystal ball, and in it Parcelsus was thought to have bound a familiar spirit, whom he called Azoth or Zoth. However that may be, initiates believe that "Liber Azoth" was not a demon at all, but the term used to describe the vital mercury of the alchemists.

The swords used for magic had to be especially scoured and cleaned and made from virgin steel or iron, and usually had a copper handle in the form of a crucifix. The blade was tempered in the blood of a bird, animal or human according to its uses, and anointed with the juice of magic herbs. Swords were pre-eminently part of the insignia of black magicians, and did not always form a part of the accessories of the ordinary conjurer of spirits. Variations of the sword and knife were daggers, and a particular knife with a curved blade more like a sickle, called "Andamcos."

Magic tridents were also used by witches and sorcerers, cut out of hazel or almond wood. Both swords, wands and tridents had to be "consecrated" by a magician who already owned one. The knives were to be made on a certain day, at a certain time that was propitious according to the planets. In black magic the haft was often made of ebony or jet, and in white magic of ivory; both the blade and handle being engraved with magical inscriptions, the word "Agla" often appearing on the blade.

The parchment upon which pacts and inscriptions were written was often composed of the skin of embryonical animals, while the "ink" was the blood of black animals or birds, though sometimes a special variety was used made from the juices of herbs.

Censers were made of bronze or silver, and lamps of gold,

silver, brass or iron. The chalice used was composed of different metals according to the rites ; those used in black magic being black engraved with symbols of the Moon. Human skulls were used for this purpose, too ; containing the blood of the sacrifice, which was to be drunk. Candlesticks were of gold, brass, silver, copper or iron, and in the case of black magic of ebony and shaped like the crescent moon. The candles were of virgin wax, or human fat if the practices belonged to the black art.

The magicians often had as many as four assistants, all of whom were provided with magic rings and swords and to whom were allotted different tasks. One had to carry the incense and its censer ; another books, pen and ink ; a third was entrusted with the knife ; the fourth carried the receptacle for fire. No woman could take part in the ceremonies, and to admit one was to nullify results.

It was held in ancient magic that the sexes could not mix as a rule ; sorcerers very rarely conspiring with witches, and *vice versa*. Some magicians required a virgin for acts of divination, but she appeared solely as an instrument and not as a participator.

Male children were employed for the discerning of spirits, or as we should now say—clairvoyance. They were chosen for their innocence and freedom from evil, and were dressed for the occasion in white silk, the head and eyes being covered with a white veil, upon which the name "Uriel" was written. The magician was clothed in black vestments, with a black veil upon which was woven the name "Adam."

The fires at ceremonies of necromancy and black magic were made up of cypress, alder wood, laurel, broken crosses and the blood of snakes. The ungents with which sorcerers and witches anointed themselves contained human fat, the blood of corpses, aconite, belladonna and poisonous fungi. Oils for anointing the Karcist in white magic were made of olive oil, myrrh, cinnamon and galingala.

Incense, or perfumes, were made from a very large variety of woods, herbs and flowers, and each day of the week had its special magical perfume. For instance, that used on Sundays was composed of mastick, musk, labdanum, amber, ammoniacum, benjamin and storax. All sweet woods were used for the middle days of the week, and on Friday the petals of roses and violets with sandalwood and frankincense. To raise spirits suddenly, "Sperma-a-Ceti, consisting of sperm oil, red storax, the blood of a bird, pepperwort and saffron" was recommended. For black magic, assafœtida, garlic, dragon's blood, sulphur, and such-like vile-smelling concoctions were used.

The incense and fumigations that the ancient magicians employed included among them several powerful drugs and narcotics, whose effects they well understood. The fumes from these substances must have influenced those present, and most certainly produced hallucinations and a partial release of the astral body. Such things as poppies (opium), henbane, hellebore and mandrake were known to incite people with spurious courage and produce strange sights and sounds to the senses. Sorcerers claimed that the knowledge of these things was obtained through Hermes Trismegistus, who discovered a book of herbs hidden in a stone by Abel the son of Adam.

The altars used for magical purposes were of carved wood or, if made of stone, had to be a natural slab, unhewn and untouched by hammer or chisel.

The underlying principle of the use of magic rings was practically the same as in case of the circle. Rings were employed to bestow protection and various supernatural qualities upon the wearer. According to old Hebrew manuscripts a ring of copper and iron, engraved with magic signs, rendered the wearer invisible at will. Most commonly rings were formed of copper or lead, and were about three inches wide. They had the word "Tetragrammerton" inscribed upon them, and a hole so that the ring could be tied upon the finger. In "good" magic, they were consecrated with Holy Oil before being worn. Another variety was made of gold, engraved with the name of a spirit and bearing the symbol of the Sun. When nearly completed, they were fumigated with mastick, red storax, benjamin and musk. A piece of marigold or bay leaf was imbedded in the metal, and over it a carbuncle or chrysolite was placed.

Certain gems and stones were considered to be under the influence of the planets and the signs of the Zodiac, and were chosen accordingly. Thus, Mars was represented by the ruby, and moonstones were the emblem of Virgo.

King Solomon's ring was famous in tradition, and had the magic word "Schempamphorasch" written upon it, which gave him command over spirits. By his ring's power

Solomon procured the aid of the wonderful Shamir, which helped him to build the Temple, and was enabled to foresee future events.

The potency of magic rings was universally believed in, as is demonstrated by the gift of four of them by Pope Innocent to King John of England. He requested the King graciously to study the symbology and magical significance of the stones with which the rings were set, rather than have regard to their intrinsic value.

There are still wax impressions of various famous magic rings in existence. A notable example is that of Dr. Simon Forman, the sixteenth-century alchemist and magician. This ring was of silver and on the outside edge the signet was engraved with the word *Ariel* and *Anael*, while on the outside of the circle was written: *Die et Hora*. Simon Forman was notorious in his day, and was a man of many reverses. Brilliant and clever, he was something of a quack doctor and openly practised necromancy and sorcery as well. He became involved in the murder of Sir Thomas Overbury in 1615; having provided the Countess of Essex with a philtre to alienate her husband, and another to win the love of the Earl of Somerset. It was also found that he had made wax images of the people concerned. Eventually his manuscripts and seal impress passed into the hands of Elias Ashmole, who left them to the Bodleian Library.

Of the jewels used in rings, the diamond was believed to have remarkable powers over evil spirits, being the one unchangeable substance that fire itself was unable to injure. Rubies conferred increased virtue and banished sadness, but had their darker side as the agents of Mars in stirring up strife and disharmony. The sapphire had great healing properties, and was an emblem of goodness and peace. Emeralds were believed to ward off evil spirits and bestow eloquence. They were also thought to show the fidelity of a loved one, by shining with pure green brilliance, whereas if he or she were unfaithful the stone clouded and became pale. For this reason they were favourite gems for betrothal rings and love gifts. Rubies, again, had the property of turning black or loosing colour if misfortune threatened the wearer. Opals were not considered unlucky as they are now, but had qualities of sympathy and protection like the turquoise and coral. The topaz was the emblem of the Sun, and conferred wisdom and good health. The place of the onyx in magic was an important one, and was considered potent for good or evil.

An ancient magic manuscript tells us that if we make a ring of silver or gold, having set within it a red jacinth, inscribed with the image of a naked girl, tall and strong, riding upon a lion, with six men worshipping her, and make it at midday upon a Sunday morning, with the Moon in the tenth degree, then it will confer power over others. People shall bow down before the owner of such a ring, and no man shall be able to withstand him.

If a magician were undertaking any particular experiments, he was advised to prepare himself for three or six months beforehand. He should choose a hut built of logs in a wood for his magic arts, the floor to be covered with sand that could be thrown away in a secret place after any operations had been carried out. If the magician lived in a town, he must choose a house with a balcony, part of which could be enclosed with wood to form a hut. He must keep aloof from the world and shun much company, must not on any account touch wine or alcohol and have daily baths. The latter injunction was in itself an undertaking, we imagine, in days when personal cleanliness was not regarded with favour, even by members of the higher classes, and washing was supposed to weaken the body.

Very many herbs, plants, trees and shrubs had magical significance, and formed an indispensable part of all magic ceremonies and practices.

Garlic and assafœtida were used in exorcism, and also for some rites of black magic. Deadly nightshade, henbane, hellebore and mandrakes were of evil reputation ; the latter being called the "Devil's Candles," as they were supposed to shine out with baleful gleams upon dark nights. The hemlock had been known from very ancient times as a deadly poison, being employed by the Greeks and Romans, and was used in Russia and by the Slavonic peoples for black magic. Vervain (or as it is more often called, verbena) was extensively used in witchcraft, and its properties were related to have been revealed to sorcerers by the Devil himself. Foxgloves were called "Witches Bells," and were used by them for love philtres. Sea-poppies and ragwort were plants of ill-fame, too.

The oleander tree was looked upon as malevolent to any animal who came beneath its shade, and the Italians shunned walnut trees because under them witches were thought to gather at night time. In respect to walnut trees the same superstition was found in Spain. The elder, yew, cypress, oak, hazel and others too numerous to mention, were used for magic purposes.

Brooms were connected with witches both in the East and West, and in Europe they were thought to make them of hazel or from the "broom-plant." Curiously enough, in Germany brooms were used to *keep witches off*, and in some parts were laid across the threshold at night as a protection against them.

Now and again old countrymen can be found who know all the lore of the witches' herbs and the legends pertaining to the local sorcerers who used them, and a striking fact is that whether you speak to a Dorset farm hand, a South-down shepherd, an Italian, German or French peasant, the underlying beliefs and practices are identical. Magic, indeed, was always a kind of freemasonry, but the gipsies (or Bohemians, as they were called in the Middle Ages) did much to carry the beliefs and rites of magic from one far country to another.

CHAPTER XI

BLACK MAGIC AND SEX-RITES

Is a brief outline of the sex-rites performed in connection with black magic ceremonies and sorcery in many countries.

IN early times, and among more modern primitive races, phallic worship had little or nothing to do with sorcery. On the contrary, the sex forces were regarded as protective and beneficent, and were invoked to operate against evil. They symbolised life versus death, and fertility and plenty as against barrenness, destruction and disease.

The phallus had power to subdue the attacks of demons and the Evil Eye; and the female organs were potent over elemental disturbances, thus a woman uncovering herself could quell a storm. The snake, typifying man's virility, was everywhere worshipped and accepted as the symbol of wisdom, and solar deities were reverenced with phallic rites. Celebrations heralding the spring and the sowing of crops were accompanied by rites of sexual intercourse to stimulate fertility, and in the autumn the festivals of harvest were acclaimed in the same manner in the expression of joy and thanksgiving.

Civilisation has imbued man's minds with false ideas of the evil of sex and its fulfilment. Light is dawning upon this subject at the present time, but there is still a tendency in some quarters to regard sex as an unseemly necessity, and to stifle that which is naturally grand and pure with obscene thoughts. Not so the peoples of bygone eras, and the primitive races to-day. We have ourselves to thank for the evils of sexual promiscuity and vice, which wreck the health and serenity of so many thousands.

The carving and representations of sexual acts, which cover Hindu temples especially, were probably placed there with no intention of pandering to the worst in man, but rather in honour of the great creative force which was the highest manifestation which he could conceive of the unseen mysteries. I am not contesting the fact that gross sexuality is one of the characteristics of India as a whole nor that the Hindu religion has given birth to the apparently opposed twins, Ascetism and Sensuality ; but most people who have studied the subject will agree that the primitive concept of the generative act was one of awe and worship, accorded to a force which was incomprehensible and baffling.

Nearly all amulets originally appeared in phallic formations, but gradually their significance became covered over. Thus, hands represented the male and female generative organs ; the former being commonly in the shape of part of an arm with the fist clenched, and the latter merely a hand alone and open. Most people are familiar with such little ornaments made in coral. Even the pyramid, triangle, or cone is but a form of the phallus reduced to simple lines ; and most Egyptian amulets were of this origin, with the possible exception of the Scarab (which was a symbol of resurrection) and the Eye of Horus.

Phallicism was, therefore, at the root of all religion, and was definitely the opponent of evil and darkness. However, as time went on and magic became identified with so many of the religious customs and ceremonies, the phallic aspect became considerably degraded. The original high symbolism was lost sight of, and the sexual rites became a blind outlet for men's passions—occasions upon which promiscuous indulgence had not only the sanction of custom but the blessing of the gods. From the natural and joyous intercourse which acclaimed the bounty of nature, or invoked her abundance, foul rites of unnatural sensuality crept in, stimulated by heavy feasting and drunkenness.

Religious sodomy was practised by male prostitutes in the Hebrew temple groves, which was one of the abominations of Israel that Josiah cleared away. We are told in the 23rd chapter of 2 Kings that Josiah broke down their houses which were near the temple, and drove the Sodomites out, burning their groves and scattering the ashes on the graves of the people. At the same time he " put away " all the wizards and workers with familiar spirits, and destroyed the idols and images, filling up the site of the groves with the bodies of the dead. This custom of sacred male prostitution was not confined to the Israelites, and its counterpart can be found in nearly all the ancient religions of the East. In Egypt and Assyria it appears to have been customary to make eunuchs expressly for this purpose.

The practice of having sacred female prostitutes attached to temples in Greece, Rome, Egypt and India is so well known as to require no comment.

Sorcery and witchcraft, being in themselves evil, naturally seized upon the sexual instinct and passions to pervert them to their own ends. While, since the object of Satanic worship or demonism, was to swamp the personality in evil, no better means could be found than by first arousing lust and then giving it free play. In Europe the witches' Sabbaths were the outstanding example of sexual depravity in connection with sorcery. Participants divested themselves of their clothing, and yielded themselves to every conceivable lustful impulse, this condition being further induced by the drug-like properties of the ointments and oils which were first smeared on the body.

From the end of the fifteenth century onwards small coteries, practising spells and enchantments and indulging in performances of the black mass, found an ugly fascination in lewd indulgences and a taking part in rituals which entailed entire nakedness or partial exposure. Many of the so-called rites of these secret societies were so patently ridiculous, that it is quite obvious that they were merely an excuse for men and women to indulge in sex-play and lustful gratification, frequently of an abnormal kind. We can imagine how the fashionable women of the seventeenth and eighteenth centuries, already robust to the point of crudity in their love affairs, welcomed opportunities of greater coarseness, with the added thrill of flirting with the Devil.

Love philtres were compounded of various odious substances mixed with certain human fluids, according to the sex of the would-be lover, while special charms were made after the fashion of the genital organs. Moreover, though to some extent disguised, among many peoples the nature of such charms was perfectly obvious. To-day, these phallic talismans are to be seen everywhere among barbarous races, and are worn without any concealment in many parts of India and the East.

The powdered roots of the male and female mandrake were, and still are, used to incite love in many European countries. The method of the root's use was pure sorcery; the powder being burned over a fire, with some of the operator's pubic hair and characteristic secretions. At the same time a coarse incantation was uttered, invoking a demon to draw the desired person to the operator's abode at midnight.

Hindu women make a powder of an aphrodisiacal nature by frying the genital organs of male turtles, which they also use with enchantments. Until quite recently there was a secret society in India, which possibly still exists, called Saktas. Roughly, their philosophy expounded the need of wallowing in sensuality of all kinds in order to attain perfection. This doctrine of "sin for salvation" was very popular in Russia during the first decade or so of the present century. The Saktas indulged in rites in which the men represented Siva and the women Durga, Siva's wife. They all sat in a circle without any consideration of caste, and in the centre of it, the naked wife of the priest. After feasting on meat, fish and grain and drinking wine, the Saktas gave themselves up to wholesale sexual intercourse, without even care to avoid incest. The ritual of this society became so notorious that no decent people would associate with its members.

Nearly all the sex ceremonial of which we hear so much among primitive races both was, and is, connected with the puberty rites of their youths and girls, the fertility of the soil, and in a lesser degree the celebration of marriage and funeral customs; comparatively little is related in any way to witchcraft. To say that their religions and ceremonial are consciously or unconsciously phallic is perfectly true; but, at the same time, such things are not sorcery. Certainly some of the meetings of Voodoo and Obeah in the West Indies end in a general carouse and sexual intercourse. Yet the reason for that is not so much to do with the actual ceremonial as the fact that it represents a usual ending in any country to large gatherings of men and women, when feasting and drunkenness predominate and customary restraints are removed. The same thing could be said, in a lesser degree, of the very early English May Day revels; which, incidentally, also had a phallic origin, the May Pole itself being an emblem of the phallus. All Hallow's E'en, the night of the first of November, when the souls of the dead are believed to return and witches and warlocks roam abroad, is a time for casting love spells and going through magic ceremonies. Even in Scotland, where the rites of Hallow's E'en are still kept up, the original significance of many of the customs has long been forgotten. Games with apples and candles figure very largely; but apples are a fruit with a phallic symbolism, and we need go no farther than the Garden of Eden to find that Adam and Eve had no sex-consciousness until they had consumed the tempting fruit.

From time immemorial candles have represented the phallus upon altars, although many people might angrily deny the fact, and many architectural designs upon ancient buildings have the same origin. Again, some writers have suggested that the birch brooms bestrode by the witches were but symbols of the same potent factor.

In Italy, on Midsummer's Night, many Christians keep vigil, while witches and demons are thought to hold unholy and unmentionable revelry around the walnut trees of the country districts. Peasants gather garlic onions and go about carrying them by the bulbous roots, shaking the long flowering parts in the faces of their friends, in imitation of the wooden phallus that used to be so carried at an earlier day.

Little feasts of the boiled vegetable are also made, as it is believed to incite desire for intercourse; while childless women eat certain snails, in hope of conceiving, though the parents of a child begotten on Midsummer Night would run the risk of its possessing the evil eye. Young lovers seek each other out with love potions and gifts of flowers which symbolise passion; unless, of course hard-headed Fascism has swept away all the picturesque pagan customs and "la vecchia religione" lies dead at last, which I can scarcely believe.

Sex rites were used in mediæval times and even more recently, in very gross forms of necromancy, and for invoking the presence of demons or elementals. The virile life forces of the body were believed to have an even greater potency than blood, and both were employed for demoniac invocation, together and separately, the use of these methods entailing the exercise of base forms of sex perversion. In parts of Europe, Asia, Africa and elsewhere, when necromancy was performed with the dead bodies of women, an assistant of the operator often had intercourse with the corpse as a preliminary means of revitalising it.

Women taking part in the rites of black magic were required to sacrifice their virginity to Satan, usually at the instance of the chief officiator, who was sometimes disguised as the Devil; and subsequently they had intercourse with other participants. Some black magicians, however, kept themselves severely aloof from the surrounding indulgences; merely drinking the blood of the sacrifice and diverting the animal and emotional vibrations released to their own ends, or to those of the purpose of the celebrations. Women had a special part to play at the time of their lunar periods, and among savage tribes and elsewhere, the characteristic female fluids were used in sorcery. Normally primitive peoples dread and detest the condition, many of them going so far as to banish their women from encampments and villages at those times. In any case women so afflicted are considered rigidly taboo, and may not be approached by their menfolk for fear misfortune would fall upon the latter.

Blood has been reverenced or dreaded everywhere among all nations and races, as possessing the vital essence of life and an incalculable mystic potency. It was either poured out freely so that its lavish expenditure should imbue the living with courage, strength and vitality, or else it was carefully guarded and great pains taken not to spill it, even in carrying out executions. For that reason, so many mediæval tortures did not entail the actual shedding of blood and those who inflicted punishment by burning were not held guilty of the blood of their victims.

Certain flesh-eating peoples will not partake of animal blood in any form, but require all blood to be first drained from the meat. In some such instances, the poor animal is allowed to bleed to death.

The sorcerers of the Australian Aborigines were accustomed to bestiality, usually in those instances where the magician himself was supposed to turn into an animal at certain periods. The custom was also by no means unknown among such people as the early Egyptians, Assyrians and Hebrews. In some of the cults of Isis, and the forbidden idolatries of Israel, both priest and priestess performed the horrible ritual with sacrificial animals immediately before their slaughter.

Among certain modern races these practices, for the purpose of sorcery, seem to be deliberately undertaken in order to form a link with everything vile and base; but the more primitive men did so with the object of completely identifying themselves with particular animals. It may be objected that it would normally be impossible for men to be in sufficiently close touch with the wild beasts for this to occur; yet seemingly impossible events are common where native sorcerers were concerned, many of them having an apparently supernatural influence over the animal kingdom.

Much of the so-called monkey worship in places like Cambodia bordered upon open phallicism; the sorcerers casting their enchantments and spells with the aid of the phallus of monkeys and baboons, either mummified or ground to powder. Women were the guardians of the simians in the temples and are believed to have entered into relationship with them.

Many native customs that appear on the surface utterly crude and repugnant were not sorcery, although the acts were done with the express purpose of using their magic potency to attain a given end. Thus, in some parts of Africa and the East Indies, where large crops of spices are grown, men will strip naked and go to the trees and shrubs by night, and there, singly or in small groups, simulate copulation with the trees, at the same time crying for more abundance.

When sorcery was resorted to as a revenge for slighted love, figures were made of wood, clay, wax or dough, according to nationality, with enormously disproportionate reproductive organs, which were subjected to various ingenious tortures, to bring about suffering in the unfaithful victim. In some of the South Sea Islands women, whose husbands have committed adultery, make such an image and fasten it to a tree with a long thorn driven through the phallus; in other cases, a lighted brand is held to the member until it is gradually burnt off. These customs are equally to be found in different parts of Europe and Asia.

Coition was, and is, regarded in many parts of the world as being fraught with uncanny dangers, and even husbands and wives before embracing had to perform special rites to prevent demons taking possession of them or causing their death. This idea of the disastrous consequences of sexual union was so deeply ingrained in some races that a youth, having passed through the puberty rites, sought out some old woman and, taking her unawares, raped and killed her; it being believed that anyone with whom a man had his first intercourse was bound to die.

In Polynesia giving birth to twins is considered terribly unlucky and ill omened, not to say a pollution to the mother. The latter consequently has ceremonial intercourse, with four men, presided over by a witch doctor before cohabiting with her husband again. These acts of coition are purposely incomplete and unfruitful, and it is believed inevitable that three at least of the men will die.

If rain-making be considered black magic, then many of the ceremonies and dances for procuring it are of a sexual character. To mention only one instance, in many parts of Africa drought is thought to be due to concealed miscarriages among the women. The witch-doctor, therefore, has a round up of the females of his district and has little difficulty in making them confess their guilt. A black ox is then killed, and the grass removed from its stomach and placed in a vessel with four openings, north, south, east and west. Little girls next pour water into the vessel, which escapes through the channels to the four points of the compass ; the girls at the same time intoning a chant. The women strip naked and dance a rain dance ; after which they proceed to dig up the remains of the abortions and miscarriages, water or urine being emptied into the graves. At nightfall the pathetic remnants are reinterred, and the rain is then confidently expected.

Among tribes where the customs regarding sexual intercourse are not rigid, the rain dance and burials are followed by general sexual licence ; the men visiting the huts of different women during the night, and a free interchange of wives taking place for the occasion.

Among certain European black magic societies circumcision is performed on male members, the flesh being consumed as a sacrifice by the participants. In some parts of Asia again, the whole or parts of the genital organs are amputated as a sacrificial offering. Ceremonial shaving of the pubic hair of both sexes is common in connection with sorcery in nearly every part of the world. After its removal the hair is either sprinkled with blood and buried, or else burnt with various other substances.

Many forms of phallic worship in older days entailed human sacrifice, especially of children and virgins. Astarte, Isis and Dionysius were honoured with offerings of blood, and children were willingly cast down the temple steps into deep ravines by their unnatural parents. The celebrations to Mithra wore a phallic aspect, and in some sects cultivating his worship the blood was obtained by most unholy means.

In Asia the phallic hand is a common feature of many idols and carvings representing Siva, and others. In India, images with a greatly exaggerated phallus are resorted to by women who desire to bear children; their methods of worship in many cases entailing acts of sorcery. In some instances the image was actually embraced. Sex rites of a foul and devilish nature are performed in order to induce erotic passion in lovers.

These pages give some indication of the general trend of sex rites everywhere. To enlarge upon the subject would only entail dwelling *ad nauseam* on man's perverse use of his creative forces.

CHAPTER XII

PRIMITIVE RACES AND BLACK MAGIC

Describes the habits and beliefs of savage races in connection with witchcraft, and some account of their ceremonies and secret societies.

AMONG the majority of primitive peoples, sorcery and magic are the prerogative of the witch-doctors and secret societies, though in a few cases solitary black magic can be performed by ordinary individuals. In such places as Polynesia, the South Sea Islands and parts of Africa, every adult male belongs to a secret society and takes part in magic rites and dances; but as a member of the group only, never as a separate individual outside it.

An example of this is the Leopard Society of Sierra Leone, whose members dress in leopard skins and imitate these animals in ceremonial dances and ritual. They are believed to be "Ju-Ju" or were-leopards, and in this guise to roam through the forest in bands, bent on evil and destruction. They are known to fall occasionally upon an unwary wanderer and kill him, or her, for sacrificial purposes. It is doubtful whether they possess the powers claimed for them; but it is certain that, when bent on killing, they are covered with the entire skins and masks of leopards, and behave as these jungle beasts rather than as humans.

An acquaintance of mine once had a remarkable experience of leopard-men, while on a shooting expedition in Africa. As nightfall was approaching, he and his "boys" entered a native village, where drums were beating to summon the men to their "Lodge." My friend's boys, although they were fatigued, and in spite of hospitality offered by the women of the village and an old man, urged him to press on. Having gone some distance from the village, the boys explained that the men were "Ju-Ju" leopards who would be abroad that night, and that misfortune and probably death would overtake anyone crossing their path. The party arranged to sleep in the trees, therefore; the boys taking it in turn to keep watch. During the

" Among the majority . . . sorcery and magic are the prerogatives of the witch-doctors, and Secret Societies."

night my friend was cautiously awakened by the man on guard and, peering out from his shelter, dimly perceived in the moonlight filtering through the branches what appeared to be literally hundreds of leopards passing silently but quickly through the forest. He was very much mystified by a certain uncanny atmosphere about the beasts, and their unusual numbers, as the leopard is a comparatively solitary creature. The next day brought the party to another village, where a great clamour of mourning and distress was going on on account of an attack that had been made by wild beasts during the night, women and children having been killed and carried off. Was the presence of the strange leopards moving in that direction pure coincidence?

In the East Indies such creatures are believed first to attack their victims in animal form, whereupon the latter fall into a sort of stupor. The were-animal then resumes human form, cuts open the body, tears out the liver and eats it. The victim is then closed up again, but subsequently gradually dies, fading away much as the victim of the European vampire is supposed to do.

The famous Duk-Duk Societies of Melanesia and other parts are not concerned with sorcery, except in as much as the whole life of the native is bound up with magic in every shape and form. On the contrary, the main purpose of the Duk-Duks is to enforce the customs and laws of their respective tribes, and to deal with the rules of Taboo, the rites and initiation ceremonies of puberty, the ceremonial dances and the social regulation of the people. They try men and women accused of wrong-doing and mete out the penalties.

There are endless varieties of rain-making practised by witch-doctors; one very interesting African method being carried out with the help of a skeleton. The sorcerer exhumes a dead body and, having boiled all the remnants of flesh from the bones, gathers them together and takes them to a cave or a hut made with the branches of trees. The skeleton is then tied together as well as possible, and suspended from the roof. Piles of leaves are placed under it, and the witch-doctor and others pour water through the bones on to the leaves. If no water is available, their own urine is used. An animal such as a goat or dog is sacrificed, its blood being drunk by the sorcerer and the carcase left outside for the rain-gods. As a matter of fact, these deities arrive in the form of the inevitable birds of prey. After that, custom decrees that the witch-doctor shall remain in the cave or hut, fasting and repeating chants until rain does fall. For some reason or other, he usually does not have to remain there many days. If, however, the clouds refuse to appear, it is due to some fault in the ceremony, which takes place all over again ; with additions such as a rain dance by the young men accompanied by much lunging of spears and shouting at the skies.

"Bull-roarers" are used in Africa and Australasia to encourage rainfall, besides being employed in other rites of the secret societies. The bull-roarer is merely a thin oblong or oval piece of wood, with pointed ends and a hole in the centre through which a string is passed. If it is correctly pulled the roarer whirls round, giving out a loud booming sound. Small ones are made for children to play with, but the very large ones used by the men make an immense noise, that can be heard at a distance.

The African witch-doctor casts his spells chiefly by means of sympathetic magic. That is, he requires some article belonging to the victim, or some actual part of his person, on which to work. Hair, toe or nail parings, saliva, urine or excrement, and best of all a tooth are used. When such has been obtained the witch-doctor may either mix it in the blood of an animal which has been especially killed and cast it in the fire, or he may bury it in the ground, wrapped up in the leaves of poisonous shrubs if the article is substantial. If, on the other hand, the article is liquid it must be placed in a small bowl in a hole in the ground that has been half-filled with blood. This will infallibly cause death or illness ; particularly if the victim gets to hear of what has transpired, when his psychological reactions do the rest.

The bones of the dead are also used ; being ground to powder, and blown towards the victim or in the direction in which he lives. Skulls are used for divinatory purposes, the walls of the witch-doctor's hut being sometimes literally festooned with these grim-looking relics. A man very anxious to get in touch with his parents in the spirit world will occasionally dig up their earthly remains and, taking their skulls home with him, sleep with one on each side. The dreams that visit him are then supposed to be direct portents, sent to guide or instruct him ; though it often takes the local sorcerer to supply the exact meaning—if any.

On the banks of the River Amazon and elsewhere boiled heads (examples of which can be seen in London and Continental museums) are employed by the natives for divination and sorcery. The heads are those of children or adults, from which the bony structure is very cleverly removed without cutting or injuring the face or scalp. They are treated with a certain process and boiled, finally shrivelling to about the size of a large orange. They, too, are hung up in the witch-doctor's hut or adorn the walls of the "lodges."

The African sorcerer works with curses, personally delivered, and sometimes accompanied by an act such as blowing bone-dust or salt or pointing a bone at the person. These curses are generally of a character calculated to cause the victim so much discomfort and distress that he or she is willing to pay the witch-doctor anything in reason to have the spell removed. Thus, the "snake curse" may be laid on a man, and everywhere he goes these reptiles will appear to dog his path. They will be found coiled in his sleeping place, and lurking in the receptacles for his food. Growing desperate, the victim resorts to the sorcerer to remove the spell for the consideration of gifts, or else employs a rival witch-doctor to operate a counter enchantment. The latter course often results in some very heated feuds between some magicians and their followers.

Totemism, or the tribal adoption of a certain animal to represent them, is not strictly speaking sorcery. The totem animal is respected and seldom killed, the humans of the tribe claiming brotherhood with it. In some places marriage must not take place between men and women of the same totem, and children are bound to respect the totem of their mother's families. The custom of totemism is found in North and South America, Africa, Polynesia and Australasia; many peoples erecting totem poles adorned with carved images and faces at the entrance to their villages. There are, also, an innumerable number of totems acknowledged in India and the surrounding countries.

In Annam, "Oñg Cop," the tiger, is deeply reverenced and has special priests and sorcerers in his honour. Many temples have no representation of any deity, except the image of a huge tiger on the altar. Nevertheless, "Oñg Cop" is hunted just the same, the natives apparently making some sort of distinction between tigers in the spirit and those in the flesh. Indeed, these peoples' lives are constantly overshadowed by dread of various well-known types of evil spirits. A particularly malignant one is " Ma-lai," who appears as a pretty young girl to mislead travellers and the unwary. At night a hideous transformation comes over her, the head detaching itself from the body and rising into the air, with only the alimentary canal still connected with it. The dreadful thing then glides among the haunts of men and animals, feeding on excrement and even seeking for it in the bowels of sleepers. The demon is also believed to attend vile revels, in the company of every variety of witch and demon.

The natives of Annam believe in earth and other elemental spirits, particularly those who guard mines and fiercely resent men attempting to wrest the treasures of earth from them. The same beliefs are found in Europe, in the legends of gnomes and goblins. Welsh miners have many tales to tell of the beings encountered in the depths of the earth, some of them puckish and even willing to be of assistance, others terrible in their stony malignity.

The Annamese believe that the spirits of the drowned lurk in the water, waiting to seize upon swimmers and give them cramp. In order to avoid this state of affairs, a sorcerer and a kind of mediumistic assistant are called in to trap the errant soul, by providing another body for it to be properly buried in. The first task is to make an artificial body, the bones of which are the branches of the mulberry tree, the entrails strong-coloured threads, the flesh and viscera earth and wax, the skin a sort of pancake-like substance made principally of flour. This macabre image is dressed in the best garments of the deceased and placed in a coffin, ready for the spirit to enter into it. The sorcerer and his assistant then go in a boat to the place where the deceased is supposed to have drowned, and the assistant holds out a coat that belonged to the departed, rather as the douser holds the hazel-twig. When the assistant's arm and the coat begin to tremble, he declares that the man's spirit is rising up to put his garment on once more. After which the assistant dives into the water himself. In a few seconds he rises again and announces that he has got the spirit in the coat, which is quickly taken back and placed in the coffin. The magician recites some incantations and the burial takes place, the spirit having been placated by the funeral arrangements.

Many of the native tribes of Burma, such as the K'Chins, practised cannibalism in connection with their sorcery until quite recent times ; they probably do so still surreptitiously, although every kind of human sacrifice and torture has been sternly suppressed by the Government. The Burmans proper are Buddhists, nevertheless they were very fond of propitiating the powers-that-be with offerings of living victims. They greatly dread evil "Nats" or spirits, to whom they attribute every possible misfortune or illness. Like their Western brothers, groups of native youths from outlying places set out cheerfully on Saturday nights to visit the nearest "Bioscope," as they call the cinema, but on their return along the tree-shadowed roads or jungle pathways they blow feverishly upon reed pipes and bang drums and little gongs to keep the Nats away. In particular are feared those malevolent ladies with their feet turned back to front.

The more barbaric tribes perform divination by entrails, and make sacrifices of blood to procure rain. Some of the tortures which the natives of Upper Chindwin used to inflict upon children in this respect are too terrible to mention. The K'Chin sorcerer kills a dog, in order to cast a spell of illness or madness upon a man. The carcase is placed at a cross-road, and the magician and young men cast spears over it in the direction of the victim's home.

In Cambodia the sorcerers place great faith in the fœtus of an unborn child for producing magical results. This fœtus is believed to possess as developed a spirit as any child born in the normal way, but as it is regarded as malevolent if frustrated in its effort to be born, any woman who has a miscarriage calls in the sorcerer to deal with the unlucky event. Burning incense and chanting incantation, the sorcerer seals the abortion in a jar, to prevent its escape. He is then supposed to take it to the nearest stream or river and, having broken the jar with his wand, to leave the contents in the water. More often than not he takes possession of the fœtus himself, and roasts it over a fire protected by seven cotton threads. He then proceeds to blacken it with soot and varnish it, after which it is sewn in a bag which he keeps, as a familiar spirit that will regard him as an adopted father. Sorcerers visit the Cambodian burial-grounds, and command the spirits of women who died in pregnancy or early labour to give up their children. They then dig the bodies up and remove the fœtus, or still-born child, as the case may be, for the foregoing purposes. Sometimes the body is magically revitalised and the tongue bitten out of the women before re-burial.

The powers of the embryonical body are supposed to be so potent that, formerly, a wife carrying her first child was not safe from attack by her husband, should he require an invincible amulet. The fœtus of the first child of a couple was believed to be doubly protective, and the spirit attached to it even more useful than that of others. A husband with such designs would enquire jokingly of his wife, about the fifth month or so, if she would give him the child she was bearing. If she was unwary and replied to the effect that it was his already, he would take her away to a secluded place and kill her. When he had removed the child he took it to the sorcerer to roast and blacken, and henceforth used the remains of his child as a familiar and an amulet that rendered him invulnerable. Even at the present, the parent of a young wife keeps her under surveillance as much as possible during her first pregnancy, in case of such attacks upon her.

Among all the different inhabitants of the Malay Peninsula, magic is brought into every aspect of the daily life. Omens are consulted, and divination practised even before setting out on hunting or fishing expeditions. The official medium between the material world and that of the spirits is the "Pawang," who employs a familiar to cope with demons and ghosts on his behalf, but who is not above casting spells himself occasionally, principally by "pointing the kris" at the intended victim. This act is designed to inflict agonising suffering, and when the spell is beginning to work the kris or dagger is supposed to drip blood. The "Pawang" also inflicts death from a distance, by burning the cordiform top of a newly opened bunch of bananas on the tree. This, too, is a recognised method of causing exquisite torture, and when the sorcerer finally cuts the top through, the victim suddenly dies from hæmorrhage of the lungs.

Certain cults and individuals of the West look towards Tibet as the abode of mysterious Mahatmas and "Masters," and the home of the Great White Brotherhood. However that may be, it is undoubtedly true that some of the Llamas of the monasteries possess great occult knowledge, which is for the most part hidden to the world in general, but on the other hand, many of them are comparatively ignorant and undeveloped, and never get beyond the first stage of their elementary initiation.

Black magic is extensively practised in this part of the world, a prominent example being the well-known Bon cult. The symbol of these people is the swastika with its arms reversed, which indicates its lunar origin. They secretly make living sacrifices, accompanied by horrible blood rituals, and wandering members of the cult, travelling in remote places, carry out the rites of their Order with devotees collected in the desolate villages.

In this connection it is rather suggestive that the German Nazis have presumably unconsciously chosen the same reversed aspect of the swastika for their emblem; the sign which represents to most occultists the sinister "Soma" influence of the moon, and the dark and blood-stained emanations from it.

Coming to Japan, we find those strange aboriginal people the Ainus, steeped in magic, which always brings sorcery in its train. The Ainus hold the bear in remarkable veneration, not to say worship, but strangely enough do not hesitate to make deliberate living sacrifices of their deified pets, who become at once the god and the votive offering. Nearly every humble Ainu family has its own bear, kept with every mark of affection and fed on the choicest morsels. A day comes, however, when the poor creature is made into a public sacrifice, and its owners ask their friends to come and share the festivity. The bewildered animal, accustomed to being petted, is seized upon by four men and strung up on horizontal poles in a very cruel position. The local sorcerer presides over the sacrifice, the bear's throat ultimately being cut and other wounds inflicted. As the blood pours out, the sorcerer and men rush forward to catch the blood and drink it warm from the body. None must fall to the ground; if so much as a drop of the blood is spilt, misfortune will come upon the owners, if not upon the entire village.

In Northern Africa—Tripolitania, to be exact—there is a tribe of women with the reputation of being able to turn into foxes on a certain night of full-moon every month. They live in cave-like dwellings in the sides of hills and seldom see the light of day, preferring to live in the darkness of their caverns and only coming out as a rule at sundown. The well-known woman traveller and explorer, Rosita Forbes, recently published the story of a visit she paid to these women, and according to her own account witnessed occurrences which would seem to be undoubted proof of their claims.

One of the chief African secret societies that actually practise black magic is the Ngil society of sorcerers. The initiation into this "Order" is accompanied by many obscene and disgusting rites, together with excessive gluttony. Strange to say, however, these men also practise exorcism and act as witch-finders; since although the fetish-man, or witch-doctor, is an almost indispensable adjunct to most barbarous tribes, the witch is looked upon with fear and loathing, and the official sorcerers hate her as a rival and are only too glad to have the opportunity of "smelling her out." One of the witches' supposed activities is to catch the wandering souls of sleepers at night, and prevent them from returning to their bodies. Other magicians are, therefore, employed to frustrate the witches' work. In the past very few of the negro secret societies were free from the taint of cannibalism; even the famous Duk-Duks ate human flesh on certain occasions, though less with the deliberate intention of sorcery than to imbue themselves with bravery and free themselves from the spiritual onslaughts of deceased enemies.

The same theories and practices of magic and witchcraft are to be found with little variation among the aboriginal inhabitants of Australia, the adjacent islands, Melanesia and Polynesia. The sorcery of the Australian aborigine is closely bound up with the animal and reptile kingdom, the black magicians there also claiming the ability to turn into animals at certain seasons. These men are known occasionally to practise bestiality, in pursuance of their magic rites.

The Maoris also have many customs in relation to the black art. They apparently have a theory that the indefinable psychic gift that they call magic, and which we might designate "psychicism," can be acquired by accosting the soul of a murdered man in a burial ground at midnight.

Sorcery is not the exclusive prerogative of the fetish-man, but is practised haphazardly by anyone who wishes to cast a spell upon another. The official enchanter may be consulted as to the propitious time for the casting of the spell and to acquire various substances in connection with the sinister performance.

Salt is a very favoured ingredient of spell-binding concoctions. Thrown after a man, it causes him irritation and excessive unrest, so that he wanders by day and cannot sleep by night. Sprinkled with the blood of a black cock, and thrown across the threshold of a dwelling for three nights in succession, it will cause the inhabitants to leave. Mixed in love philtres it will arouse passion; and placed in the bed of a desired lover or sprinkled upon the hair during sleep, it will irresistibly draw the subject towards the operator. The coloured peoples, wheresoever found, connect salt in some mysterious way with the forces of sex, and it often takes an important place in the marriage rites for that reason. The inherent qualities of salt are stimulating, and excessive stimulation for the release of physical and emotional forces is the underlying principle of orgies.

Alum and sulphur are also employed for magical purposes, and the primitive man uses bitumen ochres and coloured clays. Iron is considered protective, and hence in many tribes we find the people wearing heavy iron rings on their arms and legs as amulets.

In New Guinea and the adjacent islands the natives firmly believe in the magic power of various stones and animals, but to a large extent they make their own magic. For instance, if a man comes across a stone or similar object that appeals to his imagination, he decides to appropriate it for his own "fetish." He then brings money (formerly blood), and scatters it in a circle around the chosen object, announcing to others that that place is henceforth "rongo." Sometimes there is a living creature involved as well, such as a snake in a hole or an octopus sheltering in a rock pool; in which case the creature is fed, and induced to remain in that particular spot.

To the peoples of the Pacific Islands all success in life depends on inciting the forces of nature with magic. They realise that the elements do their work independently of mankind, and are excellent weather-prophets; but they appear to think that they can add power to the natural phenomena by singing and performing ritual dances, and so on. As the men build their canoes they sing certain songs in rhythm, and unless these are sung correctly the canoe will be sluggish in the water, while, again, wind and rain are invoked by dances and sacrifices.

The sorcerers of the islands are called "balubualata," and give the fetish-men as much trouble as anyone else, the latter being expected to undo their machinations. Their main activities take the form of causing illness, parting lovers and married couples, making canoes heavy in the water, withholding rain, causing pigs to run away.

In some of the islands it is considered terribly unlucky to mention the name of a man who is away fishing or hunting, as to do so will recall his spirit and cause him misfortune or even death. Wives have to be particularly careful of their smallest actions and words, on account of the magical sympathetic link which is believed to exist between them and their husbands. The theory is that the husband depends to some extent on the quality of the magnetism exchanged between him and his wife, no matter how great the distance between them ; and *vice versa.*

Until comparatively recent years human sacrifices to obtain rain were common among the natives of the Pacific Islands, and also among those of the West Indies. The women stripped naked and took part in a rain-dance, a girl being chosen for the sacrificial victim. Sometimes she was clubbed to death and her blood offered to the rain-gods, but occasionally a more lingering and terrible death was inflicted. Travellers have testified to seeing women tied to the tops of trees (so that the guardians of the elements can see them), and being eaten alive by birds of prey. The rain-dances are still performed without the element of human sacrifice, although in remote places it is very difficult to say that the custom is entirely suppressed.

Fetishism is inextricably bound up with native magic and totemism. As we have seen, any object may become a fetish ; the actual thing itself not being reverenced, but the spirit which is believed to have taken up its abode within it. The fetish is seldom regarded as a god ; its spirit being looked upon more in the light of a familiar that can be cajoled and propitiated, like the djinns of the Arabians. Fetishism is very often erroneously identified with sorcery ; generally speaking, however, it is nothing of the kind, only ordinary magic. Even so, the primitive sorcerer does occasionally use a fetish in performance of his enchantments.

Within the space of one chapter it has only been possible to touch very briefly on the magic customs of peoples who are dispersed over a very wide area of the earth. Consequently, there has been chosen those which are as far as possible representative of the whole.

CHAPTER XIII

SORCERY IN NORTH AND SOUTH AMERICA

Is a brief account of sorcery in North and South America from earliest times up to the present day.

THE sorcery of the primitive peoples of the great American continent has naturally always been connected with the beliefs regarding the spirit world and its manifestations, and has centred chiefly round a form of Shamanism.

Eskimos of the Far North deal with the Unseen through the Shaman, or Tun-gha-lîk. This man's power is judged by the number of spirits he is able to subjugate to his will; not necessarily all of them evil, though their controller's method of gaining his position is by means of sorcery. The would-be Tun-gha-lîk directly murders, or causes the the death of, a new-born child and steals the body. He next dries and embalms it and keeps it always with him, thereby gaining control over the spirit of the child, which becomes his familiar and does his bidding and divines the future for him. When fully fledged, the Tun-gha-lîk can call upon both the spirits of men and animals, change the weather, cause or cure disease and illness. But the Shaman who fails in his claims, or misuses his gifts, risks his life at the hands of the tribe to which he belongs.

Some of the Eskimo peoples practise a kind of spiritualism; the "medium" sitting down in a darkened hut, from which strange noises subsequently emanate. The "medium then entertains his familiar, who can be asked questions by the seekers sitting respectfully outside, but not before gifts of tobacco and the like have been pushed into the hut. Occasionally the Shaman claims actually to go away to visit the spirit world with his guardian, bringing back with him disturbing information of future events that will certainly come to pass unless his commands are strictly adhered to.

The Tun-gha-lîk supplies amulets and charms of every

description, particularly for the protection of hunters and children. The charms are composed chiefly of parts of animals, such as teeth, claws and ears, and the skin from the roof of the mouth of bears. The Eskimo fears and dislikes all storms and disturbance of the elements, and the Shaman accordingly provides a jacket made from the skin of a still-born seal. If a thunderstorm occurs, the hunter must take off this coat and beat it upon the ground, whereupon the thunder will stop.

The "medicine-man" of the Red Indians was only a rather more advanced Shaman, but the Red Indians' form of Nature worship was infinitely superior to the very elementary beliefs of many of the native races of North and South America. I say *was*, because unfortunately civilisation has robbed the Red man of much of his former dignity and simple grandeur.

The Red Indian "medicine-man" was also a spirit-medium like the "Tun-gha-lîk," and erected a special tent in which to operate, upon the same principle as the cabinet of the séance-room. This tent was cone-shaped, and supported by three poles covered with skins and mats. Only a very small aperture was left in the front, through which the medicine-man had to crawl. The subsequent phenomena were very similar to that of the Eskimo ritual; the tent creaking and groaning as if assailed by a furious gale and voices that sometimes seemed to speak from high up in the air, and sometimes to proceed from the depths of the earth, issuing from it. Those consulting the spirit had to make offerings of tobacco, beads and the like; though it seems more probable that the medium benefited rather than the spirits.

In some tribes the "medicine-man" kept a mask to represent each of his different familiars, and these he donned before entering the hut or wore alternately on ceremonial occasions. The duties of a "medicine-man," in addition to his being the official link with the Unseen, were to heal, to influence the weather, to interpret omens, to divine the the future, and so on. In healing he made use of hypnotism, magnetic passes with the hands, blowing or breathing upon the afflicted, besides having a very wide knowledge of the properties of herbs.

Sorcery does not seem to have been the exclusive prerogative of the "medicine-man," nor does it appear to have been carried out on any large scale as a rule. It was, rather, a matter of isolated individuals casting spells and enchantments, or obtaining the services of the "medicine-man" to operate for them. Disease was sometimes thought to be caused by the absence of the soul, and it was the duty of the "medicine-man" to charm the soul back to the body; though in the practice of sorcery he also expelled souls, to cause illness and death. Both results were obtained by wild dances, accompanied by the beating of drums, tambourines and rattles.

Necromancy was extensively practised among all tribes of the North American Indians. The bodies of the dead were arrayed in ceremonial costume and seated within a special hut, to be consulted regarding the future by the local "medicine-man," who was operator and interpreter. Lycanthropy also was common, in early times at least, and belief in werewolves and werefoxes existed among all tribes. A curious means of communication with the dead was established by the Ghost Dance of the Paviotso of Nevada. By this a state of hypnotic trance was induced, during which the people were believed to discourse with their departed friends.

The Sioux Indians induced visions by removing the skin from a freshly killed animal and tying it so tightly round the neck that consciousness was lost. The hallucinations thereby invoked were believed to have particular significance. These people also used the symbols of the supernatural powers painted upon their war-shields, both to strike fear into the enemy and to invoke protection. Their "totems" or tribal symbols were animals, birds or reptiles, such as the bear, wolf, eagle and turtle; while their amulets were composed of the teeth, claws, skins and feathers of these creatures. In addition, the Sioux made powerful charms from the navel-strings of newly-born children in the shape of turtles. Children, too, were frequently provided with their own navel-strings, placed in small bags made of bearskin and slung round the neck. The "medicine-man" supplied a special amulet, composed of the dried body of the blue bird with the ears of a jack-rabbit attached to it.

Hunters believed that by chewing the sinews of a deer that had been "charmed" by a sorcerer, the muscles of wounded quarry would contract so painfully that it was bound to fall into the hands of the pursuer.

A very strange hunting sorcery was practised by the natives of Alaska, for capturing the sea-otter. The preparation for this lasted for a month, during which time the hunter had no intercourse with his wife and must take great care that no one but himself touched the receptacle for his urine. At the end of the month he killed an eagle and cut off one of the bird's feet. To the claws of the foot he attached some of the plant called "grabbing medicine," which had very potent magic properties. The next thing was to make a clay canoe, with an image of himself taking aim, and to fasten the eagle's foot to the seat of the craft. The next day, fortified with his charms, the hunter set out in his canoe. Directly he sighted a likely otter, he blew some of his urine which had been saved towards it, and was thereby supposed to confuse the creature. After that, the hunter fired. If he had not abstained from intercourse with his wife as was required, his arm would tremble and his aim be weak. Otherwise, however, the "sympathetic magic" between the clay canoe, with its eagle's foot and "grabbing medicine" would ensure the hunter's success.

If they wished to secure a doe, the Alaskans took the pubic hair from one already killed, and tying it up with some of the "grabbing medicine" plant attached it to his arrows.

All Red Indians had implicit faith in love charms, and believed that by means of them they could obtain the love of any woman they desired. One of the simplest methods was to take two plants, male and female, and, after tying them up with the hair of the lover and the beloved, to bury them in the ground. A fire had then to be made over the spot, and certain incantations uttered as the smoke arose. Another process which brought many gifts and dollars to the "medicine-man," was to take a plant and a small flat-stone supplied by him and, having tied them together, throw them at the woman concerned. The woman, after the lapse of three days and nights, would come to visit the lover. Certain tribes made a peculiar magic effigy, as a means of obtaining money. This figure was composed of two pieces of sheet-copper, stuffed in between with broken remains of valuable articles that had been stolen, and was kept secretly among its owner's blankets or in some other hiding-place. It was offered food, and possibly had prayers addressed to it, and was supposed to bring not only money but other material gain to the possessor.

The greatest charm of all, perhaps, was the sacred cord made by the Shaman—composed of malachite, pieces of lightning-struck wood, claws, teeth, and so on—which was supposed to render the wearer invulnerable to the attacks of enemies, man or animal, and to endow him with the power of covering great distances without fatugue.

The Botocados ate their enemies in order to be protected from the revenge of their relatives and tribe, and to make them invulnerable against hostile arrows. Other tribes ate pieces of their murdered victims, to prevent their ghosts haunting them; evidently working on the theory that when the body was eaten and assimilated, the spirit was rendered powerless.

The Cherokee sorcerers worked by means of spiders and their web; the spider being regarded as a representative of evil. Having obtained one, complete with its web, the sorcerer repeated incantations for destroying the life of his victim, entangling his soul in the web of spells or enticing it away from its body.

The Red Indians had a very important secret society for the development of "medicine-men" called the Midiwiwin, their initiation passing through various stages and grades. They practised fasting and offered prayers to the Bear Spirit; and at a later stage entered initiation through the Serpentine Gateway, which was symbolised by the materialisation of an immense snake, under the archway of whose coils the initiate had to pass. Those who passed through all the various degrees attained the power to see events in other places and in the future, and to live in the spirit world as well as on earth. The cult was originally supposed to have been inaugurated by a god, who revealed his secrets to a sacred otter, giving it a mystic drum, rattle and sacred tobacco.

A great deal of the magic of the native Mexican tribes was founded on the remains of the old Aztec religion, many of whose deities were magicians. In the days of the Aztecs' supremacy, there was a striking resemblance between many of their customs and those of the Egyptians, one of them being the official status of their sorcerers. The Aztecs possessed a college of Augurs, whose members divined the future by the flight and songs of birds, and their sorcerers were believed to have power over life and death and the elements. They interpreted dreams, and claimed that they could visit distant lands in the spirit. According to them all sorcerers, necromancers and evil-doers were born under the baleful influence of the seventh calendic sign, and all enchantments were operated within the number seven.

Following in the Aztecs' footsteps, Mexican magicians chose an evil planetary influence under which to work their enchantments, and, after having prepared their spells for four consecutive nights, they finally set out in animal form actively to put them into operation. These men were called "naualli," and appear to have been also dreaded as vampires. On ceremonial occasions they displayed remarkable powers, such as cutting off their own hands or feet with no loss of blood and restoring the limb without injury. They caused fire to ignite spontaneously, and even burned their huts, renewing them immediately without damage.

Most of our knowledge of these people is gained from the early Spanish traders and missionary priests, who, while condemning their witchcraft, seem to have had no doubt as to its reality and potency. Most Mexican amulets had some relation with their deities; especially Tezcatlipoca, the magician, who was supposed to have driven the aboriginals crazy, by beating upon a magic drum which caused thousands of them to perish by throwing themselves into a deep ravine. A favourite Mexican symbol was a staff carved in serpentine form, like that of Quetalcoatl.

Like the Hindus, the Mexicans dreaded the ghosts of women who died in child-birth, which were to be seen by night at cross-roads, wailing and weeping for their children. They were thought to be vampires, and such a woman was usually decapitated before burial. At certain times of the year such creatures were supposed to attempt to enter houses, in order to steal the children or suck their blood, and every opening and crevice was accordingly stuffed up, to the accompaniment of incantations and protective spells.

Serpents were regarded everywhere with great respect and treated with a reverence little short of worship, rattlesnakes being used as "familiars" by the "medicine-men" of some tribes.

The deer, or goat-god, of north-west Virginia was believed to lie in the mountains of that State, where there was a huge slant-eyed image of him in the Blue Ridge district. He was worshipped with sorcery, while offerings of both fresh and dried blood were made to him.

The Cherokee Indians placed great importance on the symbolism of colour, and divined omens from the colours of lakes, of the sunrise and sunset, and so on. Colours, for them, corresponded to the four elements and the four points of the compass. Thus: the North was represented by Blue, which meant trouble or defeat; the South by White, which signified peace and happiness; the East by Red, which meant success and triumph; the West by Black, which was Death. Yellow had practically the same evil significance as Blue; Brown was propitiatory; Green was the colour of nature and magic.

The Red Indians, generally, made drums and tambours from the skins of slain enemies, and at certain seasons, or before war, held wild dances with the "medicine-man" as the most prominent figure. Huge fires were made and young warriors, caked with pigment and clay, danced half-naked around them, from time to time seizing brands with which they touched themselves and the bare backs of those in front of them without apparent injury. Orgies, again, were held, in which the spirits of evil were propitiated and invoked by means of the Shamans and warriors falling upon each other with terrible blows and sharp weapons; so that the blood flowed and the flesh hung down in strips. Sometimes the celebrants died of their wounds, and from their exhibitions of swallowing sticks and knives. The warriors of Arikaras and Gros Ventres tribes, when preparing for war, made incisions in their bodies and thrust pieces of wood through them beneath the shoulder blades, allowing themselves to be thus suspended over river chasms and the like.

All tribes of Indians were proficient conjurers; so much so that the early French settlers called them "Jongleurs," and believed that most of the manifestations of the Shamans could be attributed to the same art. The more intelligent Indian tribes, however, worshipped the Great Spirit, whom they considered was served by all the forces of Nature. Indeed, even the more ignorant and undeveloped of the race do not seem to have been so overshadowed by the belief in unseen evil as many primitive peoples.

Indian sorcerers and "medicine-men" induced visions and ecstatic states by drinking the juice of tobacco and poisonous herbs, and used shiny flat stones as crystals, which they "fed" by smearing them with blood. A form of black magic was practised by obtaining the hair or tooth of a victim and burying it in a hole under a tree. A fire was next made over the spot, and the spirit of the tree was invoked in the flames and smoke. When the spirit duly appeared, it was "sent out" to injure the desired person.

Bones, too, had magic properties, and he who could obtain the "finger bone" of an enemy would have unlimited power over him. This belief may have been at the back of the strange custom of the widows of the carrier Indians taking about the bones of their husbands with them for a period of four years after death. Such widows anointed themselves at the funeral pyre with the fat that ran from the roasting bodies of their husbands, often getting seriously burned in the process. When nothing more remained but the charred bones, the women gathered them up and placed them in a bag made of skins, and this they afterwards carried continually strapped to their sides, or upon their backs. When four years had passed, the spirit of the husband was supposed to be secure in the happy hunting-ground of all good warriors, and his bones could safely be buried.

Many tribes, however, merely left the bodies of the dead on high scaffolds erected outside their villages, or in the branches of trees. The spirits of suicides were greatly dreaded, and their bodies were disposed of as quickly as possible without ceremony; the "medicine-man" in some cases shooting arrows over the corpse to scare away its ghost.

Nearly all Red Indian sorcerers claimed the power of turning into foxes, bears or wolves, and practised the universal form of magic by which life was transferred to material objects to accomplish the magician's end. Thus, the clay figure of a buffalo or wolf would be made and blood smeared over it to the accompaniment of incantations, which process was thought to imbue it with life to go out to kill the sorcerer's victims. In the same way the Shaman made life-size clay figures of infants and sold them to sterile women in order to induce child-bearing.

The magic practices of all the native tribes of North America bear a striking similarity; but two important kinds of black magic are practised in the United States, as well as in the West Indies and Guiana, by the Negro population who were originally imported from Africa. These two branches are Voodooism and Obeah, and both are carried on to-day, though not to the same extent as was formerly the case.

Voodooism is Devil worship pure and simple. In past days it entailed the sacrifice of a girl-child who was called "the goat without horns," although the natives declare that no such sacrifice has now been made for over fifty years. We hope this is true, but the author's opinion is that both Vodooism and Obeah have probably claimed human victims, quite apart from still-born infants, much more recently than that. Nowadays a real goat or young kid has been substituted, and whether the sacrifice was human or animal it was the custom to administer a powerful drug composed of herbs, so that no pain was felt at the moment of death. However, beside the goat, black cocks and hens and sometimes dogs were sacrificed, by the cruel process of ripping open the stomach so that the bowels and other organs fell out.

The Voodoo rites were carried out in lonely and desolate places, when the moon was full, the participants joining hands and dancing round the altar. Sometimes these dances were in honour of the moon as representing the "Old Master" or Devil, and sometimes they were "Fire" or "Snake" dances. In the latter case those taking part brought their own snakes and placed them in the centre of the gathering, where they usually remained torpid under the charms of the Voodoo priest or priestess. As the dances grew wilder, the victims were killed and pieces of the quivering flesh given to each of the celebrants to eat, which spurred them on to even greater delirium. They shouted invocations to the "Old Master" and the "Sweet Moon," piled the fires of wood and tar higher and higher, until eventually the dancers sank to the ground exhausted with their revelry. Such scenes were usually, though not always, accompanied by drunkenness and debauchery.

The Voodoo priest or priestess was usually chosen by an existing one, and if they were naturally epileptic or hysterical so much the better. Sometimes whole families were Voodoo priests by descent. The training was exceedingly difficult, and calculated to test the endurance and will power up to the hilt. It included fasting, going without sleep, eating offal and drinking foul ooze, the endurance of terrible dreams induced by drugs, solitude in the jungle and extremes of heat and cold. Having successfully passed these tests, the priest or priestess had to learn how to make love charms and various objects to cause enchantments ; such as fingers-of-death, hands-of-love, luck balls and tricken-bags, the names of which adequately express their purpose. They had also to be numerologists, fortune-tellers, interpreters of omens and, above all, hypnotists.

The excessive power that Voodoo exercised over the Negro races was largely psychological, working through the fear instilled into credulous minds by the sorcerers. At the same time, the results of Voodoo cannot always be denied. Obeah and Voodoo became considerably intermingled, but originally the former was the worship of the fetish of the snake-god Obi, the spirit of evil. Like Voodooism the rites of Obeah took place in groves and mountain caves, where Satanic orgies were carried out. Nearly every village of the Southern States and the West Indies had, or has, its Obeah-Man, who practises sorcery of every description. Nowadays he is usually a very shabby and dirty old Negro, who claims to have known slavery days and who will undertake any dubious commission for money. He will cast spells and enchantments on enemies, and still claims the power of the jungle Obeah-Man to kill at a distance. In outlying places some of the original Shamanistic Obeah-Men are to be found.

Usually the sacrifices of Obeah were confined to animals and birds, but where it mixed with Red Voodooism it openly practised human sacrifice. In the old days both branches indulged in wholesale poisoning, the favourite being the fine hairs of bamboo cane mixed with food to produce acute dysentery. In the actual ritual of the ceremonies the priest and priestess dressed in red and danced a snake dance before the altar, drinking at intervals the blood of the sacrifice.

As these two kinds of sorcery were practised both in the United States and the northern portion of South America around the basin of the Orinoco River, Guiana, they formed a superficial link between the magic of the north and south, though even among the aborigines there was no very marked difference between the " medicine-man " of the north and the witch-doctor of southern tribes.

Among the native Indians of Brazil and Patagonia there was a form of sorcery called Nagualism, whose participants worked witchcraft against the Whites. Like the devotees of Voodoo and Obeah, its members met in dark caverns and indulged in rites founded upon the ancient religions that had been at any rate partially suppressed by the White man. Part of the ritual consisted of impersonating various anmals, who were looked upon as the familiars of the participants ; each member having the spirit of a bear, wolf, bison or snake, and the like, consigned to him on initiation.

A particular tribe in Brazil worshipped a demon-god called Jupurari, to whom the young men were dedicated at certain seasons of the year. This god was inimical to women, and when the drums began to beat and the pipes to wail in what was known as the Jupurari music, all women and girls hid themselves away. Any female who ventured into the light from curiosity, was apt to become a living sacrifice.

The majority of South American peoples, such as the Chiquitos of Bolivia, believed that the souls of the dead incarnated into animals. With them evil spirits who had once been humans were supposed to dwell in the water in the form of huge serpents or crabs, and even material objects were thought capable of being imbued with spirit life. In Patagonian tribes the Shaman, or witch-doctor, held an important position, second only to the Chief. His primary purpose was to cure the sick, but he also occupied himself with all the usual duties of sorcerers, his works being beneficent or evil according to the requirements of those who consulted him.

The usual treatment of the afflicted consisted of making as much noise as possible, in order to drive away the attacking demon, and of the Shaman sucking a part of the invalid's body and subsequently displaying a stone, stick or insect which was supposed to be the evil spirit. Sometimes the stricken person was strapped naked on a horse, and forced to ride out in the cold amid a great clamour. Next to noise, cold was considered of invaluable assistance in bringing about a cure. If a disease threatened to be fatal, a mare was brought to the hut of the sufferer and sacrificed on the spot ; men falling upon it with their knives, and the Shaman dealing the fatal blow to the heart. This organ was then removed, and carried round and round the poor creature as it died in convulsions. The whole company afterwards fell to and ate the whole body, including the entrails, until nothing but the head, hoofs and bones remained. The head and feet were attached to a pole, and a party of horsemen galloped with it to the nearest hill-top, where it was erected. If this ceremony did not effect a cure, the case was considered hopeless.

At birth a child was placed inside the carcase of a horse, which had been ripped from throat to tail and the entrails removed. This was believed to ensure that the child would live to be a good horseman.

Those who practised sorcery exclusively kept aloof from the rest of the tribe as a rule, living alone on hill-sides or in caves. It was believed that their magic power was concentrated in small rough stones, which they inherited from father to son, mother to daughter, and so on. If these stones were lost or damaged, the magician lost his or her power.

With the South Americans, the smallest particles of hair, nails, teeth and even rags of clothing, were thought to have the property of turning into evil spirits, and so such things were always carefully burnt. At death all material possessions were either buried with the body, or burnt separately as quickly as possible.

The Chilian sorcerers also lived in caves, and were served by men who claimed the power of transforming themselves into animals at will. Such men visited the sorcerers in their animal form, but mixed among men in their human shape to accomplish the requirements of their Masters. The sorcerers themselves were supposed to turn into nocturnal birds, and fly through the air after dark, shooting arrows at those who had incurred their displeasure. In many parts, again, they were believed to be vampires.

The training for these sorcerers was everywhere exceedingly arduous ; including the usual test of going without food and sleep, and in the case of the Chilian natives eating alive toads, snakes and small birds, and other practices too revolting to mention. By the time the aspirant had successfully passed through all the horrors of his initiation, he was usually half-demented. Yet even then his path was fraught with difficulty ; he having to provide and arrange the weather to suit his tribe, to bring about their victory over enemies, and so on. Fortunately it is the prerogative of oracles to be obscure, and witch-doctors were usually no less so in their weather prophecies, seldom committing themselves until various signs in nature indicated the coming of rain. One of their spectacular rain-making ceremonies consisted of the slaughter of a particular kind of duck, and the throwing of its blood towards the sky; but the appearance of these birds was in itself an indication of the coming deluge, as they did not migrate south until certain that the swamps would be not merely barren wastes of hardened mud and sun-cracked earth but filled with water.

In Guiana the native Red man practised in early times very much the same sort of magic and sorcery as was to be found in other parts of the continent. He believed in the transmigration of souls, propitiated demons and evil spirits, and sometimes made human sacrifices to them of his enemies —eating the flesh with great relish himself, and offering the blood to the demons. Unlike many other peoples, the Red man of these parts never made sacrifices of their children; the latter being regarded from a very personal standpoint, as actually part of their fathers, and protected accordingly.

In course of time, however, and particularly after the discovery of gold deposits in rivers, the imported Negro population began to make an impression on the primitive beliefs of the Red man, and Obeah and Voodoo became inextricably mixed up with their own witchcraft. These quasi-Obeah-Men, or witch-doctors, of Guiana were distinguished by the calabash that they carried thrust through with a bamboo stick. The interior of the calabash was scooped out, filled with flat white stones which were rattled to summon the spirits, while coloured threads and feathers were attached to the protruding end of the stick. This affair was used by the witch-doctors in the same way as the mediæval magician used his wand.

Originally a certain amount of inter-marriage took place between the Red men and slaves who had escaped to the forest, and in later times with some of the less-developed Negroes, resulting in a form of magic consisting of the worst and crudest practices of both races. The author knows that not more than twenty years or so ago ceremonial black magic was practised by the Red man in the forest of Guiana, and the banks of the Essequibo River, large numbers of West Indians attending, although they actually took no part.

In conclusion, the witchcraft of the white settlers and the subsequent European population cannot be overlooked, but this ran so much upon the lines of the black magic and sorcery of the Old World that details would be superfluous.

During the seventeenth and eighteenth centuries the persecution of American witches was as acute as that of their European contemporaries; a man named Cotton Mather gaining an unenviable reputation for the extreme cruelty of the punishments he inflicted upon them. Americans have been renowned as the originators of freak religions and peculiar sects, and until recent times the United States was certainly the home of various Satanic societies and groups devoted to black magic, and quite possibly still is.

PART II

CHAPTER I

THE LESSER YOGIS AND FAKIRS OF INDIA

Deals with magical practices of the lesser Yogis and Fakirs, and Indian black magic as a whole.

THERE is a prevalent idea in Europe that Yogis and Fakirs are one and the same thing, which has caused many people to ignore Yoga philosophy when it has been presented to them.

The true Yogi is a man of culture, has developed his powers through a long and arduous training, and is one who devotes his time to the upliftment of mankind physically, mentally and spiritually. He is not to be found by the roadsides of India, and the thousands of mendicants and charlatans who throng the great roads and busy streets calling themselves "Yogis," have no real claim to the title at all. Nor have the deluded men, who sit by the wayside with uplifted arms that have become fixed and withered and perform similar feats of self-torture.

There are many people who evidently believe that Yoga practices are a form of black magic, but I can assure them most emphatically that this is not so. Presumably, the idea springs from this confusion between the so-called Yogis and Fakirs and the true ones. The former are usually beggars and performers of petty sorceries and conjuring, and occasionally hypnotists.

There are, of course, many practices in the various branches of Yoga (especially Hatha Yoga) that are distasteful to the intelligent mind and which would only be attempted by the credulous. On the other hand, the Yoga philosophy as a whole offers an immense field of development, both of mind and body, as those who have studied the subject and learnt the breathing according to Yoga principles will readily agree. Many, it is true, who start upon the path do not complete it and, falling by the wayside, use the knowledge and powers they have gained for the practice of black magic and sorcery. This applies equally to Oriental and Occidental students; though, fortunately, the highest wisdom and greatest attainments can only be gained by those who have earned these closely guarded treasures, and those who turn aside achieve only a modicum of power.

The wandering Yogis and Fakirs usually perform their magic by means of elementals, and have what is called in the West "mediumistic powers" which produce phenomena. These men are often snake-charmers and jugglers as well, and are feared and despised by the natives as workers of malicious evil which they are willing to perform for a few "pice." The spirits they work with are called "Afrits," and they employ the agency of the Evil Eye. Generally speaking, this type will deny that he works with elemental spirits, even as the higher variety claims to do. The evolved Yogi and Fakir also has power over the elementary spirits, but he very seldom uses it. When he does, it is as a Master summoning obedient servants. The former kind, however, court the aid of spirits on the same rate of vibration as themselves.

Fakirs make frequent reference to the "Pitris," and attribute much of their powers to the influence of these spiritual beings. The latter are not elementals but spirits of the Genii order, and correspond to the inferior "gods" of the invisible worlds. It is these that the orthodox Christian world calls "Angels."

Most Fakirs possess mediumistic powers in a marked degree, but they do not use them in the same way as a European "sensitive" does. Indeed, the average Fakir considers attempts to converse with departed spirits as little short of blasphemy, regarding it as the prerogative of the Yogis and Gurus only, to consult with spirits; though there again it is difficult to make an entirely definite statement, some Brahmin Fakirs admitting that they depend on the aid of disembodied human spirits.

The actual status of the Fakir is a most complicated one, depending upon degrees of spiritual evolution and progress. Broadly speaking, however, they are confined to the lowest path of a course of initiation whose highest adepts are members of the "Ancient Supreme Council of Seventy." They are constantly under the will and supervision of their "Gurus," and very frequently serve as "mediums" for a power which emanates in reality from this master and is often handed on to them by a sort of hypnotic suggestion. On the death or transition of the "Guru," the Fakir frequently loses his powers, which he is in the habit of gathering to himself from this master during meditation in the Temples.

Although he cannot pass beyond the first degree of initiation, the Fakir is nevertheless the agent and a link between the "Silent Brothers" (who may not pass the threshold of their sacred dwelling) and the material world. He carries their teaching and makes known their wishes in some instances, and always accomplishes his "magic" through their instruction or actual assistance.

The genuine Fakir lives a life of unbelievable sacrifice and self-abnegation, which to Europeans appears so much fanatical madness. To the Fakir, on the contrary, it is all a means of quickly accomplishing "Karma," and will enable him to make rapid progress in initiation in his next incarnation.

Every Fakir is attached to a temple, and never acts except under the orders of the temple. Moreover, unless he has attained an extraordinary degree of sanctity, he is never freed from the influence of his Guru, from whom he receives the small bamboo wand with seven notches. This wand is his protection from contaminating influences, and is designed to shield him from debasing elements. None the less, he is still liable to contamination from the magnetic emanations of profane people and also from unclean objects.

I remember a travelling Fakir from India, who was reported among the Burmans of our district to be very clever at producing magic. Some army officers of our acquaintance were very anxious to see some performances of the "rope trick" order, but were intensely sceptical of any real result. The Fakir was approached and at length consented to come to our bungalow and give a demonstration. He arrived clad only in his scanty loincloth, with a wooden whistle attached to his hair and the seven-notched bamboo wand in his hand. He was accompanied by a small boy who carried his mat, which was placed for him to sit on. The room in which we received him had been previously cleared, and we ourselves were seated on rugs.

The Fakir explained that anything that occurred should be received calmly and without disturbance, and particularly enjoined that when he entered the trance state no one must touch him or place a foot over his circle.

Having given one or two minor displays, the man consented to make a plant grow for us, and showed us the well-known trick of a mango springing up before our eyes from a seed placed in ordinary earth and a pot which we had provided. Having first "magnetised" the earth with his hand, the Fakir caused slowly to appear the first green shoot of the tiny tree. The shoot gradually grew larger; developed leaves, a flower, a fruit; and then withered and died—the whole process probably taking about half an hour, or so.

The Fakir next had water provided, and this he poured into two of our glass jugs and proceeded to colour by breathing over it. One lot of water became a rosy pink, the other blue. The man then poured the contents of both jugs back into the large bowl in which the water had been brought, the two portions remaining separate and retaining their colours one upon another. Finally the water was restored to its usual appearance by the Fakir inhaling over it.

After that we gave our visitor a piece of chalk, with which he drew a wide circle upon the floor. Sitting cross-legged upon his mat in the middle of the circle, the Fakir recited three mantrams and then gradually became entranced. His complexion turned livid and his body gradually relaxed from his position, until he was lying stretched upon the ground. Thereupon he slowly rose in a horizontal position to about four feet from the floor, where he remained for several minutes suspended in space. Without placing our feet whithin his circle or touching him, we were able to stretch over and pass our hands around him. One of the officers, however, disobeyed the Fakir's command and tried to cross the circle. In an instant the young man received a violent blow on the chest, from some invisible force, that sent him reeling back against the door. He described it afterwards as like having been "hit by a blast of wind." The Fakir then descended from his levitation, and soon recovered his normal state. Shortly after which he departed, having refused to accept anything from us other than a bowl of rice that had been specially prepared for him.

As all travellers in the East know, wherever crowds gather there are to be found *Guni*, the snake-charmers, "Fakir" mesmerists and jugglers, and those who will often predict the future with marvellous accuracy. There are, of course,

" He remained for several minutes suspended in space."

snake-charmers who are charlatans; but many go about literally festooned with some of India's deadliest serpents, and certainly very many of these reptiles have not had their fangs removed. The Fakir has knowledge of a particular mantram which prevents the serpents from biting, and also has power over wild animals.

How the Fakirs and Yogis are trained to their attainments in the temples and pagodas is a secret that lies hidden with the adepts and the Brahmins and can never be divulged. Occultists of both the Left Hand and the Right Hand Path refuse to divulge their secrets to the uninitiated.

Fakirs are to be seen occasionally seated in dangerous proximity to wild animals and reptiles, while engaged in contemplation and meditation. For example, they will remain lost to the material world by the side of pools seething with alligators, who crawl out and sun themselves on the banks. The reptiles remain quite harmless so long as the Fakirs are present, but ordinarily it would be fatal for anyone to approach.

Witchcraft is universally feared in India and the adjacent countries, and various forms of Devil worship are to be found everywhere. Even in parts where demons are not worshipped, the eternal struggle between the forces of dark and light are everywhere typified in the religious rites, with a distinct tendency to propitiate evil. The temple dancers of Burma, Java and Indo-China all have their representations of grotesque devils; who war against the gods and their followers or against mankind, sometimes with defeat, but often with triumph, when the god's attendants feign suicide.

The women of India, especially, are overshadowed by the fear of sorcery, and every important occurrence in their lives is accompanied by rites to shield them from demons, witches and the evil-eye. Children, again, are looked upon as the prey of sorceries and devils, and are all protected by amulets and talismans. The ceremonies attending birth and marriage are often intermingled with rites for the prevention of witchcraft.

The Kangalins and Jadügar (witches and sorcerers) are believed to possess almost unlimited powers, and are dreaded accordingly. It is thought that they can inspire love or hatred at will, send devils to take possession of men and torture them, cause sudden death or cast incurable disease upon their victims. The Jadügar are believed to have the power to expel a man's soul from his body and to cause sterility, to arouse unbridled passions in both men and women. The very sight of a supposed sorcerer or Master of Darkness causes the most extreme terror.

In this respect it is certainly true that sorcery is practised, but probably many men and women (particularly those attached to the temples, or who are connected with any of the multitudinous religious sects) have a reputation for witchcraft that is undeserved. All supernatural powers are not necessarily evil, but the ignorant and fearful of all nations are inclined to regard that which they cannot understand as being of the Devil.

Away from the cities, particularly, the bodies of the dead are guarded until cremation. Sorcerers are always anxious to obtain parts of the body for the practice of black magic; especially in the case of pregnant women, as the human fœtus is much coveted for working the black art. In the cremation grounds of Burma and Java the towering funeral pyres are carried round and round in circles, to avoid the evil spirits who are thought to be hungering for the souls of the dead.

I have mentioned elsewhere the dreadful ghost of the "Churel," who walks at night with her broken feet turned back to front. She is the wraith of a woman who died in child-birth, and stalks abroad to wreak her vengeance upon man.

There is also the Yakshini; who lies in wait for men and arouses their passions, with the ultimate object of delivering them over to demons or of feeding upon them as a vampire. This class of witch-spirit has the power to stretch her limbs abnormally; so that many a man having married one has been terrified to see his wife suddenly stretch out her arm the length of a room, to extinguish a light or perform some similar act. There is an account of a poor man who married a Yakshini and in due course was borne a child by her. One day the wife was busy cooking, when the baby became hungry and began to cry. In order that she might both suckle the child in comfort and attend to the cooking, the Yakshini assumed gigantic proportions, stretching from one part of the room to another. The husband, on returning home, was horrified to witness the spectacle and at once realised the kind of woman he had married. The creature, however, immediately vanished away, leaving behind only the child as a memento of her existence.

In Persia, and further West, beyond India, in the regions around Asiatic Turkey, there are some people called Yezides who are notorious for the cult of black magic and witchcraft. They are divided into tribes, under sheikhs noted for their knowledge and powers in magic. Of Mohammedan origin, the Yezides appear to believe that Satan, though at present at enmity with God, may at any time become reconciled with Him, and so in the meantime it is best to cultivate His arts and acknowledge His powers. Their practices rank them among the cruellest and most degraded of Black Magicians.

In Burma it is well known that there is a city whose inhabitants are given over entirely to the practices of sorcery and devil worship. It is cut off on one side from the inquisitiveness of travellers by a swamp, infested with alligators and other reptiles. Burmese sorcerers indulged in the practice of consulting bleeding heads as oracles, usually those of infants. A woman on the point of child-birth was chosen, and the sorcerer and his assistant remained with her during her labour. The instant the baby was born, its head was literally wrung or torn off and placed in a dish. Amid volumes of incense the sorcerer bowed repeatedly and rocked backwards and forwards, calling upon the evil spirits to answer him through the mouth of the newly born.

Closely allied with black magic in India is serpent worship, which is to be found in every province, although not all the sects who worship snakes are sorcerers by any means. In thousands of gardens all over India shrines are to be found reserved for the serpents, but probably their more intellectual devotees regard them purely symbolically.

The members of a religious sect in Persia practising black magic are the Yakuts, if they still exist. Their ancient temples are now mostly ruined, and they have to meet in secret places. They hold their celebrations with delirious dancing, until they reach a point of mad exultation. With shaven heads and long white garments they whirl frenziedly around, cutting and wounding themselves and each other, until they are bathed in blood and the ground beneath their feet becomes saturated. It is reported that this devilish performance entices evil spirits, which can be seen dancing with the celebrants, every man having his fiendish companion, who is distinguishable from the shaven Yakuts by hair on the head. Other rites are too revolting and terrible to relate.

This custom of dancing and wounding is a very ancient one, having had a place in early Greek and Roman cults. Again, similar rites took place in the Jewish temple groves; young men dancing themselves into a daze, stabbing themselves and their companions with knives until they fell on the ground, bathed in each other's blood. Obviously sadistic, such ceremonies had a homosexual aspect as well.

The Indian Yogis have a world-wide renown for their wisdom and so-called supernatural powers. Many people, of course, believe that their claims are greatly exaggerated and are the result of self-deception; but the greatest of these men hardly ever come in contact with the outside world and their powers are very real indeed. The Yogi cannot be surpassed for majestic calm, simplicity, infinite wisdom and utter self-mastery. At the same time there are scores of different varieities of Yogis, including those who have no real claim to the title at all. There are some who lead a celibate life in the monasteries, or live alone as hermits; and again sects who do not practise a very rigid austerity, but who marry and, while treading the Path, bring up a family, the sons often to be Yogis in their turn.

The female cult, called Yogini, is looked upon with suspicion. Its members are regarded as witches and sorcerers, but there does not seem to be any substantial proof to support the belief.

A very important branch of what may be termed the Lesser Yogis is that of the Kānphatās, who can be distinguished by the enormous ear-rings they wear and which are inserted on Initiation. They have no cast prejudices, including among them men of every grade. Some of them are attached to monasteries, but they have permission to live in market-places, by the road-side and beneath trees. This is rather an elastic rule, too; many being married, pursuing ordinary occupations and even becoming soldiers. The ordinary people on the whole fear and either despise or respect them, with the possible exception of the Brahmins. They have a reputation for sorcery, astrology and soothsaying, which is often true of those who live by begging or travelling about singing the religious songs. In their yellow robes, with horn whistles around their necks, a satchel slung on the left side, a begging gourd in the right hand, and the famous ear-rings, they are a feature of both the Indian cities and country-side.

Those known as the Western Kānphatās live in monasteries, although they occasionally mix with their fellow-men. As a sect they are very rich and are noted for their charity, distributing food three times a day. The most depraved of these Yogis are to be found in the hills, where they are reputed to follow the black ritual of Tantras in orgies that belong to the Left Hand Path.

There is an increasing interest in the cult of Yoga in the West to-day. Many people fear it, and not altogether unreasonably. This is so not because it is evil, but because generally the western temperament, the western physical body and western vibrations are unsuited to it. Nevertheless, the European or American student can with advantage acquire some of the Yoga practices, and a knowledge of their various forms of mental development.

CHAPTER II

BLACK MAGIC IN THE BRITISH ISLES

Describes witchcraft and black magic in the British Isles, and some of the superstitions and legends in connection with it.

BRITISH magic of which there is any record begins with the Druids; though magic itself was a feature of the lives of all Celtic peoples before the dawn of history, and must therefore have existed in some parts of these islands from the remotest ages.

The Druids, were, of course, a sect of priests whose philosophy was primarily a pantheistic one, and whose influence extended among most of the Celtic peoples of Western Europe. They were well established in Gaul, for instance, but their "headquarters" were in Britain; other Celts sending men over to be initiated into their learning and rites. Such men as Julius Cæsar and Pomponius Mela spoke of the Druids' philosophic science and their school of learning; but their terrible human sacrifices were mentioned, also, which Suetonius described as being savage and cruel. So that, in early times at least, the barbarity of the Druids' ceremonies probably outweighed their philosophy.

There are many relics of this mysterious fraternity in various parts of the British Isles. They appear to have held their ceremonies within circles composed of huge slabs of stone, arranged at intervals both in perpendicular and horizontal positions, after the manner of the famous Stonehenge. The position chosen for the site of these circles was usually in a barren place, on the tops or slopes of hills, which probably had a Solar significance. However, many Cromlechs and Dolmins are carelessly called "Druid's circles," when in reality they were the burial places of ancient chieftains and their households, although the Druids may certainly have influenced their construction.

There are several such Cromlechs in the Channel Islands; one in Guernsey bearing upon its walls a remarkable carving of a face that is called "Le Gardien du Tombeau." The crude markings present a face of remarkably vivid expression, particularly about the eyes, and the likeness was probably placed there by some prehistoric artist (possibly even a Druid), to represent the Spirit which had been invoked to guard the sleeping bodies and their possessions.

Another relic of Druid times in Guernsey is the roughly chiselled figure of a woman in a stone, found on the site of St. Martin's Church graveyard. Its true origin is entirely mysterious, some people having even identified it with very early rites of Isis worship. However that may be, the figure was originally placed upright in the church porch, where there were so many votive offerings brought to it by stealth, that the authorities decided to have it removed to its present position as a pillar of the church gateway. And even then, as recently as a few years ago, offerings of coins and flowers were found in a hollow on the top of the image's head.

It is not improbable that in the early days of the figure's discovery, the peasantry regarded it in the light of an image of the Virgin, but nowadays it is irreverently referred to as "Granny" and the "Old Lady" of St. Martin's Church. Who knows but that in dim ages of the past, this stony figure may have been the centre of wild orgies upon moonlight nights. Sacrificial fires may have lighted up its crude enigmatical features, while it received libations of the victims' blood. Now village children carelessly play around it, and regard "Granny" as little more than a variety of giant doll. In jocular spirit the author once presented "The Old Lady" with a libation of wine in memory of former homage, probably the last she will ever receive.

But these remains of the Druids' days are not unique; their counterpart are to be found in various parts of the British Isles. The Druids themselves were links between simple shamanism and the magic of mediæval times. The sect had a profound knowledge of herbs, both for magic and curative purposes, and gathered them with great ceremony, clad in white and with bare feet. A sacrifice was made and the herbs plucked in a certain way, at a propitious time which was ascertained by astrology.

The solar and lunar positions were particularly important to the Druids' activities. Mistletoe figured largely in their ceremonies, and sprigs of it were attached to their staves or wands, or in some instances grafted on to them.

The female Druids especially were seers and diviners, but some of them appear to have held positions as prophetic poetesses. The chief magical attainments of the Druids were their power to change their shape, to become invisible, to cause prolonged sleep by enchantment, to overcome distance, and to cause sterility or fertility to human beings, animals, or land at will.

The legendary Merlin, the magician of King Arthur's Court, may have been a Druid in reality. Merlin is certainly one of the oldest British sorcerers of whom there is any record, being one of the original Welsh Bards. Anglo-Saxon magic, which made its appearance much later, was naturally of Teutonic origin; its practitioners being called "Wicca" (a wise woman, or witch) and "Wiglaer" (wizard). The Romans do not seem to have made much impression on native British magic, though some few practices and beliefs are traceable to that origin.

The early British witches seem to have excelled in necromancy and divination, and to have made a speciality of love-philtres. By their art they not only bestowed but alienated affections, which in many instances led to deeds of cruelty and murder. As early as the seventh century A.D. laws against witchcraft existed, and in the year 696 the Council of Berkhamsted condemned to severe physical punishment those who had intercourse with evil spirits.

The first trial for witchcraft in Britain took place in the reign of King John, when the wife of a merchant accused a Jew named Guideon of sorcery. Guideon, however, underwent the ordeal of trial by red-hot iron without turning a hair, and thereby established his innocence. The latter conclusion in such cases always seems somewhat paradoxical, as the ability to pass through terrible trials unscathed was surely a sign of superior powers, if not of sorcery itself.

There is a very early Scottish record of a witch named Iona, who lived in the reign of Natholocus in the second century A.D. This King sent one of his captains to consult her about a rebellion that was troubling his kingdom. The witch declared that the king would very shortly be assassinated by one in whom he placed implicit trust. This disturbed the captain considerably, and he pressed her to name the friend who would do so foul a deed. The witch replied simply that it was himself. The captain, who had had no thought of disloyalty to his king, was terribly angry and distressed, and protested that he would see the witch burnt before he did such a thing. However, after leaving her, he considered matters carefully and came to the conclusion that if he related the witch's prophecy to the king, the latter would certainly have him put to death as a precaution. On his return, therefore, the captain lured Natholocus into a quiet place, and falling upon him slew him.

In every part of the British Isles the witches were believed to attend the witches' Sabbaths, or midnight Satanic gatherings. These assemblies were so named because, being held just after midnight on Friday, they coincided with the Jewish Sabbath, and popular prejudice identified the witches' orgies with the Jews' Holy Day.

The Sabbaths were held on lonely moors and deserted wastes or in fields adjoining cross-roads, while it was believed that on the exact spot where the orgies took place no flowers or herbs would grow. Other accounts relate that such places were surrounded by poisonous weeds and creeping plants, and that excessive numbers of worms, toads, slugs and vipers were to be found there among the roots and stones.

There was a noted sorcerer in England in very early times named Eudo de Stella, who had a large following of people given over to the practice of black magic. It was related of him that he collected disciples by travelling about the country-side, and holding miraculous feasts in forest glades. Whoever tasted his food, or accepted any gift from him, was henceforth his faithful follower. William of Newbury relates that a neighbouring knight, accompanied by his squire, once visited Eudo de Stella, to try and persuade him to abandon his evil deeds and sorcery. De Stella received his admonitions politely but non-committally, and on their departure offered the squire a beautiful hawk. The knight advised his companion not to accept the gift, but the bird's strength and gallant bearing appealed to the squire too forcibly for him to refuse. As they rode back to the knight's castle, the hawk's talons gripped its new owner more and more strongly and he became alarmed. The hawk then suddenly rose up into the air with the unhappy squire in its clutches, and he was never seen again.

Ireland was the home of many witches and wizards, as a country so steeped in the belief in magic and the supernatural might be expected to be. The Irish witches were adepts in changing themselves into wild animals, cats, dogs and bats, and were able to travel amazing distances by magic means.

Dame Alicia Kyteler, or Le Poer, was notorious in her day for being a sorceress of the deepest dye. About 1324 it came to the ears of the Bishop Ossory that the people of Kilkenny were given up to witchcraft, and that their leader was none other than Dame Alicia herself. The Bishop forthwith ordered her to be placed on trial for sorcery, and she and her friends were accused of a long list of crimes.

It was said that Dame Alicia Kyteler and her friends had abstained from church worship for varying periods, according to the requirements of the Devil, from whom they obtained favours ; that they had made sacrifices of living animals, tearing them limb from limb and offering them at cross-roads to a demon named Robert Artisson ; that it was their practice to seek answers and oracles from demons. It was further alleged that Dame Alicia used the rites of the Church in a degraded form to excommunicate her husband, and the husbands of her friends ; attending the altar, candle in hand, and systematically committing each part of the excommunicated person's body to Hell, naming them from crown to heel and at length extinguishing the candles with unholy cries. It was believed that Dame Alicia had made horrible offerings of the entrails of cocks, together with disgusting worms, poisonous herbs, the nails and hair of dead men, the brains, hair and clothes of unbaptised children, and other dreadful things, which were all boiled with the skull of a robber who had been beheaded, over a fire made of oak sticks. Dame Alicia was also accused of having invented ointments and powders, and of making candles of human fat boiled in the same skull, which were used for enchantments to cause love or to torture the bodies of true Christians.

This lady had been married four times, and the sons and daughters of her different husbands complained to the Bishop that she had beguiled and enchanted their respective fathers into parting with all their property to her and the son of her first husband (William Cutlawe) ; and that she had reduced her last husband, John de Poer, to a wreck with her magic potions and incantations. It was believed, furthermore, that she had had unholy relations with the demon Robert Artisson, who came to her in the form of a black dog, or a very tall negro, accompanied by two others.

In spite of John de Poer testifying against her, Dame Alicia escaped Bishop Ossory's clutches by the aid of her rich and influential friends, and so turned the tables on the good Prelate that he himself got into trouble and was forced to withdraw the interdict that he had laid over Kilkenny. However, the Bishop persevered and some time later succeeded in having the case brought up again. This time Alicia Kyteler fled away to England, and the brunt of the accusations fell on her friends and finally upon her maid Petronella of Meath.

The unhappy Petronella had no money to get her out of difficulties, and under severe flogging she made a confession. In her confession she declared that Dame Alicia was the greatest sorceress in Britain; that she offered sacrifices to the Evil One; and that she made unguents with the disgusting substances already mentioned, which had the magic property of turning women's faces into those of horned goats. Petronella further stated that she and her friends joined Satan in unholy revelries, and that her mistress had damned the souls of her husband with the rites of the Black Mass. According to the maid's admission she had been present when Dame Alicia held her assignations with the demon, and had seen foul acts of unmentionable immorality pass between them.

But, of course, her asservations only served to betray the unfortunate Petronella herself, and after being found guilty of witchcraft she was sentenced to be burnt alive. Of Dame Alicia herself we hear nothing more.

Ireland abounds in tales of fairies and goblins, leprechauns and banshees, and sorcery had as great a hold there as elsewhere. According to legend, poor St. Patrick was driven out of Scotland by the Devil, with demon hounds, and even when he was settled in Ireland the saint had to contend endlessly with the onslaught of the Evil One and his demons.

In Ireland tales of werewolves and lycanthropy are not rare. In one instance a priest was journeying with a friend, and was forced to spend the night in a dark forest. As they crouched round the fire they had lit, a wolf approached and bade them not to fear. The good priest crossed himself, however, and enquired what manner of wolf it was that spoke in human tongue. The animal replied that he was in truth a man, but that he and his wife had been cursed by an Abbot to appear as wolves for seven years. Now, the man's wife lay very ill, and he requested the favour of the priest's attendance upon her, as she did not wish to die without confessing her misdeeds. In some trepidation the priest and his friend accompanied the wolf to his den, where lay a she-wolf on the point of death. The first animal tore her skin down with its paw, and disclosed the face of an elderly woman. The poor priest, although he felt that all these circumstances were very ungodly, received the she-wolf's confession and ministered extreme unction. However, nothing untoward occurred, and when the priest's errand of mercy was accomplished the human wolves allowed him and his friend to depart with their blessing.

In October, 1925, the *Occult Review* published an account of the strange appearance of an Irish priest after his funeral.

The priest in his lifetime had been studious and unsociable, and his parishioners had respected rather than loved him. He was taken ill, somewhat suddenly, and died within a few days, the body being carried back to the home of his old mother, to whom her son's death was a great sorrow.

When the time for the funeral arrived quite a large procession of relatives set out, leaving the old lady behind alone in the house, as was the custom. It was a long way to the cemetery, and the Burial Service was conducted as quickly as possible as dark was already approaching. The company of mourners were all sober (they were not always so at Irish funerals), and had not stopped at public-houses on the way, in view of it being a priest's burial. This explanation is necessary in the light of what occurred.

The *cortège* rapidly drove away from the cemetery, and had proceeded some miles of the homeward way, when a priest's figure was seen approaching from the opposite direction. Now this was strange, as those who had officiated at the grave-side lived near the country, and all the priests around were known. As this one approached the procession, he turned his face away towards the hedge; nevertheless, the horrified relations clearly recognised the gait and features of him they had buried an hour or so ago. Instead of the grave clothes the spirit wore the dead man's usual garments, but the face was livid and corpse-like and bore the appearance of that of a vampire.

The terrified mourners egged on the horses to travel

faster than ever, but when they reached the priest's mother's home again they were uncertain what to do. At length they entered, to find the house in darkness and the old lady unconscious on the floor. When they succeeded in reviving her, she related how thunderous knocks had come upon her door, and when she opened it her son stood there, but changed, a horrible expression distorting the livid face, while the glaring eyes would not meet her own. He pressed forward to enter, but the mother was so horrified at his appearance that in her terror she lost consciousness, until revived by her relatives.

Here, then, is a little puzzle for psychic investigators. Did the priest return as a vampire, or was it the impersonation of an evil spirit ?

In Scotland, in or near Pendle Forest, there was a lofty ruin called the Malkin Tower, which was the meeting-place of all the witches and warlocks of the neighbourhood ; and the Forest, incidentally, apparently teemed with them. They were led by two rival cronies, Mother Chattox and Mother Dundike, who caused so much trouble in the district by their supposed spells and quarrels that a local magistrate had them arrested. Accordingly, on the night of Good Friday, 1612, a quaint gathering of witches met to hold their Sabbath, celebrate the Black Mass, and discuss what sorcery or plot could be set on foot to free their leaders. However, a child, named Janet Device, attended the meeting, and betrayed the witches' secrets, with the result that most of the band were subsequently arrested and went to the stake. Malkin Tower, nevertheless, continued to be regarded as the centre of sinister occurrences and dreadful hauntings, and no one would approach its grim walls after nightfall.

All Celtic witches were believed to have the power of turning themselves into hares, and in this form sucked the milk from cows, leaving them dry. An antidote for this activity was to make a fire of cow's dung, and place a pan of milk full of pins over it. As the milk boiled, the witch would be troubled by the pricking of the pins, and in some instances would appear at the window and request the operator to cease from tormenting her. In many cases, the cows would be troubled no more.

Irish witches, in particular, had the gift of turning common objects into red pigs ; though why red, it is impossible to say. They sold these creatures on market days, but if they were subsequently driven across a stream or over a bridge they disappeared, and in the ordinary course of events creatures so created could not last longer than three days.

We have mentioned the famous Earl of Desmond elsewhere. He was credited with performing terrible sorceries in his island castle, and with changing himself into any desired shape, frequently taking on the form of a vast bat and flitting about the country-side. Slavonic sorcerers who changed into bats were always connected with vampirism, but this does not seem to have been the case with Gerald Desmond.

An Irish prophetess forewarned James I of Scotland of his impending fate, on the very night that he was assassinated in Perth. The prophetess herself had been previously informed of the catastrophe by her familiar spirit, named Huthart. Teutonic witches had dealings with familiars of the goblin order, who were called Hudekins of Hildekins, and Anglo-Saxon witches in Ulster may have introduced these sprites to the Celts. The familiar, "Huthart," was probably therefore of this order.

Irish mythology naturally contains many gods and heroes possessing magical powers, but few of them can be identified with actual persons. One at least, however, Dagda the god of agriculture and fertility, was worshipped with rites that bordered on sorcery. Images of this Dagda were called Cromm-cruaich (bloody head) and at certain seasons many children were sacrificed to the deity. The blood of the infant sacrifices was smeared over the god's image, in order to obtain an abundance of corn and milk, while the children's bodies were buried in the ground to promote fertility.

Mannanen, the son of the sea, who gave his name to the Isle of Man (formerly the Isle of Falgar), was also accorded homage that in some respects smacked of the black art. There is a legend, too, that the English sorcerer Merlin, who was himself enchanted by the Lady of the Lake, removed the Druid's Circle or Giant's Dance by magic means from Ireland to Stonehenge.

To return to more recent times, a volume could be filled with accounts of the witchcraft and sorceries of Florence Newton, the witch of Youghall, and many others, did space permit.

All Hallows Eve, which was celebrated everywhere on the First of November, but especially in Scotland and

Ireland, was originally one of the great fire festivals of Britain in the time of the Druids. The latter built huge fires around their altars on the hilltops, but every other fire had to be extinguished, the people renewing their own fires by "buying" them from the Druids at the price of a sacrifice. In very early times this probably took the form of a goat or cocks and hens, and rather later an offering of the fruits of the harvest. In Ireland All Hallows Eve was celebrated purely as a Solar festival, called the Samhein; while in Scotland it became identified with the return of the spirits of the dead, and was believed to be a night on which witches and demons mingled with visitants from beyond the grave.

Strangely enough, All Hallows Eve was also the night upon which youths and maidens performed magic ceremonies to discover their future marriage partners. In the darkness they besieged their neighbours' kitchen-gardens, to "pluck the Kail" or cabbage stalk growing there. If a girl found that she had pulled a fine upstanding stalk, with fresh leaves and strong roots, she would be married to a handsome husband who would give her bonny children; but should she pluck a poorly developed and twisted one, her husband would be small and sickly and she herself would be barren. The phallic symbol in the superstition is obvious.

While the young people were flirting and enjoying their matrimonial magic on All Hallows Night, the older people were carefully guarding their homes from the attacks of the witches and demons. This they did by smearing the windows and doorways with garlic, and hanging bunches of St. John's Wort on the entrance. Usually the good folk did not go to bed till cock-crow, when all foul shapes, vampires, ghosts and the "pestilence that walketh in darkness" would have vanished away.

A little known magic gift among both Irish and Scottish peoples was that of "horse-whispering" or charming, although this art is also known to the gipsies of Europe and in South America. A common superstition of these people is that it is fatal to praise a horse or any other animal, unless you add "God save it." If any misfortune occurs within three days to a horse that had been praised, the person who commends it must be sought out and, when found, must whisper the "Lord's Prayer" in the animal's right ear.

There was an Irish horse-whisperer in the last century named Con Sullivan, who was noted everywhere for his marvellous skill with ferocious horses. He was quite an ordinary uneducated peasant, who did not know himself the source of his power. A Colonel Westenra (who later became the Earl of Roscoe) had a horse named " Rainbow " which he was attempting to train for racing. However, " Rainbow " was exceedingly vicious, and attacked his would-be jockeys by tearing their legs with his teeth. Sullivan was called in and, after spending a quarter of an hour alone with the horse, succeeded in making him perfectly docile, although both horse and man were utterly exhausted. This is only one instance of this otherwise insignificant man's peculiar gift of charming and training horses.

In the North of Scotland there existed a secret society called " The Horseman's," whose members claimed that its origin lay far back in the Dark Ages. Only those who earned their living exclusively by the care of horses were eligible, and men of education and means were jealously excluded. Farmers looked upon " The Horseman " with suspicion and prejudice, but were forced to admit that their services were of more value than those of the ordinary veterinary surgeon. These men were skilled in the knowledge of herbs, and the society possessed an " inner circle " given up to the practices of the black art and the study of spells, incantations and charms. Initiates were able to smite horses and cattle with disease and cause wild animals to attack them, as well as having the power to overcome intractable horses and miraculously cure them of disease. They were masters of hypnotism, at least as far as animals were concerned ; but the root of their powers of fascination probably did not lie in magnetic influence alone, though their exact secrets were never divulged. Possibly, like Sullivan, they could not explain their own gifts, though the society probably taught some of its members how to develop their faculty of " charming."

The curious feature of the art was that " horse-whisperers " actually talked to the animal, usually from mouth to ear, in an unintelligible tongue ; which, however, the horses appeared to understand. It is possible that such a society may still exist.

Scottish witches appear in literature from Shakespeare's *Macbeth* down to the Waverley Novels of Sir Walter Scott.

Those in high places were accustomed to consult witches and soothsayers, and practise sorcery themselves for political purposes, in instances too numerous to mention. Many of the famous "hauntings" of Scottish and Irish families, also, were due to a curse laid on an ancestor by witch or sorcerer.

The sorceries of any country are connected quite naturally with the particular industries of the people, and thus we find ancient Scottish witches weaving spells as they work at their spinning wheel, and sending good winds or contrary ones to mariners and fishermen. This art of "raising the wind" must have been quite a profitable one for the old crones, as in some parts they actually sold winds to seamen.

A certain Scottish fisherman, having a sweetheart whose mother was a witch, begged this old dame to raise him a good wind to take a catch of fish to a northern harbour. In response, the witch gave him a thread from her spinning distaff, with three knots in it. The first knot the fisherman unloosed as his boat put out to sea, and a fresh little breeze arose; then, farther out, the man undid the next knot, which produced a strong wind that carried him nearly into port. As the boat entered the harbour, however, the fisherman was unable to resist untying the last knot to see what would happen, but with that a tidal wave suddenly towered up and, carrying the man's craft and many others with it, dashed them to pieces upon land.

Witches were believed to cause storms and shipwreck by the simple process of setting a pailful of water, in which was placed a small dish, upon the floor. They then said incantations and spells over the pail and as the water grew agitated, a storm sprang up at sea. When the dish filled and upset, a certain ship would be wrecked.

Sometimes, too, the witches were in league with the wreckers, who lured ships to destruction on rocky coasts to obtain their spoils. The witches on the wild east coast of Jersey were supposed to do the same thing, and on stormy nights the villagers declare the witches can still be heard singing and shrieking, their cries mingling with those of their victims far out to sea.

"Witches wailing" is believed to be heard before deaths in Scotland, just as the "Banshee" is in Ireland. The "Banshee," though, is an actual spirit which is supposed to attach itself to certain families, and to give warning of death by its plaintive cry. The "witches wailing" is a dreadful sound that is heard at the place where grief will soon be felt, a mixture of grim mirth and mournful dirge.

Gaelic witches were thought to be able to find the bodies of drowned persons, by casting some of the deceased's clothes upon the sea or wherever they had met their death. The garments floated on the spot where the body had sunk. The same belief is held in parts of India, and some Fakirs find bodies by similar means. The Normans and Bretons believe that if two persons drown together, and one body is cast upon the coast, the other will follow to the exact spot within three days.

There is an amusing story of an English mediæval witch, who hoped to defeat the Devil on her death-bed. This beldame was called "The Old Woman of Berkeley" and, according to William of Malmesbury, she had made a pact with the Evil One but was extremely anxious that he should not claim her, body and soul. As her end was approaching she confessed her sorceries to some Monks, who conveyed her to a convent. She prayed that her body might be encased in a stag's skin, and placed in a stone coffin with iron bars, and that fifty Masses might be said for her soul. Her wishes were faithfully carried out after her death, but the Monks had to struggle with demons each night for the possession of her body. On the third night Satan himself appeared riding upon a black horse, and in a voice of thunder called upon the Old Woman of Malmesbury to rise out of her coffin. Her corpse replied that it was bound down by chains and bars. The Devil thereupon repeated some words, at which the coffin burst asunder, and, seizing the witch, the Devil placed her on his horse and rode rapidly away.

Both horse-shoes and horses were believed to have protective qualities, and anyone riding through witches' revels on horseback was thought to be able to dispel their power. Another superstition was that no one riding upon a horse could be assailed by a demon. One legend relates that a certain man was brave enough to ride a horse to a Scottish Witches' Sabbath and, without dismounting, snatched away "The Red Book of Appin" from the clutches of a sorcerer. This Red Book was a sort of Scottish Grimorie, and without it the wizards and witches were at a loss to work their enchantments. The luck and protection attributed to horses was probably a legacy of the gipsies, who impressed their beliefs very strongly in Scotland, whence the idea was conveyed to the English. The amulet of the horse-shoe itself, though, was ingrafted on to a much earlier symbol of protection, and was of no use unless it had been accidentally found.

A sorcery practised all over the British Isles among the country witches, was that of roasting a black cat alive over an open fire, to the accompaniment of incantations. A demon, usually in animal form, was believed to appear before the creature was dead, in order to answer questions about the future or to bestow favours. Another method was to sacrifice a bull, and, having removed the entire skin, to wrap oneself up in it and lie down by the bank of a river or stream on a moonlight night. Evil spirits would then come up from the water and impart secrets or carry out commands.

In the Middle Ages, Friar Roger Bacon had the greatest reputation for sorcery, though it is more probable that he was actually merely an advanced scientist for his time. He manufactured a head of brass, and made various experiments to endeavour to make it speak. There is a very quaint satirical account of his troubles with it, written by a contemporary of the Friar's, which relates how Bacon enlisted the help of a Friar Bungay.

The two friars were at their wits' end to endow the head with motion without which it could not speak, and decided to consult a spirit in the matter by necromancy. Accordingly, on a certain night they both repaired to a wood and, by means of the usual conjurations, raised a spirit of whom they enquired the right method of setting the head in motion for it to speak. The demon told them that "with a continued fume of the six hottest simples, it would have motion in one month and speak; the time of the day he knew not, also he told them that if they heard it not before it had done speaking, all their labour was lost." The two friars carried out these instructions to the letter, watching the brazen head night and day for weeks. At length, they grew so weary and worn out for lack of sleep that they placed Bacon's servant, Miles, to watch instead, with strict injunctions that they should be awakened if the head spoke.

Now, Miles was a merry jocular fellow, who found the time hang heavy on his hands. In consequence, he played upon a tabor and sang, to keep himself awake. Until finally, all of a sudden, there was a whirring sound inside the head, the brazen jaws opened and a voice intoned: "Time is." Poor Miles was very taken back, but thought the unmeaning statement was not sufficiently important to justify his waking Friar Bacon and Friar Bungay. He began, therefore, to jest and make merry at the expense of the head, and composed a rhyme on the spur of the moment about it.

At the end of half an hour the head spoke again, saying impressively: "Time was." "Well, Marry," said Miles, "we all know that, and if you speak no wiser, Master shall not be waked by me. To think he has been working upon you all this while, and all you can say is 'Time was.'"

Miles then went on merrily singing. Until, after another interval, the brazen head said in funereal tones: "Time's past," and fell to the ground with a terrible crash and a flash of fire. Terrible noises thereupon broke out all around from an invisible source, and Miles nearly died of fright. The two friars, awakened by the din, rushed to the scene of disaster and, seeing what had happened, demanded to know if the head had spoken. Miles tremblingly confessed that it had, but to no purpose; a parrot being able to speak better in three weeks than the brazen head. At which poor Friar Bacon cursed the man with admirable invective, and a grandeur that is unfortunately lost to these superficial times. So potent indeed were his curses that Miles was reputed to have been struck dumb for a month.

Quite a number of people famous in English history were accused of sorcery and necromancy from time to time.

In 1441 a man named Roger Bolingbroke, an astronomer, and Thomas Southwell, who was Canon of St. Peter's Chapel, Westminster, were charged with conspiring against the life of Henry VI with sorcery. They declared that they had performed the Black Mass at the command of Dame Eleanor, daughter of Lord Cobham, and that she, in her turn, had enlisted the aid of a witch named Margery Goodmayne. Bolingbroke and Southwell were committed to the Tower, where the latter died, and Dame Eleanor had to make public penance for her crimes. Margery Goodmayne was burnt at the stake, while Bolingbroke was finally fixed to a hurdle and dragged through the streets at a horse's tail, before being hanged and quartered.

Again, in the reign of Edward IV the Duchess of Bedford consulted a sorcerer named Thomas Wake, in order to make the King fall in love with her daughter, Elizabeth. Whether or not the Duchess' success was due to the black art, Edward married Elizabeth, who later became the mother of the unfortunate little Princes murdered in the Tower at the instigation of Richard III. The charge against the Duchess of Bedford in this respect was finally withdrawn. After the death of Edward his one-time mistress, Jane Shaw, was convicted of witchcraft against Richard, together with another lover, Lord Hastings, whose implication with Jane Shaw cost him his head.

During the Middle Ages, and up to the time of the Commonwealth, various men made a profession of "Witch Finding" and hunting down individuals suspected of sorcery. The most noted of them all was Matthew Hopkins (1645), who by various means—some of them grossly unjust and ridiculous—secured the convictions of hundreds of people; many, if not most, of whom must have been entirely innocent of wrong. The tortures imposed on these poor creatures were hideous, and under them they confessed to the most wildly improbable actions; often retracting their confessions on the removal of the torture. The fires for destroying the wretches were kept continually burning, while death was frequently made even more excruciating by disembowelling the victims when still alive before they were tied to the stake. It is almost incredible, but life even then still lingered in some of the remains.

The boot, thumbscrews, the shackles, and a contraption called the "warm hose," were only a few of the inflictions that faced those accused of witchcraft; some of the tortures being too terrible to mention. Hopkins secured no less than two hundred and sixty convictions in two countries alone. Scotland was not behindhand in burning her witches, the flames of their fires reddening the skies of Edinburgh and Aberdeen in particular. In London the favourite place for the execution of witches and sorcerers was at Tyburn Gallows, which stood near the present site of the Marble Arch, and they were also burnt nearby.

The character of British sorcery had changed somewhat by the end of Queen Elizabeth's reign. Little was heard of Sabbaths and witches' gatherings, of transformation into animals, and the more fantastic operations of Black Magicians, but necromancy flourished and divination and enchantments were still used for personal motives and political aims.

Nevertheless, towards the end of the sixteenth century witches seem to have made as good a business out of so-called " cures " and counter-spells as some folk do to-day in out of the way nooks and corners of the cities and country-side. A certain Thomas Gale mentions that he visited St. Thomas and St. Bartholomew's Hospitals in London about that time, and saw there many people in dreadful bodily and mental states, who said they had bought cures from the witches or, having fallen under enchantment, had sought a counter-spell, only to become more deeply poisoned.

At all times it was thought possible to draw upon the power of the moon by certain ceremonies, and to divert this force for personal gain, such as love, revenge, money, or to back up some particular enterprise. This sorcery probably made its appearance in Britain through the Romans, who had themselves learnt the art of drawing down the moon from the Greeks. In England the rites accompanying it required the slaughter of a young animal or female child, or that the blood of an adult virgin should be offered. Most of us are familiar with the " magic " word ABRACADABRA, but in the Middle Ages it was seriously regarded as being extremely potent against demons, having in fact a phallic origin which can be traced back to the Egyptian Toth. It was invaluable if written in the following formation, and used as an amulet :

ABRACADABRA
BRACADABR
RACADAB
ACADA
CAD
A

But it also found a place in evil incantations accompanying certain rituals used by necromancers, treasure-hunters, and the like.

It was believed that Welsh witches and bards had the power of " rhyming people to death." That is, a sort of curse in rhyme was said or sung at a certain person, who would later fall ill and perhaps die. Alternatively, a wax or leaden image might be made and the verses sung over it, which would have the same effect. Much of Welsh magic carried on the most ancient Druid customs into comparatively recent times.

Wookey Hole in Somerset, only a short distance from the Welsh border, was once as noted for being the abode of a witch as for the archæological discoveries that have been made there. The vast caves situated in the Mendip Hills, that go by the odd name of Wookey Hole, were evidently the abode of primitive man in the age of flint and stone, and remnants of wild beasts who have long disappeared from Europe have been found in that spot. In the Middle Ages, however, the country folk greatly feared a Welsh witch who was believed to dwell there. They attributed all sorts of disasters and illnesses to the influence of her evil-eye, and believed that she caused demons and other malign spirits to roam the neighbourhood at night. A priest accordingly went to Wookey Hole and, on entering, saw an old woman seated in the cave. What formula the priest used is unknown, but the hag fled away into an inner cave and was seen no more. Later, when a search was made, after excavations a large stone was discovered having the appearance of the huddled form of a woman, and legend declared that the witch had been turned into stone.

It is interesting to note that the tale of the witch of Wookey Hole, which has been handed down from generation to generation by word of mouth, in course of time became discredited, until not so long ago fresh excavations brought to light the skeleton of an old woman within the third chamber of the caves. With her were the remains of a young goat and sheep ; while relics of paraphernalia remained, too, in the shape of bowls and utensils used for fire. In consequence the existence of the witch of Wookey Hole was re-established. Perhaps the old woman really was a witch ; perhaps she was merely a lonely strange creature, who had fled from her persecutors into the inner caves, and died there eventually of privation. The truth will never be known, but the Witch's Stone is still pointed out to visitors.

Witchcraft, both in England and Scotland, had a bitter enemy in James VI, afterwards James I, the successor of Queen Elizabeth. James wrote an exhaustive work on Demonology, and vehemently denounced sorcery. Yet the original cause of the king's hostility to the black art seems to have been altogether fantastic. In 1591 James was to marry a Norwegian Princess, but when the time came for the king to sail terrific storms prevented his ships from putting out, and on the slightest grounds a man named

Johanne Fane was accused of consorting with witches to delay the king. When the latter did eventually sail, tempests still pursued him and Johanne was then reported to have thrown an enchanted cat into the sea to produce them. Only the king's natural piety was supposed to have saved the man. In any case, the alleged enchantments resulted in a round up of the witches of Oslo on James' arrival. On James' return to Scotland with his bride Fane was arrested for sorcery, and under torture confessed that he had broken into North Berwick church at night by means of a magic candle (or "Hand of Glory"), had there taken part in a mock service conducted by the Devil with a congregation of demons, and had conspired for the destruction of the king. On being released from the torture, Fane recanted all he had said, and the most excruciating inflictions could not subsequently force from him any further confessions. Fane was finally burnt on Castle Hill, greatly to the relief of King James.

The gipsies believed in a strange evil spirit called Chagrin or Cagrino, which took the form of a hedgehog-like creature and specialised in riding horses almost to death. These spirits were sometimes thought to be the agents of "chov-hanis" or witches, and it was always easy to recognise the symptons of their nightly activities. The afflicted animals appeared utterly exhausted, covered with foam and sweat, their manes tangled and caked with mire. For protection the gipsies tethered their mounts to stakes rubbed with garlic juice, and marked the ground with a cross made of red thread. Sometimes a dough was made of meal mixed with the horse's hair, salt and the blood of a bat, and smeared over the animal's hoofs, for the same purpose.

It is interesting to speculate whether the secret language of the British tinklers, or tinkers, could have any connection with the hidden tongue of the witches. This "Shelta Thari," as it is called, is believed to have descended directly from the Celtic Druids and Bards, and is not a form of the Romany tongue. The wandering tinkers of the British Isles kept their language closely hidden until the last century. The true witches spoke an unknown language among themselves, and it is at least possible that it was a form of this "Shelta Thari" which would be conveyed to them by the nomadic tinkers, just as much of their magical knowledge was carried by the gipsies.

Again, it is possible that witches originally derived their use of flint-arrow-heads in sorcery from a purely Celtic basis; the instruments called elf-arrows, that is, which were used for "shooting death," though some people thought they sped from the bows of malicious goblins and elves.

There seems to have been practically no outstanding magicians in England after the reign of Elizabeth and James, and certainly none of repute after the Reformation. Nevertheless, witchcraft and sorcery existed in isolated cases, and the persecution and execution of witches continued until the beginning of the nineteenth century.

William Lilly, 1602, who was himself an astrologer and prophet, has recorded the activities of many occultists of his day, and seems to have been quite blithely engaged upon investigating the unseen amid the horrors of the Plague.

Rather earlier than Lilly, in Elizabeth's time, Robert Fludd introduced various continental theories and doctrines into England, and is credited with having founded the first branch of the Rosicrucian Brotherhood in Britain. This mystic society at no time had anything to do with sorcery, and so a detailed account of it is irrelevant here. Suffice it to say that the Rosicrucian doctrine was, and is, transcendental, and that the early Rosicrucians at least made very large claims which were difficult to prove. Fludd was not, strictly speaking, a sorcerer; but he was an ardent follower of Paracelsus, besides being engrossed in theories of the powers of magnetism. One of his great enthusiasms was for a "sympathetic" weapon salve, an idea originating in Paracelsus. With this preparation the weapon that had caused a wound was to be anointed, and the wound itself was to be merely washed and bandaged. To make the salve, one took "moss growing on the head of a thief, who had been hanged and left in the air, of real mummy one ounce, of warm human blood another ounce, of human suet or fat two ounces, and of linseed oil, turpentine and Armenian Bole two drachms each." This revolting concoction was to be mixed together, and then kept in a narrow urn till required. It was supposed to be remarkably efficacious for healing, so long as it was confined to the cause and nothing more harmful than water contacted the actual wound!

Sir Keneln Digby later used the same substances but reduced them to a powder. A certain Pastor Foster, however, publicly condemned the use of such things; declaring that it was neither more nor less than witchcraft both in mixture and application.

During the reign of Charles I a certain Dr. Lambe flourished, who had the reputation of being a sorcerer and was certainly a quack doctor and a very evil-living man. It was reported that on one occasion two men went to visit him, and on entering his room Lambe immediately produced a vision of beautiful trees hung with fairy fruit. As the astonished gentlemen gazed entranced, two little mannikins trundled in with minature axes and proceeded to cut down the trees! Chips flew about, and one of the visitors picked one up and placed it in his pocket. When the trees were disposed of, the gnomes vanished again. Later on, after the inquisitive visitor had returned home, a terrible hurricane arose, the windows rattled and wind shook the house, while the man related to his wife the happening of the evening. His wife implored her husband to throw the chip away, as she felt sure they were the cause of the storm, and on his complying with her request the hurricane immediately died away.

Dr. Lambe was the confidant of the infamous George Villiers, Duke of Buckingham, and undertook various nefarious commissions for him. Ultimately, however, Lambe's connection with that gentleman cost him his life. Rumour reported that he supplied Buckingham with love philtres, by means of which the notorious rake seduced the many victims of his fascination. Eventually, on an occasion when the populace had become bitterly enraged with Buckingham and with Lambe as his abettor, they seized upon the latter and, though he fought desperately, he was overcome by numbers. In a short time Lambe was little more than a mangled heap of flesh and bones, one of his eyes being beaten out of its socket by cudgel blows. He was rescued by soldiers and constables while still a small spark of life remained, but he died of his injuries almost immediately. Charles I was very disturbed on learning of the occurrence, as it indicated the hatred that was felt everywhere towards the Duke of Buckingham, who would have fared even worse had the people been able to get at him.

William Lilly, referred to previously, was able to maintain a position of importance and standing up to the last. He was widely consulted as a prognosticator of the future, and was commonly regarded as a magician; but he was also a very shrewd man of affairs, who understood the art of keeping on the right side of the law—a very difficult feat in those days, when a thoughtless word of spiteful implication could send a man to the gallows.

Gradually sorcery became discredited, and although the rigid views and bitter austerity of the Puritans during the Commonwealth period had much to do with this change in public opinion, the cynicism of the Court of Charles II had more. From time to time there had always been famous outbreaks of accusations of withcraft, such as those of the Lancashire witches and the witches of Salmesbury; but gradually the actual convictions and executions for sorcery grew less. In 1703 a labouring man, named Richard Hathaway, declared an old woman had bewitched him. Hathaway himself, however, was prosecuted for having made a false accusation, which indicates the altering trend of opinion. Actually, none the less, persecutions did not entirely cease until the dawn of the nineteenth century.

Witchcraft has continued to be practised by the ignorant and undeveloped in out-of-the-way places until recent years, but the more intelligent varieties of sorcery tended to operate in various secret societies, which pursued it under the cover of "Brotherhoods" and outlandish religious sects. From time to time the people took it into their own hands to "lynch" so-called witches and wizards, but of the thousands who lost their lives either by the law or by the unreasoning fury of public hatred only about one in a few hundreds deserved their fate. The secret societies were more or less safe from prosecution in the eighteenth century, and when accusations of black magic grew too numerous and pointed, they merely dissolved, to rise Phœnix-like elsewhere under another name. In the British Isles these societies were comparatively few. They flourished mostly on the Continent, and boasted many English members who could afford to travel or who lived abroad.

Secret societies of a magical nature often began quite innocently, as coteries for the study of animal magnetism, Kabalism, astrology, and so on. But their practices of ceremonial magic sometimes drifted into the black art, or some of the members broke away to form fraternities given up to sorcery and black magic. Some of the original societies had wonderfully impressive names; such as the Academy of Ancients and the Mysteries (1767), and the Society of the Universal Aurora at Paris in 1783.

Nevertheless, the belief in witchcraft even to-day is by no means dead, especially in such counties as Devon, Cornwall and Somerset ; while black magic, true or professed, is still to be found in every part of the country.

CHAPTER III

NECROMANCY AND SPIRITUALISM

Necromancy and spiritualism show the relation between very ancient magical practices and modern mediumship and spirit communication.

A VERSE in Deuteronomy says: "There shall not be found among you anyone that useth divination, or an observer of the times, an enchanter, a witch, a charmer, a consulter of familiar spirits, or a necromancer." If we are going to take this text seriously and literally, I think it would have to be applied equally to sorcerers of the past and modern spiritualists. It is quite clear that the whole Bible, with the exception of the Acts and the Epistles, frowns upon intercourse with those who have departed from the material world. And, indeed, as spiritualism stands to-day, I think there is much to be said for those who are antipathetic to it, although I have often spoken on spiritualist platforms myself and shall probably continue to do so.

Necromancy is the practice of calling up the spirits of the departed; not always, of course, for an evil purpose, although in the past it did figure very largely in black magic. Elephas Levi said: "Evocations should always have a motive, and a becoming end, otherwise they are works of darkness and folly, dangerous to health and reason." I wish it were possible to impress this truth upon people who rush into spiritualism from curiosity, or who try "table rapping" or some similar phenomenon "for fun."

Necromancers of the past were looked upon with fear and loathing, as their art seemed the most ghastly of all the categories of black magic. Most commonly spirit beings appear in their etheric bodies, but there are many accounts of these old sorcerers calling up spirits in the fleshly bodies which they had inhabited during life, frequently at tombs and in graveyards. The gruesome visitants thus invoked can only be imagined as most horrifying spectacles. There is a print extant, showing Dr. Dee, astrologer to Queen Elizabeth, and his assistant, Kelly, calling up a spirit in its corpse in an English graveyard. The invokers were protected by the usual magic circle and pentacles, and Dr. Dee, who is holding a torch to see the ghastly visitor more clearly, seems, notwithstanding his experience as an occultist, distinctly horrified at what he beholds. The raising of Samuel by the Witch of Endor is an historic instance of necromancy; apparently Samuel appeared only in the spirit, as he seems to have been invisible to Saul.

The sorcerers who constantly invoked the dead had an elaborate system of conjurations, evocations, symbols and spells, as we have seen in a previous chapter. And no necromancer would embark upon calling up a spirit unless protected by his magic circle, from which he must not move on any account. Herbs and incense of various kinds were burnt on such occasions. The systems employed were practically the same all over the world, sorcery being a sort of freemasonry among all nations.

In Europe Latin evocations were the most common for obvious reasons. Words of power and the names of spirits and angels taken from the Kabala were inscribed between the inner and outer hedges of the magic circle, interspersed by crosses in the case of "good" evocations. In Spain necromancy was taught as an art in Toledo, Seville and Salamanca. It was practised commonly in caves specially reserved for the purpose, and which Isabella the Catholic subsequently had walled up. Both witches and necromancers of the past were frequently nothing more than mediums as we know them to-day, and in some aspects the methods used have not altered so greatly. "Familiar spirits" coincided with the "Guides" of modern mediums, and a circle is still required as a necessity for protection and power. Nowadays the circle is composed of people sitting in a ring, often holding hands; but the principle is the same. Prayers called "invocations" are usually offered, and hymn singing is customary. In the Reginon de Prüm's *De Ecclesiasticis Disciplinis et religione Christiana* we find a passage dealing with "diabolic songs sung by the ignoble and vulgar over the dead at night time"; the analogy being obvious. Musical instruments are often placed in circles for physical phenomena, while a certain necromancer of past days possessed a Necromantic Bell for calling up the spirits and which they could use themselves for manifestation.

The witch-doctors of barbaric peoples are mediums and necromancers in Australia, New Zealand, Polynesia, Africa, and indeed wherever primitive races are found. It is not to be disputed that high intelligences can be contacted through various kinds of mediumship, but only too often séances degenerate into pure sorcery or necromancy, attracting all kinds of undeveloped and earth-bound entities.

Mediums should study occult laws, and know the power and possibilities of their own minds, before embarking upon their calling. They should also realise that it is essential to lead a particularly abstinent life, and to conserve their magnetism. In failing to do this, they suffer in health and cannot rely on the validity of the spirits they contact. Psychic gifts do not necessarily presuppose spirituality, and it would be a very good thing if seekers in this direction recognised the fact. Some time ago I came across a woman who practised as a medium. She was looked upon as gifted, and was widely consulted by people wishing to get in touch with those "beyond." I found, however, that while the woman in question possessed psychic gifts, they were very much abused by their owner living a life incompatible with spiritual laws. The woman, in fact, was not above participating in Satanic practices, and at the same time continuing her mediumistic work in connection with a spiritualist centre. Now, the "Guides" of such people cannot be what they represent themselves, and those who "sit" with a medium should be immensely careful of the vibrations they are contacting, otherwise disappointment and possibly disaster are bound to follow in the end.

Many circles and séances only attract the most undesirable elements of the astral world. The result is the moral degeneration of those who attend, accompanied by ill-health and mental troubles which they seek to have cured by "Healers," who, in many instances, are themselves suffering and unhealthy. Not so very long ago I was consulted by a lady who had become obsessed by an entity of the incubus type, which had attached itself to her at a "Healing" meeting.

In nearly every respect the séance room can find its prototype in the Lodge of the Witch-Doctors. I do not dispute the fact that spirit communication has brought comfort and conviction of survival to thousands of people, but I do contend that many of the methods in connection with it should be abolished, and that none should venture on this ground without knowledge, preparation and, above all, sincerity. The peoples of past centuries were wiser than we are in this respect, and, whether they were "good" necromancers and astrologers or occultists of the Left-Hand Path, they investigated and studied their art diligently. We know that it required great patience and practice, and that no one rushed lightly into these matters; and the same is true of primitive peoples to-day.

There is a very amusing account in Wrexall's *Memoirs of Courts of Berlin, Dresden, Warsaw and Vienna*, of a little adventure in necromancy by Prince Charles, nephew and heir of the Chevalier de Saxe, in his palace at Dresden. The good Chevalier had died, leaving treasure hidden or buried about his palace according to rumour. Friends urged the heir, Prince Charles, to try and call up the spirit of his uncle, so that he might divulge the hiding-place. Accordingly they called in a necromancer named Schrepfer, and arranged a night for the attempt. The company assembled in one of the rooms of the palace, the necromancer going away in a corner by himself to pray and to manipulate his sorceries. After a time weird sounds were heard outside the windows and within the room, which Schrepfer said were good and evil spirits assembling. Suddenly the door burst open, and there whirled into the room a large black ball surrounded by a cloud, in the middle of which appeared the face of the Chevalier de Saxe, wearing a very angry expression. A voice then shouted: "Was wollte du mit mich, Carl?" (What do you want with me, Carl?) Everyone was so terrified that most of the company fled, and the necromancer only restored order among the Satanic outburst of yells and cries by frantic exorcisms, leaving the purpose of the meeting entirely unachieved.

The test of the ancient occultist lay in his power of necromancy. By that means alone could he prove his abilities, as he had to be in the position to summon and command spirit entities without fear or danger to himself. Not all necromancers were black magicians; they frequently tried to contact the departed for the same purpose that draws people to spiritualist séances to-day—the hope of communicating with someone dearly loved, or for information that would be helpful to those in difficulties. Nevertheless, their work did associate them with sorcery, and it was

" Psychic phenomena . . . where materialisations . . . are sought."

believed that no one could practise necromancy without a pact with the Devil. Quite a large majority of the conjurations and incantations extant in old manuscripts are of Christian origin, calling upon the names of Christ and the Virgin Mary, and commanding the spirits by the power of Light, especially when it was desired to get in touch with a spirit in order to exorcise a " Haunting."

The place chosen for the practice of necromancy does not seem to have been of any great importance, though in the case of invoking one recently dead the room which they chiefly inhabited was regarded as favourable. The darker kinds of this art were carried on in gloomy caves, ruined churches and buildings of all kinds, or in dark woods. Darkness is certainly considered necessary for psychic phenomena to-day, in a greater or lesser degree ; particularly where materialisations or any physical manifestations are sought, and modern necromancers, both civilised and barbarian, use cabinets for consolidating the power for the spirit to " build up." " Cabinets," of course, is not quite the word to use for the means employed among some savage tribes. None the less, the apportionment of a special hut is common in the wilds, and I have frequently seen a kind of arbour erected for a witch-doctor or sorcerer to sit in while entranced, and from which subsequently issued phenomena similar to those obtained in Western séances.

The object of this chapter is not to decry sincere spiritualists in their effort to form a link between this world and the Unseen. It is rather to point out the difference between mere psychism and true spirituality, and to emphasise the dangers of ignorantly handling practices that inherit a vibration of darkness from time immemorial, and even now, in their less evolved aspects, put them on *en rapport* with barbaric customs.

CHAPTER IV

THE BLACK MASS

Is a full account of the chief ceremony of black magic and the methods employed in its ritual.

THE Black Mass is the most important and blasphemous ceremony in the whole performance of black magic. Festivals of evil and witches' Sabbaths were held long before Christianity became a power, but the mass, being essentially a perversion of the highest and holiest ceremony of the Church, was evidently introduced later, as the predominant feature of the Sabbaths and the supreme ceremony of evil performed by sorcerers and workers of the Left-Hand Path.

We must first consider some of the aspects of the great Christian Sacrament.

From the earliest dawn of humanity man was obsessed by the idea of propitiating his deity or gods with the sacrifice of life and blood, and frequently of human beings. Even in the Bible this idea of the worthiness of human sacrifice is evident ; as is shown by Abraham's readiness to offer up his son to the supposed wishes of an omnipotent God, and the requirement of the first-born sons of the Egyptians on the eve of the departure of the Jewish people from slavery. And, while making due allowance for the occult symbology of these matters, the Jewish sacrificial ideal rose in a crescendo, until it culminated in the belief among the followers of the Nazarene that the universal Creator required the life of His own Son as a fleshly sacrifice—a scapegoat for humanity.

With the understanding that He always displayed, and with His readiness to use the formulas to which His people were accustomed, the Master said to them symbolically at the Last Supper : " This is my body which is given for you," and " This cup is the New Testament in my blood which is shed for you." It is very much open to question, however, whether Our Lord intended this ceremony to be anything more than an act that should be imprinted on the disciples' minds It was probably His intention that, when He returned in His spiritual body and repeated the phrases, His followers should immediately recognise their significance; the Master having undoubtedly foreseen there would be some hesitation over His recognition. The doctrine of transubstantiation, in fact, is going right back to the most primitive ideas regarding communication with the Godhead and the theory of propitiation for sins, because such a transmutation could be nothing else but magic and, in its gross aspect of flesh and blood, black magic. Nor is it reasonable to suppose that the Master Christ could have been speaking in any other terms than the symbolism of the times, and drawing an analogy between His own impending fate and Jewish sacrificial rites. To the evolved personality the sacrifice of even animal flesh and blood is revolting, and entirely inharmonious with a conception of the Divine Consciousness. From the occult point of view the redeeming blood so frequently mentioned is the force of the Red Ray, through which humanity has been, is still, and for many ages yet will be working. But as very few whose feet are not upon the Path of Initiation have any idea of this aspect, the matter becomes confined to its lower material issues and cut off as it were from the higher significance. Wherein, then, lies the power of the Holy Sacrament? Very briefly, its power operates through the very life force of this Red Ray, manifesting through symbols and backed by the creative thought of the Master linked with the vast thought-form of centuries and generations of believers. Christian mystics and occultists may consider this explanation very inadequate, but this work is chiefly concerned with man's evil perversion of the Sacrament in the ceremony of the Black Mass, the chief feature of which was originally human sacrifice—flesh and blood. The performance of the Black Mass could only be accomplished by a renegade priest, one who had taken the vows of the Holy Mother Church, but had either been unfrocked or had turned his back upon her. When witchcraft was at its height in the Middle Ages, the ceremony of the Black Mass was celebrated almost openly and the priests and clergy had to guard their churches closely against sacrilege. As it was, the graveyards were frequently the scene of witches' Sabbaths, and the church of North Berwick on the borders of England and Scotland was notorious for the celebration of the "Sacrament of Hell." In the ceremony the officiating priest was usually accompanied by female assistants, clad in a travesty of the garments of the Church, and the Host itself was made in the form of small black wafers, mixed with revolting substances and stamped with obscene images or the impress of Satan. Sometimes, however, the wafers were of a darkish red colour, resembling dried blood. The Chalice used was occasionally of wood and metal, but frequently the hollowed skull of a criminal served this purpose. The fluid within the Chalice was blood mixed with vile substances; or in another variation of the ceremony the urine of the participants, especially that of women, would be substituted.

There were many slight differences in the form of procedure, and even in the appurtenances employed, but the main features of the blasphemous ceremony remained the same. In some cases the altar was covered with a black linen cloth ; in others it was left bare, or was merely a rough slab of stone on which were placed the candles, bowls or skulls to be used. The candles were composed of human fat mixed with sulphur and other substances, and were always black. The candlesticks represented the heavenly bodies—sun, moon and stars—and were made of ebony. The "incense" used was a mixture of assefœtida, sulphur and alum, or other herbs of obnoxious odour. The priest's vestments were sometimes black, with a white silk cape embroidered with fir cones, while on other occasions he and his assistants wore violet or scarlet robes.

Henri de Valois, son of Catherine de' Medici (herself no mean sorceress), practised the black art in one of the turrets of his castle in the Bois de Vincennes, where he evidently celebrated the Black Mass himself. After his death a most interesting collection of articles used for the altar was discovered. There was a cross, and two silver figures of satyrs turning their backs upon the cross and carrying behind them large crystal bowls that were evidently used for drugs or libations. A good deal of controversy raged about the exact purpose of these articles, but they were undoubtedly the appurtenances of sorcery. Among the relics the dressed skin of a child was also found.

Again, when King Charles IX of France lay dying, Catherine de' Medici decided to consult the oracle of the Bleeding Head. Of all her infamous family she was probably the most cruel and implacable, and among other atrocities she instigated the massacre of St. Bartholomew. She had in her service an apostate priest, who was an adept in the black art and accustomed to working sorcery for Catherine by torturing people through their wax simulacra, and so forth. For the oracle in question a child was required, who was both good-looking, pure and sweet-natured. A boy was accordingly chosen and prepared in secret for his first communion by the palace chaplain. Then, at midnight on an appointed day, the Black Mass was celebrated by Catherine's sorcerer in the chamber of the dying King, the Queen-Mother also being present. In the room an altar had been erected, with the figure of the Devil above it and under his feet a reversed cross. The sorcerer-priest first consecrated two wafers, one black and one white, after which the child victim was brought in, dressed as for baptism, and given the white wafer. Immediately after having received his first communion, the little victim's head was struck off with one blow from a sword upon the very steps of the altar. The head was placed, bleeding and quivering, upon the black wafer, and then transferred to a table upon which lights were burning. The priest next pronounced an incantation, and the demon was commanded to speak through the head of the poor little victim, in reply to a secret question of the King's that could not be spoken aloud. It was recorded that a strange voice did, in fact, speak ; but what it said is unknown, and the sorcery failed in its main object, as the King died.

A similar form of black magic is found in many parts of the world, practised by primitive peoples with the heads of newly born infants placed in a bowl of blood.

Most of the sacrificial victims of the Black Mass were women, but young children and even babies were not exempt, and occasionally men were butchered as well. All were slain with ingenious torture and cruelty, their bowels and entrails being literally torn out, while, when women were the victims, the reproductive organs were chosen as the point of torture. Little children were treated in the same way ; the Devil, or at least his followers, evidently taking an unholy pleasure in the sacrifice of the young.

Reading of these atrocities, we feel that those who participated in them must have been so sunk in evil as to be almost devils themselves. Nevertheless, the horrors performed in the pursuance of black magic were not worse than those perpetrated upon so-called sorcerers and witches by the Church itself. In the course of their persecutions neither Church nor State discriminated between the true and the false, the innocent and the guilty. Even children were burnt by them, and the tortures they inflicted were the equal of any evil performed in the honour of Satan.

Cruelty is not absent from the world to-day, but in the West at least the type of mind that can endure such abominations is fortunately becoming rare and its possessor looked upon as abnormal. The Black Mass was always performed between eleven o'clock and midnight, but the subsequent revellings lasted till dawn. As a further perversion of the Holy Sacrament, which should be taken fasting, enormous quantities of food and wine were consumed before and after the main part of Satan's banquet. There does not appear to have been any fixed rule for the time of the sacrifice of the victim; that is, whether it took place before the actual celebration of the Black Mass or during its rites. Some early accounts place it before, some as the culminating point of the whole hideous ritual.

Accompanying the candles and receptacles on the altar, there was frequently an inverted crucifix and a missal bound in the skin of an unbaptised infant. The number of the candles was seven, nine or thirteen, and they were occasionally arranged to form an inverted triangle. All being in readiness, the priest would sprinkle his followers with wine mixed with the blood of the victim (if he or she had been already killed) and proceed to open the service of the Black Mass by an invocation of praise to the Devil and a repetition of the Lord's Prayer backwards. This was followed by a mock confession, the celebrant making an inverse sign of the Cross with his left hand. The Chalice would then be passed round, to be filled with the urine of the participants or dipped in the blood of the sacrifice. Next came the elevation of the Host, which was received with wild screams and hideous yells from the congregation. The priest then stabbed the Host with the same knife which he had used for killing the victim, and the wafers composing it were dipped in the blood. The Host, after that, was thrown upon the ground, where the priest spat upon it and all the participants rushed forward with growls and screams to trample it underfoot. The final desecration was the outpouring of the contents of the Chalice upon the crushed remains.

It was believed that if anyone had an enemy, and at a celebration of the Black Mass secured a portion of the blood-stained Host and holding it aloft called out the name of the person with curses, he or she would surely die or be injured. As nearly everyone possessed an enemy, or at least someone to whom they wished harm, the dreadful scramble for the trampled Host was feverish in its intensity. The ceremony ended in feasting (often upon the remains of the sacrificial victim) with every imaginable exhibition of gluttony, after which all possible forms of sexual licence were indulged in by those who were not too overcome by excessive eating and drunkenness.

As we have stated before, there were many variations in the performance of the Mass. Where the celebration was held more or less privately, by a few persons or by the members of some secret society, it was often confined to the sacrifice and the Satanic ceremony alone, without the features of debauchery. Very often on such occasions as those the Black Mass was performed with the special purpose of cursing some particular person, or bringing about disaster and downfall to individuals and systems, and its actual character depended largely upon the intellect, class and development of its inaugurators. But all forms were alike in the utter debasement of their cruelty and sadism.

The Black Mass became the chief feature of the witches' Sabbaths, and if the witches did not actually attend them in any magical manner they certainly participated in the abominations of Satan's Sacrament. This last replaced earlier pagan rites connected with Isis, Diana or Astarte—all different aspects of a single conception of the female deity. Those taking part in these orgies abandoned clothes entirely or donned strange cloaks resembling the wings of bats and wore hideous masks representing birds, animals and reptiles. A time arrived, however, on all such occasions when all possible coverings were stripped off, and naked men and women, joining hands, danced in a ring around the altar with their backs turned to it. At the Sabbaths the Devil was either impersonated by his priest or an evil materialization, who received neophytes and children, and presented his posterior for the kiss of his followers, with unprintable additions. During the performances of the sexual orgies that followed, there are many accounts that the Devil had intercourse with people of both sexes.

It is, of course, easy to understand how the sexual element became so interwoven with the Black Mass and the witches' Sabbaths; quite apart from the obvious reason of giving fullest expression to humanity's lowest passions. The true origin is to be found in the old phallic worship, which has never been obliterated from any religion. Man from the earliest times worshipped the creative force, and its material vehicle the Linga and Yoni, seeing in them a mighty mystery and realising dimly the power behind them.

The mystic and high occultist knows the potentialities of the serpentine force and the Kundalini vibrations, by which all things may be accomplished; and recognises that pure sexual union of the positive and negative (male and female) forces has an immense creative power on many other planes than the physical. In effect it unlocks the gates of initiative wisdom. Man, dimly groping after truth, worshipped the material physical vehicles and expression of the dynamic element. As a result, there grew up the system of sacred prostitution in temples and sexual orgies in relation to the worship of deities. Humanity had not learnt to conserve and use its creative force intelligently, and often with no impure motive could see no other way of invoking the blessings of abundance and increase to the land than by a wholesale outpouring of creative energy. Unfortunately man is almost as ignorant to-day of the esoteric nature of his reproductive force as he was in centuries past.

The inaugurators of the Black Mass and witches' Sabbaths were undoubtedly steeped in Left-Hand occultism, or the black art, and knew how the great generative power might be abused and perverted both on the psychic and material planes. By inciting lust, and devising every imaginable means for its expression, they turned the great force and power of creation towards the energising of foul shapes, disease and destruction in every possible form. The ordinary participants, inflamed with drugs and drink, maddened with blood and sadistic excitement, would certainly have had no thought but of expressing their lowest and filthiest impulses, and of wallowing in a mad phantasmagoria of sexual lust. On the other hand, the officiating priest, or sorcerers, undoubtedly used the degraded release of man's highest potency with deliberate intent.

The sorcerer of the seventeenth and eighteenth centuries constantly performed the Black Mass for reasons of political intrigue, especially in France. On the night of the murder of Louis XVI in 1793, a large number of these people and their followers assembled to celebrate the Eucharist of Hell. Towards the end of the eighteenth century there sprang up a society at Linburg, calling themselves "The Goats." They met at night in a secret chapel to perform the Black Mass, after which they put on masks of goats with long gowns and set out in bands to commit rape and murder, plundering and robbing everyone who was unlucky enough to cross their path. The tribunal of Foquemont over a period condemned four hundred of this society to be hanged, but the Goats were not stamped out till 1780.

In Gascony there was a similar ritual to that of the Black Mass, called the Mass of St. Sécaire. This form was used exclusively by priests who wished to avenge themselves on those who were their enemies. They conducted their evil ceremonies in ruined or deserted churches, ancient vaults and dungeons beneath castles, or in caves. At eleven o'clock precisely the officiating priest began the Mass backwards, ending on the stroke of midnight. The Host used on these occasions was black and three-pointed. No wine was consecrated, but the priest drank filthy water or, according to some accounts, water in which the body of an unbaptised child had been thrown. He used no crucifix, but formed the sign of the cross on the ground with his left foot. It was supposed that this ceremony caused injury or death to the person against whom it was directed, who would begin to wilt and fade away from the time of its first performance. People were sometimes described as "dying of the Mass of St. Sécaire."

CHAPTER V

ELEMENTALS

Is a description of the spirits known as elementals, their origin, appearance and field of manifestation, and how they are dealt with by the black magician.

ELEMENTALS are the most elusive form of spirit beings of which we have knowledge, and can be roughly divided into three categories. First, there are the strange quasi-intelligent thought-creations, usually of an evil and malevolent character, that dwell upon the lower regions of the astral plane. Secondly, there are the so-called Nature Spirits. Thirdly, there are the "Shells," or astral simulacra of those whose actual spirits have become sunk in evil to the extinction of the ego.

We will turn our attention to the first group, to begin with. Just as man materialises his thoughts in the objective world, in the form of buildings, sculpture, art, clothes, ornaments and possessions of all kinds, and the harmonies of sound in music, so do his unexpressed thoughts create upon the mental plane. Creations of extreme beauty result from harmonious mind-vibrations, but evil and destructive thoughts produce ugly and revolting forms as malevolent and harmful as any "demon" could be. The life of these creatures depends, therefore, upon the continuation of the individual or collective thought that begat them, feeding and growing strong upon the lusts and evil passions that emanate from mankind.

Men and women build elemental beings up and support their existence, and they in turn influence the weak-minded and obsess those who do not control their thoughts. The same applies, also, to those who neglect to guard themselves from evil on the mental plane. There are thousands of people who refrain from doing wrong outwardly, for various reasons, but who entertain the vilest guests in the house of the mind. Then the day comes when these thought elementals take command, and the result is crime in some shape or form.

There is no such thing as a completely unpremeditated act, since the whole accustomed trend of thought leads in some particular direction, which is bound to culminate in action sooner or later. Thus, the man who had been nursing feelings of enmity or hatred, when suddenly faced with the opportunity of murder will most probably take advantage of it. When his passion has passed the man may be astounded at his own act; but it is only the outcome of a long period of a similar trend of thought, even if not actually directed at the ultimate victim.

The drunkard, the profligate, the murderer, the sadist, the thief, the hypocrite, the miser, and so on *ad infinitum*, are surrounded by their own abominable elementals; who feed upon them and in turn influence them, until, growing powerful, they become capable of a wider range of activity within a limited radius and grow into a menace to others.

There is a gigantic elemental of war, formed by the thoughts of individual men and nations. This, of course, is a creature centuries old and still powerful; though men are beginning to realise that it must be slain. It is, however, still being animated by the crude and undeveloped, and is accompanied by a host of other thought-creations as foul as itself. The Four Horsemen of the Apocalypse are no picturesque figment of the imagination, but an elemental reality. Battle-fields are the breeding ground of millions of elementals, which spread over the earth inciting men to further deeds of cruelty, lust and violence. Beautiful and creative thoughts naturally are equally potent for good and protection; but as we are dealing with black magic our present concern is with the darker side, and the fact that the black magician obtains many of his results by the use of evil elementals.

These beings are dependent entirely on thought forces for their existence, and if the thoughts that nourish them are withdrawn they begin to die away. Nevertheless, they do not actually become extinct until their source of maintenance is completely and utterly cut off. During their "life" period they are possessed of a semi-intelligence of their own, actuated on the mental plane, and become drawn to persons whose auras and emanations are similar. Clairvoyants can perceive elementals clearly, but occasionally such spirits achieve sufficient power to materialise objectively on this plane of existence.

In times when men were intensely evil and given up to wickedness and cruelty, as during the Dark Ages, elementals received so powerful an impetus that their appearance was comparatively common. They were called demons, and it is doubtful whether even occultists knew the difference between them and actual evil spirits. At Satan's gatherings elemental materialisations took place and do so still, the resulting form being the embodiment of the thoughts and actions of those present. Spiritualist séances which are not carefully conducted, and whose sitters are not practising self-mastery and spiritual development, give great impetus to these beings; making them frequently manifest themselves, though not always in their true form but masquerading as departed human beings.

In some instances certain houses or districts are haunted by elementals, who still receive their force from some act of violence or, more often, continued evil deeds, in a given place. As an illustration of this, my wife was once alarmed by the appearance of a malevolent elemental form in a bungalow we were inhabiting. The two Airedale dogs who were with her also perceived it, and showed the greatest terror. On another occasion we both saw the same figure built up in the garden. The reason was that the whole district for miles, and our little domain in particular, had been the scene of the activities of French smugglers about two hundred years previously, and they had been noted for their revolting cruelty to anyone who was unfortunate enough to fall into their hands.

Every scene of horror and debauchery, then, every brothel, every asylum, every prison, every slaughter-house, attracts and creates these vile beings. To a certain variety of them blood has a powerful attraction, so that they congregate around abattoirs and all places of violence and bloodshed. Paracelsus says that with the fumes of blood spirits can be called up.

The elemental is one of the types of spirits especially attracted by acts of sorcery, and contacted by means of human sacrifice and bloodshed. In appearance these creatures vary very greatly. Sometimes they are semi-human, or half-animal, and again may have a completely grotesque aspect or a huge slug-like form. They frequently seem shapeless and indefinite in outline, and their presence can be detected by a terrible smell that is sometimes noticeable

"He (the magician) clothes such forms in the shape he desires."

even to the material sense. Being dependent upon man for their existence, they can be made his slaves, and by them the sorcerer often works. On the other hand, they can become so powerful that they swamp the whole human personality in the case of pronounced evil-doers, and the body becomes nothing but the house of a host of elemental creations. Such a one was Mary Magdalene, out of whom the Master cast seven devils.

Thought forms can be deliberately built up in any aspect we choose, and sent out to do our bidding. This power can be used for good; but the black magician employs it to injure, destroy and cause bitterness, hatred, strife and immorality. He clothes such forms in the shape he desires to influence people in accordance with his own will, and for whatever end and purpose he desires. But in this form of black magic, as in all others, there is a price to pay, and the time comes when the sorcerer has to deal with the creatures he has created, and only too often they turn upon him to his destruction. Being of the sorcerer's own creation and substance, elementals return to him with the dregs of the injury or desires inflicted on his subject. For a time, therefore, the sorcerer might not be outwardly affected by the poison within him; but eventually the accumulation of wrongs sent out will injure him vitally, if a more powerful thought-form or elemental does not earlier destroy him mentally and physically.

The magician should be able to control elementals; the man or woman who is merely a medium, however experienced, cannot do so. Unless a medium leads an exceptional life, has a pure mind and carefully guarded thoughts, he or she can only attract undeveloped or evil human spirits and elementals. To sit, apparently open to any influence that may be present, is to furnish these beings with the power and shape to manifest.

The medium's thought, and the thoughts of those present, become reflected in the astral elements, enabling them to appear as individual intelligences drawing from the sitters the forces necessary to produce various phenomena. Thus, those who attend séances can easily be depleted of their magnetic energy, to bring about the resulting manifestations.

In a case where elementals are suspected of being the origin of the phenomena at a séance, their presence can be tested by bringing fresh blood into the circle. Should elementals indeed be responsible, the power and variety of the forces would thereupon increase. As has been already said, elementals literally feed on the emanations of blood, that fact being the groundwork of all black magic in which blood is used.

The elementals known as Nature Spirits can be used for the purposes of black magic and conversely for beneficent ends, but they are far more elusive and difficult to contact. All miracles that entail conquest of the elements are performed by mastery of such beings' essential spirit. Many people disbelieve that this form of spirit has any existence outside the pages of myths and legends. The explanation is simply that everything is imbued with spirit in a greater or lesser degree of individualisation and development, and some persons gifted with clairvoyance have the ability to "objectivise" elemental life. In other words, all spirit existence has form on its own plane of manifestation, and clothes itself from the thought forces of man with recognisable shapes.

There are many legends and accounts of how man has united himself with elemental beings, conferring immortality on them by so doing. But such tales are either pure myth or else symbolical of esoteric truths. It is true that there is much evidence of men and women having union with spiritual beings, especially in the course of the practice of sorcery; but such alliances could not be with Nature Spirits, only with beings of the Incubus and Succubus type. Any spirit manifesting sex inclination should be looked upon with the gravest suspicion, as their influence can only be of evil origin and has an obsessing or depleting effect. Spirits, who are literally vampires as far as the magnetic forces of the body are concerned, are not so rare as might be imagined. Naturally they present themselves to their object as pleasingly as possible, so that their origin is unsuspected by the uninitiated. I am not overlooking the fact that an advanced spiritual union is possible between a soul on the higher planes and one who is still a dweller on this earth. Such cases, none the less, are exceedingly rare and are altogether another matter.

In addition to those already mentioned, there are two other varieties of elemental: the "group-soul," to which the spirits of animals belong; and what some occultists term "Psychic Embryos," the forms of humans yet to be. These latter never manifest objectively in the usual sense, but are sometimes seen by women who are about to conceive, or who are expecting the birth of a child.

There are people walking our earth now whose spiritual self is already dead or has detached itself from being sunk in matter. Some souls cast themselves so wilfully into the pleasures of the material world, living only for its power, its luxuries and riches, bodily beauty, intellectual brilliance and wit, that they loose even the smallest link with the Divine Spark within. Starved and ignored, this gradually detaches itself and returns to the Divine Source, leaving a living and intelligent corpse behind it. Others live lives of physical, moral and spiritual evil; until the ego or soul is literally lost and becomes swamped in darkness. At death both these kinds of "living corpses" expel a shell or simulacra of the living person, which is animated for a time by an intelligence usually very inferior to that possessed on earth. They gravitate to the lower astral regions, and there become the instruments of actively evil spirits. They themselves are cunning and malicious, and are responsible for many adverse spirit manifestations. In Indian philosophies they are known as the "Brothers of the Shadows." Gradually the vibrations and impetus received during earth life die away and with it the empty wraith. The small spark of the ego, which had long ago departed, returns to be embraced in the Absolute before going forth to incarnate once more.

The magician who wishes to subjugate elementals, must be free from vices or besetting sins himself. There is an erroneous idea among some would-be occultists that, in order to work with elementary beings, it is necessary to place oneself on their rate of vibration. The truth is that the magician must be above them in every respect, and in full control of the trinity of his personality—that is, body, mind and spirit. Thus, a man of changeable temperament could not hope to control the element of water, and the ruler of fire must be calm and the governor of his temper. He who desires the world's goods must not be covetous or greedy, and must be pure within and without. Paracelsus has given lengthy exorcisms for the spirits of the earth and elements, but admits that they are based on other rituals which have been lost in antiquity.

CHAPTER VI

MODERN BLACK MAGIC

Gives an account of sorcery as it is practised to-day in all grades of society.

IN approaching the actual practices of black magic to-day we are only concerned with what are called the civilised parts of the world. Everyone recognises that sorcery and magic are a natural part of the lives of barbarous peoples, but many find it difficult to believe that black magic has any reality in advanced countries, or that it is actually an evil to be reckoned with in contemporary society.

European sorcery has changed but little since mediæval times; the structure and framework have altered in some degree, according to the development and intellectual attainment of the individuals participating, but the groundwork is the same. There are probably fewer isolated people who practise witchcraft (except in country districts, among the peasantry of all countries), and real sorcery is more consolidated in groups and societies. Magic is, of course, less common than in past centuries; but that is partly due to the fact that there are more outlets for occult curiosity now than formerly.

There are a few sects to-day practising black magic who more or less openly announce their perverted religious views, but most of these societies exist ostensibly for astrology, mystic development, and so on, while a few of them call themselves private spiritualist groups. In many cases members join in all good faith, and it is some time before they realise the true nature of the organisation. Gradually hints of secret rites come to the ears of the associate, and if he or she shows no inclination for such things, ways and means are found of getting rid of them before they have discovered anything conclusive; that is, if they have not already withdrawn in disgust. I know of one lady who became a member of such a society, and it was not very long before it dawned upon her that it was very far from being an organisation for mystic attainment. She decided, however, to stay on in order to discover the exact nature of procedure in the Inner Circle. But the "high priestess" of the fraternity soon informed the lady that she was not sufficiently evolved and enlightened to become an initiate, and that in effect many were called but few were chosen. Having, therefore, become an associate for three months, she was not allowed to extend her membership.

The first line of procedure is always an insidious undermining of the neophyte's moral standards. Doctrines are expounded to the effect that evil is only a relative term; that people have to be evolved, to see the beauty in so-called wickedness; that sin has no reality, and that the only way to a full life is to ignore ordinary standards of honesty, purity and kindliness, because the exercise of these qualities prevents people yielding to all their impulses and limits their material attainments. Until, at length, the individual who is not strong-minded begins to believe that his or her previous standards were foolish and non-progressive, and to think that black is white. Usually someone who is already an initiate is singled out to unfold the new member; cleverly finding out their weakest points, such as love of money, jealousy, repressed sexual desire, and so forth, and dangling before them tempting suggestions as to how they may achieve their ends by entering into the full membership of the society.

Of course there are many, unfortunately, who need no such gradual encouragement, but who are ready and on the look out for any centres where they may find people who like themselves are secret worshippers of the decadent. Once the neophyte shows an encouraging adaptability to the body's doctrines and methods of conduct, he or she usually passes through a more or less impressive initiation, presided over by a "High Priest" or "Priestess"—sometimes both. The staging of these affairs naturally varies; but it is often accompanied by the sacrifice of small animals, such as cats, dogs, or goats and birds, such as black cocks.

The would-be initiate frequently has to strip naked, drink some of the blood of the sacrifice, and sign a pact or agreement to uphold the doctrines of the Order, written in his or her own blood and signed with the new name accorded to him on this occasion. Sometimes it is not a name, but a number; the members having a collective name, followed by an individual number chosen sometimes in rotation, and occasionally in a vibrational sequence, such as "beast 77." It is usually enjoined, also, that they will do their best insidiously to spread the theories of Satanism; but it is not always so, as many of these coteries prefer to remain exclusive and depend on those of a like disposition gravitating to them.

In London, Paris and elsewhere numbers of such groups are only open to the wealthy, who must pay large sums before being initiated. In this connection it may be said that some of the so-called black magic societies, especially those run by a single individual, are but a trap for the unwary to lose their money. The decadent's search for depravity, therefore, becomes his or her own undoing.

In certain centres that genuinely deal with the occult, the members are promised the assistance of a "familiar" or "guide." These will help them in all their outside undertakings, and in the attaining of unusual powers, such as attracting money everywhere, the ability to see and know what is going on at a distance, hypnotic powers, and so forth. An added impressiveness is given by displays of genuine psychic phenomena.

Once membership of a society of this kind is undertaken, it is a very hard matter to get out of the clutches of such people and their cult; both materially (as ex-members open themselves to guarded blackmail) and spiritually. The evil vibrations created by disgusting rites, sexual depravity, malicious thoughts, and warped and perverted imagination, leave impressions on the mind and soul that are tremendously difficult and in some cases "wellnigh" impossible to shake off. Melancholia, loss of vitality, delusions, suicide and positive insanity are some of the consequences of having dabbled in the black art. Very few dare to "break away" and still fewer do so with impunity, becoming sucked into the irresistible vortex of Satanic influence. Some organisations tempt members with financial successes to be attained by astrological calculations, and, blinded by cupidity or the desperate need of cash, the victims do not realise the seriousness of the step they have undertaken.

A large majority of people will be inclined to think the dangers greatly exaggerated, and will either laugh at the whole matter as ridiculous or think that these centres are merely attended by those who are pathological cases of an unpleasant nature. There is certainly some truth in this theory, as far as the type of mind which is attracted by black magic and sorcery is concerned. On the other hand, the menace to society in general lies not only in the number of people who indulge in the black art, but in the effect that their conduct has upon the lives of others, consequent upon the disharmony and unhappiness caused by the breaking-down of moral standards and a plunge into debauchery. I have personally known the case of an intelligent woman who dabbled with necromancy in connection with one such organisation, whose habits became so depraved that she had no shame in confessing that she had enticed her own son, a rather abnormal boy, into having intimate relations with her, on the pretext that it would be good for him and remove some complex from which she thought he suffered.

On the Continent, if not in England, there are black magic centres whose aim is political and financial intrigue. Indeed, in certain parts of the world—on the North Coast of Africa, for instance—there are "Watch Towers," whose aim is to spread darkness and horror in the world. These centres are sinks of iniquity; constantly holding ceremonies and performing sacrifices with the object of augmenting the spirit of dissension and warfare among the nations, and of increasing suffering and moral depravity in the world.

The element of human sacrifice is still not absent from many of these Satanic orders, and in countries where murder is more difficult to trace, unimportant people who disappear have frequently become the victims of the modern Devil Worshippers. Again, it is never difficult to obtain children for this purpose in the impoverished underworld of Eastern Europe, and in the cities of Egypt and Africa.

The adepts of these organisations are highly educated men, who have concentrated all their gifts and mental qualities on the side of occultism. They may be compared with the Gun-men of America; the only difference being that the latter are well-recognised public enemies, working crudely, violently and obviously on the destructive side of life. The modern anti-social black magician is the "Mental" Gun-man of Europe and other centres of civilisation.

Many people have accused Gregory Rasputin, the Russian "Staretz," of having been a black magician. It is very doubtful whether he really was so in the accepted meaning of the word, however, though he undoubtedly had an extensive occult influence over the Tsarina and, through her, over the Royal Household. Rasputin possessed hypnotic power, a remarkable degree of animal magnetism and probably dabbled in sorcery; but the tales related of the philtres and potions he is supposed to have had administered to the Tsar are difficult to substantiate. It is quite possible that this remarkable man was linked consciously or unconsciously with the sources of darkness through his mode of life and crudely sinister mentality, and became an instrument for the operation of disaster to the Romanoffs and the Russian nobility.

The centres which operate disharmony, and work to increase all the evils of mankind, such as warfare, strikes, rebellion, famine, prostitution, and the like, find their outlet through individuals and groups who are in harmony with them, according to their actions and mental outlook. All vices form a link, and all groups working in aggression and disharmony are likewise linked.

Spiritualism, wrongly conducted, forms an excellent channel for the forces of black magic. Circles which the sitters use more or less as "petting parties," with a little thrilling psychic phenomena thrown in, are a breeding ground for moral degradation. Earnest Spiritualists of integrity may disbelieve that such cases exist, but there is a well-known male medium in London who used to hold séances of such a description, and probably still does.

Mediums, again, who drink to excess, make a focussing point for the cesspool of the astral world. Such are often supposed to have very high and wonderful guides, but in reality they are either conscious frauds or controlled by impersonating entities who at any moment may betray them with incorrect information and false teaching. Those with a real knowledge of occultism will understand how easy it is for evil centres to send out their gathered forces and vibrations for individuals and groups to unconsciously "pick up" and transmit to the world by their own thoughts and actions.

I have personally known Spiritualistic Societies in which everyone who takes part in the organisation or enrols as a member degenerates in time morally and loses all standards of morality, justice and honesty. They keep a certain hypocritical front to the world, but behind the scenes they have become completely degraded. Coming in contact with such groups, it is sometimes exceedingly difficult to avoid being influenced and swamped by their vibrations ; the only thing to be done is to withdraw immediately. While the phenomena of such places is frequently powerful, they have nothing to do with spirituality, as those who attend would realise if they knew more of the lives of the mediums and promoters. Everyone joining a circle or society should know something of their fellow-sitters and members before embarking on the dangerous undertaking of opening themselves to astral contacts in their company.

The actual procedure and ritual of modern centres of black magic are based on those of mediæval times, and of course vary in some degree according to the nationality and inclination of the promoters. None the less, all forms are alike in their sadistic and lustful practices.

At a Satanical gathering of these days the participants are of all ages and both sexes, and provide a most unhappy picture of all the vices personified—greed, lust, avarice, gluttony, drunkenness, homosexuality and the like. The room in which the Satanists meet is commonly furnished as a temple, with black or crimson hangings and long tables covered with piles of food and drink of every description in the centre. At the farthest end of this "sanctuary" an altar is erected ; dedicated to the Prince of Darkness, Isis, or any other male and female deity of sorcery. There may or may not be any actual image of the object of adoration, but the altar will be adorned with tall black candles and either a hollowed human skull or a chalice to receive the sacrificial blood. There is, also, a very sharp knife with an ebony handle for the slaying of the victim. Incense of powerful and exotic odour is burnt, except during the offering of the sacrifice, when sulphur and various resins are used instead.

The magician or priestess, as the case may be, is dressed in black or scarlet robes, while the other participants wear black cloaks. The latter are frequently surmounted with the heads of birds, animals and reptiles, so that an onlooker might think he had wandered into some strange domain of the animal kingdom.

The ritual comprises vows on the part of the members to renounce all orthodox religions and allegiance to God (in whatever form, or by whatever creed, he is worshipped), and instead to uphold the service of evil. A vow is also taken to keep the ritual of the society secret, under deadly penalties. These things having been done, a feast takes place—the members temporarily throwing back their head-dresses and consuming huge quantities of food and drink. In some societies a weird dance follows; in which all clothing is cast aside, and men and women simply, with joined hands, prance wildly, with their backs to the altar. In the end the dancers fall exhausted to the ground. After that, animals or birds are sacrificed on the altar steps, the members drinking the blood and in some cases even eating the raw flesh of the victim.

In Europe the full ritual of the Black Mass is occasionally, though not always, carried out. The orgy usually ends in complete sexual abandonment, under dim red lights or in complete darkness. All the animal passions of the participants have been previously augmented by the food and wine, which is mixed with aphrodisiacal drugs, as well as by the fumes from the burning herbs and incense. During the latter period of the orgy the principal officiator or black magician usually occupies himself with manipulating by sorcery the elemental forces released, and seldom takes part in the general abandonment.

It is not to be understood, however, that all gatherings of black magic run upon these lines. The foregoing outline is but a typical example of some of the special ceremonies analogous to the witches' Sabbaths. There are weekly or monthly meetings, at which sacrifices and evil practices take place to a lesser degree; accompanied by such serious matters as discovering propitious dates for certain activities by astrology, divining the future by clairvoyance in ink or blood or by necromancy, and discovering matters of importance to the society by means of hypnotism. In the latter case, the etheric body of the hypnotised subject is "sent out," or the subconscious mind is made to see the conditions about which information is required. On special occasions male and female members are required to make personal "offerings" from their own bodies of a sexual character, and to indulge in various practises for the purpose of sorcery which cannot be mentioned here. There are, again, black magic sects which do not introduce the sexual element, but work upon different lines entirely, many of them using the self-inflicted sufferings of extreme ascetism and material symbolism. For example, among those Lamas of Tibet who indulge in the black art, the female element is entirely non-existent.

In the past century many charges of black magic were brought against the freemasons, chiefly at the instigation of ardent Roman Catholics. Even to-day many people believe that there is an "Inner Circle" of freemasonry, unknown to the majority of its members, which is given up to sorcery. Such accusations are as manifestly untrue as they are absurd. There certainly have been societies that claimed association with the masons, but *none have any right to do so,* nor could they ever prove their extraordinary statements. "The Sovereign Council of Wisdom," or the Order of Palladium, founded in Paris, was a diabolic order claiming masonic origin. These people had a branch for women, called the "Companions of Penelope," but the whole affair was utterly fantastic and an unpardonable parody of masonry.

Satanism can be divided, roughly, into two branches: the Luciferians and the Palladists. The first mentioned seem to believe that evil is good; and that the so-called devil (or dark forces) can offer abundant material life, together with the obtaining of all material desires, by yielding to every temptation without thought of morality, self-sacrifice or duty to others. The Palladists, however, openly worship the Devil as such, taking their stand by the Goat Deity (Baphomet of the Templars) and wallowing in evil for its own sake. Both varieties had a strong following in America and on the Continent during the nineteenth century, and of course still exist in solitary groups.

Public interest in these matters was greatly inflamed about the year 1890, and onwards, by a Frenchman and ex-Jesuit, who, writing under the name of Léo Taxil, denounced freemasonry as a nest of black magicians. To support his statements, Taxil introduced the "works" of a certain Diana Vaughn, who was supposed to be an American ex-Palladist that had taken part in semi-masonic gatherings where the Demon Asmodeus had appeared in person, and other extravagances. It was further claimed that men were imprisoned in the caves about Gibraltar, for the purpose of manufacturing idols of Baphomet and other instruments of black magic and of concocting virulent poisons to be used in political intrigue. The French public became so engrossed in, and shocked by, these revelations "that they ultimately demanded that Taxil should arrange for Diana Vaughn's personal appearance. This Taxil promised to do, but eventually was forced publicly to confess that such a person had never existed and had only been used as a means of arousing interest in her creator's anti-masonic propaganda. Taxil still adhered to the statement that his charges against masonry and the Palladists were true, but naturally his word no longer bore any weight, except with those people who were equally prejudiced.

Very few people are imprisoned for witchcraft nowadays. Cases, nevertheless, do arise from time to time; especially on the Continent, where persons are accused of having received money to cast spells. Only in the last decade an Irishman murdered his wife very cruelly, because he believed her to be a witch. In such counties as Devonshire, Cornwall, Somerset, and in Ireland, the Channel Islands and the Isle of Man, the belief in sorcery and witches is particularly deep-rooted. In such parts farmers still consult "wise women" with regard to their cattle and crops, and the power of the "evil-eye" is by no means dead. Even in cities "fortune-tellers" often undertake little commissions, such as making a faithless lover return, which are neither more nor less than sorcery.

We mentioned in another chapter that an elderly American went to the electric chair in March, 1935, for having murdered and, on his own confession, partially eaten children for the purposes of black magic. Again, as recently as October 27th, 1935, the *Sunday Express* published a short account of the death of an old negro, named "Voodoo" Gray, in a cemetery at Waynesboro, Mississippi, the previous week. It had been discovered that someone was tampering with the graves in the burial-ground, and a watch was accordingly set. The negro, "Voodoo" Gray, was suspected of practising black magic, and one night he was seen to approach a grave with a spade. The guard sprang upon him, and in the ensuing scuffle a shot was fired which killed the desecrator immediately. Afterwards a belt was discovered on the body with human bones attached to it, fairly conclusive evidence that Gray did indeed practise sorcery with the remains of the dead.

The few cases that become public, however, represent many that are never heard of. And it is at least possible that some of the mysterious murders, in which the remains cannot be identified and the problem of the crime is never solved, may be due to this cause. It is less easy to prove that there are societies devoted to the black art, although there are hundreds of people who can testify to the truth of their existence.

CHAPTER VII

METHODS OF COUNTERACTING SORCERY

Gives details of exorcism, and protection against the black art, and methods of counteracting the effects of evil.

THE two most powerful methods of counteracting sorcery and evil were, and are, prayer and exorcism. They commonly went hand in hand, not only in the Christian Church but in other religious beliefs as well. Amulets, charms, protective symbols, incantations, all had their place; but exorcism stood pre-eminent, as dealing with the very demons and devils themselves.

Exorcism is, of course, a method of binding evil spirits by command, by means of ceremonies and formulas, and the word in itself implies the act of casting away or throwing out. The old time exorcist was often called a conjurer; but that word was also applied to the type of necromancer who was not a worker of evil, but an invoker of spirits for a good purpose. From the earliest times the exorcist has existed, and is the natural reaction to the black magician or sorcerer; seeking to undo the work of the latter, though it cannot be said always with success.

In Greece Epicurus and Æschines were the sons of a woman who got her living as an exorcist, and were reproached by the Stoics and Demosthenes for having assisted her in her work, which they considered dishonourable. This was a very different view from that held by the peoples of the East, for, as we have mentioned elsewhere, in Assyria and Babylon the exorcist held an important place in the temples, while the same is true of the exorcist-magicians of Egypt and India. The Jews held that God had bestowed this power upon Solomon, as one of the examples of his wisdom, in that the casting out of demons was of benefit to mankind.

There are several accounts in the New Testament of the Master Jesus having expelled evil spirits from the obsessed, while in the first verse of the ninth chapter of the Gospel of

St. Luke we read that He gave His disciples "authority over devils." The disciples thereafter practised the art of exorcism in the course of their work and propaganda.

However, the Christian Church in Europe does not appear to have acquired a body of exorcists until the close of the third century. Later, in the Council of Antioch (A.D. 341), in the Xth Canon, exorcists are mentioned in conjunction with sub-deacons, and for centuries they held quite an important place in the Church; waging war against sorcery and witchcraft in general, as well as their very particular branch of work. Possibly they had to wrestle with original sin, also as Catachumens were exorcised for twenty days before taking the Sacrament.

The exorcist forms one of the minor orders of the Roman Catholic Church, and at their ordination the Bishop addresses them upon their duties. There exists a very ancient complete manual for the Roman exorcists, who in earlier times were subjected to severe bodily and spiritual training, Their exorcisms number nine: (1) Ex-Sanctio-nominibus Dei, Schem Namphorus, Eloha, Ab, Bas, Ruachaccœia, Jehovah, Tetragrammerton, Hehije, Haja hove veyheje, Yschiros, Otheos and Athamatos; (2) Ec-ominum Sanctorum ordini; (3) Ex-pracipuis animadversione dignis, Sanctorum Angelorum; (4) Ex-actibus vitæ gloriosæ Virg. Mariæ; (5) Ex-gestis Domini Nostri Jesu Christi; (6) Ex-Vistitut venerabilium Sacramentorum; (7) Ex-Præcipuis; (8) Ecclesiæ Dogmatibus; (9) Apocalypsis Beati Jonnas Apostoli.

There are various psalms, prayers and litanies to accompany the foregoing, followed by eight Post-exorcisations. Of these the first three deal with obstinate cases of obsession by a demon. In the event of their failure, a very horrible picture of the evil spirit was to be drawn, and, after the spirit's name had been written upon it or a name considered sufficiently insulting if that was unknown, the picture was to be burnt, the whole having been sprinkled with holy water and fumigated with incense. The fourth and fifth of the Post-exorcisations were thanksgivings for freedom attained from obsessions; the sixth was used in dealing with Incubi and Succubi; the seventh was for use in haunted houses, with a special "Service" for each day of the week; the eighth and last deals with storms and tempests of a demoniac origin, or raised by sorcery. An old formula for making an exorcising fire, to deal with the latter kind of black magic, comprised the following ingredients: Sabinæ, Hupericonis, Palmæ Christie, Arthemesize, Verbermæ, Aristolochiæ rotundæ, Rutæ, Aster, Altica, Sulphuris and Assafœtida. The fire was to be banked to huge proportions, so that an immense blaze would result.

Although not so common as many other forms of exorcism and protection, exorcising fires are sometimes burnt among primitive peoples, and evidently the purifying properties of fire were dimly understood if not actively realised by all peoples of earlier times. We find fire playing an important part in many protective rites and ceremonies, as well as in sorcery and black magic.

In China the Ching-Ming Spring Festival was preceded by three days called "Ham-Shik," or "Cold eating." The meaning was that the household fires were all being allowed to die down, and fresh ones were not kindled until the end of the third day, when they were relit with great ceremony. This rite was looked upon as one of the purifications by which evil was banished; the old life of the household being renewed in goodness and purity, with every hope of happiness, health and good fortune.

In all Chinese exorcising ceremonies pure fire and pure water were intensely important. The water naturally had to be drawn from a "Holy" well, and had itself to be exorcised before use, while pure fire was obtained by burning certain woods and incense, and charcoal perfumed with incense. Until quite recent times a fire ceremony was celebrated in the province of Fuhkein, by the well-known practice of letting off crackers intended to exorcise demons and evil spirits and effect a general purification.

In the Middle Ages an exorcist addressed the demons by the worst possible names, in the hope of getting them to announce their true ones. Not unreasonably great power was thought to attach to a name, and exorcists once possessed of the name of a demon were considered to have attained a degree of mastery over the evil visitant. The latter were adjured to reveal their true names, but in many instances the demon evidently did not obey. They were then called everything vile that could be imagined, and the person affected was anointed with oil, fumigated and exhorted to patience if able to understand. I myself have known cases intensely difficult to exorcise, and have usually found that the possessed person had some queer link with the obsessing entity and did not wholly desire to get rid of it.

The last recorded acknowledgment to exorcism in the Anglican Church appears in the Baptismal Service of the Liturgy of Edward VI. Charms and amulets are, of course, the commonest form of protection used; including the relics of Holy Masters or Saints. Such things have power according to the amount of faith placed in them, and the vibration or thought form aroused by generations of belief.

There was an enormous cult and trade in relics in the early Church and during the Middle Ages. Indeed, in many instances it became a grave scandal, on account of the preposterous nature of the so-called relics. The actual sweat of Jesus Christ, the milk of the Blessed Virgin Mary, and so on, were examples of the absurdities in this connection. Many bishops and dignitaries of the Church did all they could to counteract the trade in relics, but many also supported it. And even to-day Catholics place great faith in their medals and medallions inscribed with the images of saints and martyrs.

The power of the relic lies in the supernatural grace bestowed by its holy origin, which is comparable with an inextinguishable light. This power is considered to pervade all who come in contact with the sacred object, and especially the owner. So that it is easily seen that the underlying belief in the relic is little different from the faith placed in ancient charms and talismans, and the root theory of savage magic.

Charles I of England is recorded to have carried on his person a charm against danger and poison, especially written for him by Pope Leo IX. Nowadays we give the name "charm" to little figures and symbols that are commonly supposed to be lucky, but a charm is really a magical formula that is spoken or sung. Charms were the good counterpart of the sorcerers' incantations, and were uttered on entering houses, over possessions and children, and to obtain some desired benefit. They were also written out on pieces of parchment and sewn into clothing, or otherwise attached to the person. The Burmans and others have their charms tattooed upon them.

An amulet is a material object that was worn or carried for magic reasons. Sometimes it took the form of a relic, but it was always worn to overcome disease, to give strength, to obtain love or good fortune, and as a defence against dangers.

Jewels were, and are, very favourite amulets. The Chinese and Japanese especially believe in the efficacy of jewels; red and rose coloured stones, such as rubies and garnets, being particularly favoured. Many forms of jewellery had their origin as amulets.

The Assyrians and Babylonians specialised in necklaces from which depended little images of the sun, moon, stars and astrological symbols, while ear-rings and bracelets were used both as amulets and ornaments. The amulets of Egypt are almost too well-known to mention, and appear in an amazing number and variety of forms. Among the best known are the scarab, symbol of life and resurrection; the looped cross, also a symbol of life; the snake-head amulet, usually in red stone and representative of Isis. The amulet of Menat, and the amulet of Sam, were two widely used phallic symbols representing sexual power.

Talismans were used for active benefit: that is, to bring about desired conditions and events, in contrast with the more negative protective qualities of the charm and amulet.

Barren women of all races and times have worn talismans to procure the blessing of children, such articles frequently being of phallic origin. Talismans of this description are very common among the peoples of India, but are by no means confined to them; the Phallus having always been considered a powerful token. A favourite talisman among native warriors of Mexico and the Orinoco River was to attach to their shields the hair and middle finger of the left hand of a woman who died in childbirth, to give them strength and protection against enemy arrows. In India and among Mohammedan peoples, the colours red, yellow and black are thought to be obnoxious to demons and evil spirits, while in India and China mothers tie a red thread to the hair of their children to afford them protection. In the two latter countries, again, touching fire at funerals is thought to give freedom from ghosts. The Burman believes in the efficacy of loud noises for the exorcising of evil spirits and demons; banging gongs and drums, and playing a weird "tune" upon little reed pipes to drive away the "nats" of the jungle, which is infested with evil demons and the dreaded spirits of women dead in childbirth.

In India there is no more dreaded ghost than the "Churel,"

the name by which the woman who died in childbirth type of spirit is known. She is supposed to have a great grudge against mankind on account of the manner of her death, and to appear in lonely places to lure travellers and jungle wayfarers away to destruction. She is also inimical to pregnant women and children. This spirit may be known by the feet being turned backwards.

Such a woman is buried in great haste, if not cremated; it being feared that sorcerers may attempt to desecrate the body in order to obtain the body of the unborn fœtus for the practice of black magic. Sometimes the child is removed and destroyed on this account. The corpse is then buried feet foremost, the bones having been broken above the ankle, and the feet turned round, while long thorns are struck through the heels. Sometimes charms are recited, to prevent the return of the woman spirit.

The dread of this particular kind of ghost is almost world-wide, and many savage tribes go through ceremonies of propitiation if the husband of such a one marries again. The chief means of exorcising the female demon is by the exhibition of a phallic symbol, the spirit being thought to dread the Phallus as constituting in one aspect the cause of her death and in another the symbol of fertility against her sterility.

The K'chins of Burma have a blood sprinkling ceremony at weddings, for the protection of the couples from demons and misfortune. Some Indian and Burman exorcists drink blood with this object.

In ancient Babylon there were many charms to avert the evil of a returning ghost. One of them instructs those who are haunted by the spirit of a dead man to make a clay image of him, writing his name upon the left side with a stylus; and then to hide the image in a hollow piece of horn, which must in turn be buried under a thorn bush.

Just as fire was regarded as a powerful means of exorcism, and the use of protecting or exorcising fires is found among all peoples, so water is regarded as the purifier *par excellence*. In Babylon and Assyria, once the temple exorcist had diagnosed the trouble from which his "patient" was suffering, the first thing to be done was for the latter to be purified by special water from the river Euphrates, or holy water from the Abyss. This "Abyss" might have meant the mystic waters upon which the whole earth was considered to be floating—a sort of vast ditch, whose sides were the heavens; or merely the waters from the sacred wells or tanks of the temples, which were also known as the "Abyss." The necessary purification took place frequently in the house of the priest, to which a "lustration chamber" was always attached for that purpose. The ritual was performed with great ceremony, both the exorcist and the obsessed patient being clothed in black robes.

In ancient Egypt natron was extensively used for purification and for exorcism. The whole body was fumigated with it, and a piece of natron was sucked to purify the mouth, but it was never chewed or swallowed. Any person reciting a counter-spell had to be pure in body and habits, and clothed for the occasion in linen and shod in white sandals.

The beetle was thought by the Egyptians to drive away every kind of sorcery, and for this purpose the head and wings were cut off and the insect's body boiled and laid in oil. The dismembered parts were then heated and steeped in the oil of a serpent, and the whole mixture on being boiled again was drunk by the person desiring to be free from enchantment.

Precious stones have been universally used as talismans, and the Egyptians especially attached much importance to them. The Mongolian races, also, believed greatly in the protective influence of precious stones against evil. The emerald worn on the person dispels demoniac illusions and conserves chastity. Rubies give courage, good health, and immunity from poisons. Sapphires are the emblem of peace and protection, and so forth. The Egyptians were particularly fond of amulets made of lapis-lazuli, and certain metals were regarded by them as fortunate. The Romany peoples love silver, as do also the native West Indians and various African races; probably with the idea that the metal dispels evil and is a luck bringer. And the last fact is rather curious, as the alchemist and others identified silver with the moon, whose beneficent influence is very doubtful and in some aspects definitely malevolent. However, when lunar aspects are courted as being protective and favourable, the origin is probably to be found through Isis the moon goddess; though she, too, only smiled upon her particular devotees.

A feature of all varieties of exorcism is the counter spell, and it was definitely thought that all forms of demoniac enchantment could only be removed by this means. Thus, we find that both in the East and mediæval Europe the use of articles connected with religion was considered potent against evil and sorcery. Quite an amusing little account in this connection is of how some heretics, suspected of sorcery, were seen by scandalised villagers to be walking upon the waters of a nearby river. The local priests were hurriedly called to the scene and threw pieces of the consecrated Host into the river, whereupon the heretics promptly sank and lost their lives.

Only in very rare cases did the Church ever sanction the use of black magic to overcome sorcery; the Powers of Light were depended upon to overcome Satan in the long run. However, there is a tale of a mediæval German bishop, who, on returning from Rome, had a spell cast upon him by his mistress, causing him severe pain and illness. The poor bishop implored the permission of the Pope to call in another witch to undo his mistress's enchantments, and, St. Peter's successor having consented, the effect of counter black magic was the recovery of the bishop and the death of his mistress.

An ancient story of a very different character is that known as the Legend of Ainat. This relates how the Master Jesus and his disciples, walking by the Sea of Tiberius, encountered an old witch of terrible appearance, her eyes burning with flames and fire issuing from her mouth. The disciples questioned the Master as to whom this terrible apparition could be, and Jesus replied that she was the evil demon who caused shipwrecks and disaster, flung horsemen from their saddles, and parted mothers from their children. He then confronted her, and used some words of power that rendered her helpless. The disciples, after that, seized the witch and burned her body; scattering her ashes to the four winds, with the words: "May the memory of Ainat forever be destroyed."

There are many variations in the exact methods of exorcising an obsessing spirit or places haunted by evil influences, but on the whole the groundwork is the same. Manifestations due to sorcery accomplished by means of elementals are comparatively easy to deal with, if the exorcist has an iron will. The following methods of counteracting occult disturbances due to evil spirits or black magic have been used extensively and with success; but it is well to mention here that all people troubled with such things must guard their thoughts and expel fear from their minds, otherwise good results will seldom follow.

The exorcist should be a priest, or some person versed in occult matters. The entrance to the house in question should be sealed with a wax made with wafers of the Host, and in the case of a particular room being exorcised even the windows should be treated in the same manner. Crosses must be placed or drawn with chalk upon the doors, and a large fire made upon which frankincense should be burnt. A small portion of this fire is then placed in a censer, and carried from room to room with prayers for the departure of evil. Holy water which has been consecrated in a church should next be sprinkled about the house by means of hyssop dipped in the purifying fluid, and the words: "I exorcise thee, O unclean spirit, in the name of the Father and of the Son and of the Holy Ghost," must be pronounced in each room. Possibly violent manifestations might occur during the ceremony; in which case it would be best for the exorcist and his assistant in all cases to demand the name, or source, of the evil demonstration.

Here is another ceremony, to ward off evil vibrations and occult disturbances, or to help persons rid themselves of some bad habit or obsession.

A room should be chosen for the ritual and thoroughly cleaned, and all except the essential furniture in it removed. If that cannot be done, the furniture must be pushed back against the wall and tidily arranged. The person performing the ceremony, or the one who needs purification, as the case may be, must then have a bath (cold, for preference) and afterwards put on clean clothes, or a white robe, especially prepared for the occasion. Seven small brass bowls must be arranged at intervals to form a circle, which should be nine feet in diameter, or, if the room be too small, three or six feet. These bowls must be filled with fire made of charcoal, and sprinkled with frankincense. The officiator should take his or her place within the circle, at the lower edge, standing or sitting cross-legged and facing east or north.

Jarvardi incense sticks should be burnt in the circle, and facing the operator should be two bowls, full of water—a small one on the right and a larger one on the left. Immediately in front of the larger bowl should be three candlesticks, with unlit candles. The base of the candlesticks should have three, five, or eight points like a star, but this is not absolutely necessary. The candlesticks must be arranged in a straight line or triangular formation ; *according to the inclination of the officiator*, which is important.

The time chosen for the ceremony should be eleven o'clock in the morning or eleven o'clock in the evening, but the morning is preferable. The room can either be darkened or not, but undarkened is better. The operator having entered the circle, the following evocation is recited. "I invoke the powers of light and the powers of love, and the purifying spirit that is in fire, and in water, to gather around me their forces and protection." After a pause of about three minutes, the invocation continues : "I call upon all the higher spiritual forces and beings who have the progress and welfare of their human brothers in their care, to be witness to the promise (or vow) that I am about to make to cast away those things that are unworthy and to release the spirit within, and thus become impervious to any evil vibrations that may be seeking to harm me." Then the officiator utters aloud : "I renounce so and so" (whatever evil or fault it is required to banish ; such as pride, vanity, lust, intemperance and so on), "which forms a link with evil forces."

The Lord's prayer is next recited, care being taken to say : "Leave us not when in temptation," instead of "Lead us not into." Having renounced evil, the candles should be lit and a portion of the water in the small bowl drunk. After a period of five minutes' meditation on peace and harmony, the fingers are dipped in the larger bowl of water and shaken three times. The circle is then left, the large bowl of water being removed and its contents emptied away. The circle and the rest of the articles in it are left untouched, the candles being allowed to burn themselves out. The circle must not be entered again, and the door of the room must be locked, none entering until the next day.

If the foregoing exorcising ritual can only be performed at night, when a light is required other than candles, on no account must a red light be used. Blue or green, or a dim orange, is better. The officiator must be careful not to move about or fidget within the circle, as this causes disharmony and weakens the vibrations. In most cases the participant should be alone, but if he or she is mentally distressed, another person should be present to witness the proceedings for obvious reasons. In the event of the ceremony or purification being used for dispelling an evil influence, from an individual and not from a house, the sentence "I renounce . . ." can be altered to "I exorcise the evil influence, and dispel the dark forces within this house."

The same ritual can be performed with flowers in place of fire, arranged in seven new white glass vases. The flowers should be picked by the officiator if possible, and be white, blue, mauve, pink, mixed, but never red. In such case, however, at the end of the ceremony the circle should be broken, by removing the vases of flowers and placing them in a straight row in another part of the room, which must be locked as before. After the twenty-four hours the flowers must be burnt or buried; not thrown away or used in any other part of the house.

A form of exorcism used in the Church for dealing with obsessing entities is briefly as follows. The exorcist (or priest), having first made the sign of the cross, commands the possessed person to kneel before him and proceeds to sprinkle him with Holy Water. The name of the troublesome spirit is then enquired and, having placed his hands on the demoniac's head, the exorcist repeats: "I exorcise thee, unclean spirit, in the name of Jesus Christ; tremble, O Satan, enemy of the faith, thou foe of mankind who hast brought death to the world, and hast rebelled against justice, thou seducer of mankind, thou root of evil, source of avarice, discord and envy." Prayers follow, and the spirit is commanded to leave in the name of the Blessed Virgin and the Holy Trinity.

In forming a circle for the purpose of the exorcism of sorcery, a large five-pointed star should be drawn with chalk and a circle of double lines drawn around it. Within the double lines the following words should be written, care being taken to place a cross after each word and to make the letters touch the top and bottom lines of the circle. "IN NOMINA PATRIS + ALPHA + OMEGA + ELELOHYM + SOTHER + AGIA + TETRAGRAMMERTON + AGIOS + OTHEOS + ISCHIROS +" The participants should wear garlands of assafœtida and garlic flowers, and where the disturbances are of a material nature they must on no account leave the circle until peace and harmony have been restored.

Symbols can be also used within any protective circle; the cross, for instance, and, if drawn, the cross within the circle. The triangle, again, may be employed; so long as the apex is placed upwards. From the time when man first shod horses, an unused horseshoe has been used as a protection against evil. There, however, the true origin is a sexual one; the shoe being originally representative of the female organ of generation, plenty and fertility. It is very possible that the Romany or gipsy peoples, wandering into every country in Europe, spread the belief in the protective power and "luck" of horseshoes; even as they introduced many beliefs and also practices of sorcery and the black art. In any case, in course of time the symbol of the womb became confused with the horseshoe, on account of the rough similarity of outline.

The power of all symbols lies not in the material object, but in the thought forces attached to it, and which in time form an elemental for good or ill. Thus, the ancient swastika, which was known in India at a very remote period, has a beneficent symbolism for protection and good fortune, and has been used as an amulet. It, also, has its reversed position, in which it becomes a symbol of evil significance. While not overlooking the history and esoteric meaning of the swastika, space does not permit of more than this brief mention here.

Elemental spirits can be exorcised by calling upon the spirits of air, fire, water and earth. The procedure is by breathing and sprinkling perfumes, and by tracing upon the ground the star of Solomon and the sacred Pentagram drawn with the ash of a consecrated fire. The exorcist must then pronounce the Conjuration of Four; holding the Pentacle of Solomon in his right hand, and having before him the symbolical sword, cup, and stave or wand, which he must take up in turn. This little ceremony must be preceded, and ended, by forming the sign of the Kabalistic cross.

In all Christian exorcisms for the protection of the body it was the custom to seal its nine openings with Holy Water, so that no evil influence could gain entrance. It was thought that demons could enter the body with food and drink, and even by breathing. Although this idea has become quite outgrown, the ritual is still in practice among persons preparing themselves against Satanic forces.

CHAPTER VIII

CONCLUSIONS

Consists of the author's opinion on various subjects touched on in preceding chapters and his advice to would-be occultists.

TO the majority of people the subject of black magic ranks as an impossible nightmare; an unpleasant and ridiculous phantasmagoria, at best tinged with the fascinating horror of a good ghost story, but in any case not to be treated more seriously than our childhood's stories of witches and orgies.

Others know better. Nevertheless, many, if not the worst of, the practices of the past appear to us incredible and foolish, and we wonder how many men of undoubted learning and scientific bent could have placed their faith in such preposterous magic and have worried with such outrageously foolish formulas.

Well, many people think much the same about such famous spiritualists as Sir Oliver Lodge, the late Sir William Crookes, and the late Sir Arthur Conan Doyle; to say nothing of the Hannen Swaffers and Shaw Desmonds in our midst. Yet these men and their conclusions are not to be discredited; even though the world as a whole appears to regard all psychic investigations as either a waste of time or an unwarranted interference, almost amounting to blasphemy, with matters that are "purposely hidden."

This latter argument is the most futile. Everything has been hidden in the past, and much still is hidden. It is for man to unveil the mysteries. The Divine Intelligence, which we call God, working through His creative forces, placed man in an empty world, except for the vegetable and animal kingdoms, and left him to evolve the material expressions of his own life and conquer the elements alone. I believe that nothing is purposely hidden; it is for us to invent, to design, to investigate, to claim and to attain. Everything is ours when we have earned it through effort, and have evolved sufficiently to grasp it.

To return to the question of witchcraft. I believe in black magic. I know it exists, and I have personally witnessed many incredible happenings ; but I do not necessarily believe all that I hear on the subject, and nowadays analyse any phenomena very carefully before coming to any conclusion. I have a great deal of sympathy with scientific doubters, and with those who test psychicism up hill and down dale and are not satisfied. But there are latent powers within man alone that are not yet fully understood, and until we can say definitely what are our own limits (including those of our spiritual self and etheric body), we cannot definitely state what is, and what is not, due to the interference or influence of discarnate intelligences.

Members of my race are prone to believe in magic in any case. Probably hundreds of my ancestors practised sorcery, in one form or another, back to a remote period, and more recent generations have, I know, been deeply imbued with occultism. This being so, there is all the more reason why I should be very critical of my beliefs in this respect, and especially careful to avoid being deluded or credulous. Wherefore I am become a very " doubting Thomas," indeed, when faced with phenomena of any description.

I have sat in many circles where good but credulous people have been entirely satisfied that they are communicating with those beyond, yet have personally seen and heard nothing that may not be attributed to the subconscious mind and the strange magnetic force called Pranic Energy. Likewise, I have investigated so-called black magic circles that are equally futile and non-productive of anything but delusions, except for the fact that evil intentions must always link the participators with the dark forces.

There are probably very few to-day who believe in a personified Devil, complete with hoofs, horns and " toasting-fork." What, therefore, is the force of evil with which most of us, consciously or unconsciously, wage continuous warfare ? Very largely, of course, it is our own Lower Nature. And this, while it would have been considered a perfectly presentable thing five thousand years or so ago, is quite objectionable and out of place in the present era. It has, therefore, to be sternly suppressed, which accounts for most of our nightmares and occasional anti-social lapses according to psychologists.

Apart from this undesirable double, however, though possibly including it, there is an intangible force, vibration or current of evil, eternally emanating from man's perversions of his gifts and misuse of the knowledge and wisdom to which he has attained. Man's thoughts create, and in as much as they are dark and warped they feed foul shapes of elemental beings that grow and consolidate upon the lower mental planes. These are the "Demons" of the astral world. Man, then, is the creator of his own evil, being endowed with free will in thought and action. That is to say, he possesses liberty of choice collectively, but by his tyranny and imperfect social construction he denies this freedom to all but the most rebellious and progressive of thousands of his fellow creatures.

The suffering and distress upon this earth are due to man's refusal to harmonise with the Divine Law. All the disease, cruelty, torment and injustice of the world to-day can be laid at our own door, and will continue to be so until the lesson of conforming to this rule of Universal Harmony is learnt. Another name for Universal Harmony is Love, according to the Sermon on the Mount.

We do not have to look outside this world for fiends and demons; nothing could be more cruel and diabolical than man at his worst. Death does not change him, and when such a one passes over, he lingers to impress his vileness still further upon weak humanity. Such souls can with assistance rise to better things, but it is a very arduous task and for the most part they remain rejoicers in evil.

The undoubted materialisations, somewhat approximating the popular concept of the Devil, which have been seen from time to time, can be accounted for by the fact that human thoughts have so long projected a mental image of his Satanic Majesty that elemental beings have actually built up around this mental form and become occasionally objective. All these things must die away as humanity struggles towards the Light.

In my dealings in these pages with necromancy and spiritualism there is no wish to depreciate the work of a large number of people who are seriously trying to prove to the world the truth of survival after death. But for myself I do not regard mediumship very favourably. I believe that all who have the time should so enlarge their own powers as to be able to contact the so-called "psychic planes" without any outside assistance. Unfortunately most people have not the time, even if they have the necessary patience, and so mediums remain indispensable. In my own view steps need to be taken *within the movement* to prevent anyone who feels inclined from starting a "Church" or unsupervised open circles, and the employment of untested mediums, who may be positively fraudulent or attracting undesirable or unevolved entities under the cloak of "Guides."

In Chapter VIII, Part I, reference has been made to Peter Kurten, the Dusseldorf murderer, and his case cited in connection with lycanthropy. To occultists it is evident that Kurten was at certain times the victim of a demoniac obsession, and I have since found that this fact is recognised by such experts in crime as Mr. E. T. Woodhall, late of Scotland Yard and H.M. Secret Service, who mentions Kurten in his book *Crime and the Supernatural*.

There is a good deal of interest taken in Yoga nowadays among people who have the leisure and inclination to study various cults, and I am often asked whether Yoga is really black magic. I think the chapter in this volume on Indian Yogis should have made it quite clear that Yoga is nothing of the sort. Any unfortunate results that may ever have originated from Yoga practices are probably due to the student having attempted mental exercises and postures for which he or she was totally unfitted.

Personally, I believe that the Yoga Science of Breath, and the accompanying system of self-development, can be of inestimable value to most people if suitably adapted for Western needs. To the average European student of Yoga philosophy I particularly recommend the study of Raja Yoga, which is far and away the most practical for this part of the world. There are a great many books on Yoga and its different branches, and there is no harm in reading them. But I strongly advise no one to take up practices, or to execute exercises and postures, without first consulting a teacher, who will instruct them as to what is suitable and harmless to carry out. The different modes of breathing alone need to be learnt gradually, as some can be definitely injurious physically and mentally, unless they are properly preceded by the more elementary and foundational exercises.

Altogether, the matter of Yoga needs careful attention before benefits can be attained, and furthermore it is useless for the student to take up even modified Yoga without conforming his life to the necessary principles. The prolonged one-pointed concentration, for example, is not to be advocated unless the training has started very early in life and special rules prescribed have been carried out. This form of concentration may lead to mania, and other forms of insanity.

Upon the score of the philosophy itself, however, I can only say that the Yoga system offers an expansion and a self-realisation that I have yet to find surpassed elsewhere.

It is almost certain that I shall be accused in these pages of having left out many well-known instances of sorcery, and famous witches, magicians and warlocks; but it has been impossible to give even a brief account of them all. I have simply attempted to place before the reader a gradually unfolding picture of the story of magic and witchcraft; beginning in the dim mists of antiquity, when the sun was man's greatest comfort and the moonlit darkness filled his soul with an inexpressible dread of the unknown, every shadow becoming to his uneasy fancy a monstrous being of incalculable evil. From which primitive period, down a long road of grandeur and misery, the instinct has continued until now, when often enough European magic is represented by a few elderly people waiting quietly in semi-darkness, for a Voice to speak from the same Unknown.

Among the neglected figures in this work is one who greatly captured my imagination in my younger days, the Flying Dutchman or nautical Wandering Jew. The legend which relates how that heroic form was doomed to battle round the Cape, year in, year out, till Judgment day, is too well-known to bear repetition. Even so, I have met sailors of many nationalities and differing race who declared that they had seen the Flying Dutchman's ship scudding past in the darkness with a full press of sail, though not always proving an omen of disaster.

Lastly, while there is no need to enlarge upon the profanities of the Black Mass, it is known to still take place. Occasional thefts are made from churches of the Holy Wafers, and only a few years ago a large quantity of the consecrated Host was stolen from the Cathedral of Notre Dame, by an old woman who confessed that she was procuring them for those who celebrated the Black Mass.

Just as most people wish to avoid black magic, if they

take it seriously at all, so there are others who edge up and say: "Oh, but black magic is so *fascinating!*" Possibly it may be fascinating to those who do not look beneath the surface, but surely the very word they use implies fatality? In other days, fascination betokened a glamour that covered emptiness, if not corruption, and so it is very aptly applied to the lure of black magic.

No one should ever yield to a temptation to dabble in sorcery, even if only from curiosity or the search for a new thrill. It is impossible to involve oneself in black magic in any shape or form without becoming contaminated; it is impossible to approach it and not risk losing judgment and reason. I have personally investigated it and, speaking from experience, strongly advise no one to do likewise. There is nothing of true value to gain, and everything to lose. It does not matter how light-heartedly it may be entered into as an intriguing pastime, with a tempting spice of the forbidden, the penalty is equally the same.

INDEX

A

B

C

T

U

V

W

Y

Z